VIRGIL THOMSON

Virgil Thomson, 1979. Photo by Christopher Cox.

VIRGIL THOMSON

A Bio-Bibliography

Michael Meckna

Donald L. Hixon, *Series Adviser*

Bio-Bibliographies in Music, Number 4

GREENWOOD PRESS
New York • Westport, Connecticut • London

LIBRARY OF CONGRESS CATALOGING-IN-PUBLICATION DATA

Meckna, Michael.
  Virgil Thomson, a bio-bibliography.

  (Bio-bibliographies in music, ISSN 0742-6968 ; no. 4)
  Bibliography: p.
  Discography: p.
  Includes index.
  1. Thomson, Virgil, 1896-   —Bibliography.
2. Thomson, Virgil, 1896-   —Discography. 3. Music—
Bio-bibliography. I. Title. II. Series.
ML134.T43M4   1986   016.78'092'4   86-14229
ISBN 0-313-25010-3 (lib. bdg. : alk. paper)

Library of Congress Catalog Card Number: 86-14229
ISBN: 0-313-25010-3
ISSN: 0742-6968

First published in 1986

Greenwood Press, Inc.
88 Post Road West, Westport, Connecticut 06881

Printed in the United States of America

∞™

The paper used in this book complies with the
Permanent Paper Standard issued by the National
Information Standards Organization (Z39.48-1984).

10 9 8 7 6 5 4 3 2 1

To Mr. and Mrs. Ernest O. Kartinen
this book is fondly dedicated.

Contents

Preface

Virgil Thomson is one of the twentieth century's most significant composers and, in addition, one of its keenest music critics. He has written well over three hundred musical works, and his prose works would fill far more than the eight volumes which have been published so far. This present volume organizes and often annotates the immense amount of material by and about this distinguished and influential American. It is offered in the spirit of the late Irving Lowens's dictum that "bibliography is the backbone of history," and it should be useful to students preparing analytical studies of Thomson's compositions and writings, to performers seeking sources of material and reviews, and to scholars generally interested in comparative studies of genres, style, or aesthetics.

This book is divided into the following main sections:

1) A brief biography, which discusses both the main events in Mr. Thomson's life and his major works.

2) A complete list of works and performances, classified by genre and arranged chronologically by date of composition. Each work is preceded by the mnemonic "W" (W1, W2, etc.), and each title is followed by such information as instrumentation, duration, commissions, librettist, premiere, and publisher.

3) A discography of commercially produced sound recordings, arranged alphabetically by title of work. Each entry is preceded by the mnemonic "D" (D1, D2, etc.) and includes full information on performers, date of issue, and recording company.

4) An annotated bibliography of writings by and about Virgil Thomson, each citation preceded by the mnemonic "T" in the section of writings by Mr. Thomson, or "B" in the section of writings by others. These entries usually quote directly from the piece of writing in question, and they also refer to the "Works and Performances" and "Discography" sections.

In addition, appendices provide alphabetical and chronological listings of Mr. Thomson's works, as well as a list of the archival resources, preceded by the mnemonic "A," of his manuscripts, correspondence, and personal papers. Finally, a complete _index_ of names (personal and corporate) and titles concludes the volume.

Despite painstaking research, it was not always possible to provide premiere information for several works. Readers able to supply this information are encouraged to contact the author through Greenwood Press.

PUBLISHERS DIRECTORY

American Music Edition/Presser (see Presser below)

Boosey & Hawkes, Inc., 24 West 57th Street, New York, NY 10019

Belwin-Mills Publishing Corp., 25 Deshon Drive, Melville, NY 11746; or 1776 Broadway, New York, NY 10019

Carl Fischer, Inc., 62 Cooper Square, New York, NY 10003

Columbia University Press, 562 W. 113th Street, New York, NY 10025

Da Capo Press, Inc., 227 West 17th Street, New York, NY 10011

Gentry Publications, P.O. Box 333, Tarzana, CA 91356-0333

Greenwood Press, 88 Post Road, Westport, CT 06881

G. Schirmer, Inc., 866 Third Avenue, New York, NY 10022

Heritage Music Press, 501 East 3rd Street, P.O. Box 1397, Dayton, OH 45401

Holt, Rinehart, and Winston, 383 Madison Avenue, New York, NY 10017

H.W. Gray Publications/Belwin-Mills (See Belwin-Mills above)

Keyboard Classics Magazine, 223 Katonah Ave., Katonah, NY 10536

Leeds Music Corp./Belwin-Mills (See Belwin-Mills above)

Lingua Press, 6417 La Jolla Scenic Drive South, La Jolla, CA 92037

Lorenz Industries, 501 E. 3rd Street, P.O. Box 1397, Dayton, OH 45401

McAfee Music Corp. (See Belwin-Mills above)

MCA Music Corp./Belwin-Mills (See Belwin-Mills above)

C.F. Peters Corp., 373 Park Avenue South, New York, NY 10016

Theodore Presser Co., Bryn Mawr, PA 19010

Randall M. Eagan & Associates, Publishers, Inc., 2024 Kenwood Parkway, Minneapolis, MN 55405

Ricordi (F. Colombo)/Belwin-Mills (See Belwin-Mills above)

Santee Music Press, Inc., c/o Pietro Deiro Music Headquarters, 133
    Seventh Avenue South, New York, NY 10014

Southern Music Publishing Co.,Inc., 1740 Broadway, New York, NY 10019

Weintraub Music Co., 24 East 22nd Street, New York, NY 10010

ABBREVIATIONS

The following abbreviations are used throughout:

Newspapers and Journals

AM   = Atlantic Monthly
ARG   = American Record Guide
Au   = Audio
Cal   = California Magazine
Ch   = Chicago Magazine
CR   = Consumer Research Bulletin (later Consumer's Research Magazine)
CU   = Consumer Reports (Consumers Union of U.S.)
FF   = Fanfare
FM   = Film Music: from Violins to Video. Edited and compiled by
        James L. Limbacher. Metuchen, NJ: Scarecrow Press, 1974.
Gr   = Gramophone
GS   = The Gramophone Shop Supplement
H&G   = House & Garden
Ha   = Harper's Magazine
HF   = High Fidelity
HMR   = HiFi & Music Review
HSR   = HiFi/Stereo Review
JR   = Just Records
LJ   = Library Journal
MA   = Musical America
MC   = Musical Courier
MG   = Monthly Guide to Recorded Music
MJ   = Music Journal
ML   = The Monthly Letter from E.M.G. (E.M.G. Handmade Gramophones)
MM   = Modern Music
MQ   = Musical Quarterly
MR   = Music Review
MT   = Musical Times
MWW   = Music In the Western World: A History in Documents.
        Edited by Piero Weiss and Richard Taruskin. New York:
        Schirmer Books, 1984.
Na   = The Nation
NR   = The New Records (H. Royer Smith Company)
NRe   = The New Republic
NYRB = The New York Review of Books
NYHT = The New York Herald Tribune
NYer = The New Yorker
NYT   = The New York Times
Notes = Music Library Association Notes
ON   = Opera News

Op	=	<u>Opera</u> (London)
OQ	=	<u>Opera Quarterly</u>
Ov	=	<u>Ovation</u>
PAA	=	<u>Proceedings of the American Academy of Arts and Letters and the National Institute of Arts and Letters</u>
PP	=	<u>Pan Pipes of Sigma Alpha Iota</u>
SFCh	=	<u>San Francisco Chronicle</u>
SR	=	<u>Saturday Review of Literature</u> (later <u>Saturday Review</u>)
St	=	<u>Stereo Review</u>
VF	=	<u>Vanity Fair</u>
Vg	=	<u>Vogue</u>
VTR	=	<u>The Virgil Thomson Reader</u> (See T195)

Instruments and Musical Terms

A	= alto		pic.	= piccolo
B	= bass		S	= soprano
bar.	= baritone		sax.	= saxophone
bn.	= bassoon		T	= tenor
cl.	= clarinet		tbn.	= trombone
cond.	= conductor		timp.	= timpani
Eng.hn.	= English horn		tpt.	= trumpet
fl.	= flute		va.	= viola
glock.	= glockenspiel		vc.	= violoncello
hn.	= horn		vib.	= vibraphone
ob.	= oboe		vn.	= violin
pf.	= piano		xyl.	= xylophone
perc.	= percussion			

Acknowledgements

Many persons and institutions contributed to the preparation of this volume. In particular, I should like to extend special thanks to the following:

For providing specialized bibliographical assistance:

James M. Anthony, Professor of Music, Towson State Univesity, Towson, Maryland;

Olga Buth, Music Librarian, University of Texas at Austin;

Tom Everett, Director of Bands, Harvard University;

Barbara File, Assistant Archivist, Metropolitan Museum of Art, New York City

Susanna Fink, Rare Books Assistant, Sibley Music Library, Eastman School of Music;

Eric Gordon, Publicity Manager, G. Schirmer, Inc., New York City;

Richard Jackson, Head of Americana Collection, New York Public Library, Performing Arts Research Center;

Nancy Johnson, Librarian, American Academy and Institute of Arts and Letters, New York City;

Stephanie Jutt, Nonesuch Records, New York City;

R. Wood Massi, Music Library Coordinator, Mills College, Oakland, California;

Travis Rivers, Professor of Music, Eastern Washington University, Cheney, Washington;

Charles Schille, Curatorial Assistant, Harvard University Archives;

Diane Shelton, Director, F.M. Smith Library, Graceland College, Lamoni, Iowa;

Wayne D. Shirley, Music Specialist, Library of Congress;

Anthony Tommasini, Assistant Professor of Music, Emerson College, Boston, Massachusetts;

Gregory Vaught, Librarian, San Antonio Symphony, San Antonio, Texas; and

Russell G. Wichmann, Organist and Choir Director, Shadyside Presbyterian Church, Pittsburgh, Pennsylvania.

For providing institutional support and personal encouragement:

Veva M. McCoskey, Interlibrary Loan Librarian, her assistants Bessie M. Miller and Alberta G. Virgin, and Nyal Z. Williams, Music Librarian,

Ball State University, Muncie, Indiana;

Jocelyn Mackey, Chairperson of Music History Division, Erwin C. Mueller, Acting Director, and Robert W. Sherman, Chairperson of Academic Studies Department, School of Music, Ball State University;

James L. Pyle, Director, and Serene Rubin, Program Development Specialist, Office of Research, Ball State University;

John K. Urice, Dean, College of Fine Arts, Ball State University; and

The National Endowment for the Humanities and Ball State University for research assistance grants.

For providing specialized editorial assistance:

Marilyn Brownstein, Acquisitions Editor, Greenwood Press;

Donald L. Hixon, Fine Arts Librarian at the University Library of the University of California, Irvine, and Series Advisor, Bio-Bibliographies in Music, Greenwood Press; and

Marilee M. Johnson, Coordinator of University Computer Laboratories, Ball State University.

In addition, I should like to acknowledge the generous assistance of Virgil Thomson himself, who has supported this project from the beginning. His ample and well-organized files were ever available to me through the offices of his excellent secretary, Louis Rispoli. Mr. Thomson's previous secretary, Victor Cardell, now Assistant Music Librarian at Yale University, compiled a worklist which provided the skeleton of the present volume's "Works and Performances" section. Mr. Cardell has also compiled a useful finding aid for Yale University's definitive collection of Mr. Thomson's personal papers (See A3, Appendix I).

Finally, my special thanks go to Eva Elizabeth Meckna, who assisted and encouraged me at every stage of this book.

VIRGIL THOMSON

Biography

Virgil Garnett Thomson was born in Kansas City, Missouri on November 25, 1896. On his mother's side, American roots reach back to Jamestown in the early seventeenth century, and his father's family name first appears in American records in 1717, when a Scottish forebear immigrated to Virginia to become a planter. Most of his ancestors were farmers, with an occasional lawyer, clergyman, or doctor. However, Thomson's father took civil service examinations and eventually became a post office administrator.1

With a secure and respected position, Quincy Alfred Thomson provided his family with the means which the more cultivated sensibilities of Clara May Thomson (née Gaines) converted into a genteel life. Her niece, Lela Garnett, gave Virgil, at age five, his first piano lessons. "Before that," he recalls, "I had only improvised, with flat hands and the full arm, always with the pedal down and always loud, bathing in musical sound at its most intense, naming my creations after 'The Chicago Fire' and similar events." 2 The young man also early revealed an avid interest in the theater and an unusual gift for words.

Soon turned over to local teachers, he found his way to Robert Leigh Murray, tenor soloist of Kansas City's Calvary Baptist Church and proprietor of a local piano store. Murray, a first-class professional trained in Britain, supervised Thomson's musical progress, seeing to it that he had the best instruction available. The young man now acquired his first accomplished piano teacher, Moses Boguslawski, who was followed by Gustav Schoettle, Rudolf King, and E. Geneve Lichtenwalter. In addition, he took organ lessons from Clarence Sears and occasionally served as a substitute. Murray also saw to it that his eager student earned some of the money to pay for his studies. Thomson recalls how Murray "taught me to play his accompaniments and paid me at commercial rates for doing so." 3 With all this musical activity, the fourteen-year-old Thomson one day told his parents that he planned to be a musician. Although they did not object, the vehemence of his announcement so surprised him that, he remembers, "before there was time for any replay I burst out crying and fled upstairs." 4

During this period Thomson also revealed polymath and social tendencies. As a page in the public library, he read omnivorously, including the complete works of Nietzsche and all of The Golden Bough.

Meanwhile, he befriended interesting adults, such as his sister's paint-
ing teacher, Hannah Cuthbertson, and James Gable, a well-read and
widely-traveled Englishman.   Preparing for the salons over which he was
to preside at 17 Quai Voltaire and the Chelsea Hotel, he would, with the
encouragement of his mother, invite these local lions, in addition to
members of his own age group, to dine, hoping "to create and to sustain
a symposium of the arts." 5

While all this took place, Thomson consistently earned "A's" at
Central High School, from which he was graduated in 1914. Luckily for a
talented and eager lad whose father could not afford a university education, Kansas City Polytechnic Institute and Junior College opened during
the following year.   Here the young scholar distinguished himself by
forming a literary society, the "Pansophists," founding a magazine,
Pans, and coming near to explusion for reading aloud from The Spoon
River Anthology.   He earned his keep, as he would later in Boston at
King's Chapel, by working as organist in a local church.

In the meantime, United States involvement in the European war
seemed inevitable, and Thomson was eager to see action. Although novel
experience was a major motive, the reader of Nietzsche's eighteen volumes and Frazer's ten "could only think of [war] as myth-in-action; and
acting out myths was a mystery that I had as much right as any other man
to get involved in."6 In January, 1917, several months before the Presi-
dent and Congress made their official declaration, Thomson enlisted in a
National Guard regiment, then trained in radio telephony at Columbia
University and in aviation at the University of Texas in Austin.   In
September, 1918, he received overseas orders, but the Armistice on
November 11 arrived before his troop ship sailed.

Spending little time on disappointment, Thomson now turned the full
force of his energy on completing his education. Since his ultimate aim
at this time "was to become an organist and choir director in some well-
paying city church and from there to pursue a composer's career,"7
Harvard University as well as the Boston-Cambridge environment attracted
him for the availability of good keyboard lessons, training in theory
and composition, and access to cultural life.   Thomson was strongly
influenced from the start by composer Edward Burlingame Hill, choral
conductor Archibald T. Davison, and poet S. Foster Damon.   Among his
fellow students were Walter Piston, Randall Thompson, and Leopold Mannes, who remember their colleague as "a model of industry" and "a dynamo
of enthusiasm."8 Thomson's first compositions now emerged: Vernal Equinox, for soprano with piano, to a text by Amy Lowell, The Sunflower,
also for soprano and piano but to a Blake poem, and De Profundis, for
mixed chorus a capella.

Thomson was a prominent member of the Harvard Glee Club, and in the
spring of 1921 he toured Europe with that ensemble. Having been awarded
the John Knowles Paine Traveling Fellowship, he remained behind to
study composition and organ in Paris with Nadia Boulanger when the Club
returned to Cambridge in the fall. Another decisive influence in his
life, Mlle. Boulanger was convinced "that American music was about to
'take off,' just as Russian music had done eighty years before."9
Another of her pupils at this time was Aaron Copland.   Thomson also met
Cocteau, Les Six, and Satie during this year. Moreover, initiating his

career as a critic, he sent reviews back home to the Boston Transcript.

The fall of 1922 found Thomson reluctantly back at Harvard, and three long years were to pass before his return to France. During the first he finished his degree at Harvard, serving also as a teaching assistant, and working as organist at King's Chapel. Then, with a grant from the Juilliard School, he went to New York to study composition with Rosario Scalero and conducting with Chalmers Clifton. At this time, he wrote some vocal music, a Missa Brevis, and Two Sentimental Tangos for orchestra. He also contributed articles about music to The American Mercury 10 and Vanity Fair.11

After the year in New York, and mostly for pecuniary reasons, Thomson accepted the post of assistant instructor at Harvard, also serving as organist in Whitinsville near Worcester. Growing restless and bored with, as he recalls, filling "up my waking mind with others' music,"12 Thomson left for Paris in September, 1925. He was to remain there, except for brief periods, until 1940. Already a blossoming musician, Thomson found Paris a place in which to bloom. He felt that he had left

> an America that was beginning to enclose us all, at least those among us who needed to ripen unpushed. America was impatient with us, trying always to take us in hand and make us a success, or else squeezing us dry for exhibiting in an institution...As Gertrude Stein was to observe, "It was not so much what France gave you as what she did not take away."13

Thomson did not meet Stein until the following autumn. Before then he wrote music steadily, lived frugally, and established relationships with a wide assortment of musicians, writers, and painters. As a final project with Boulanger he finished the Sonata da Chiesa, and on his own he began the Symphony on a Hymn Tune. In the first work Thomson demonstrated mastery of traditional forms as well as modern dissonance, while in the second he revealed his love for the Baptist hymnal. Both works exhibit a directness of expression and an economy of means which have come to characterize his style.

Although Thomson's Parisian circle included Darius Milhaud, Erik Satie, Jean Cocteau, André Gide, Pablo Picasso, F. Scott Fitzgerald, and others, the most important influence on his musical career was Gertrude Stein. The two became friends, saw each other a great deal, 14 and "got on like Harvard men."15 After he had successfully set several of her texts -- Susie Asado, Preciosilla, and Capital Capitals -- the two began work on the opera Four Saints in Three Acts. Stein completed the libretto in June, 1927, and Thomson had the piano score ready a year later. The work, with its stream-of-consciousness text and its crisply rhythmic, basically diatonic, and solemnly allusive setting, premiered in Hartford, Connecticut, on February 8, 1934. With Maurice Grosser's imaginative scenario, a set which included cellophane, crystal, feathers, and seashells, and an all negro cast, Four Saints was a succès de scandale. Carl Van Vechten called it a "miraculous music drama" in the New York Times,16 while Lucius Beebe recorded in the Herald Tribune that "...the field was strewn with murdered unities, decapitated conventions, smashed top hats...and Chandon magnums."17 _Four_ _Saints_ went on to triumph in New York and Chicago. Its composer's career was firmly launched.

Meanwhile, other works received performances in Paris, New York, Boston, and elsewhere. Thomson developed increased technical facility in writing for strings. His Violin Sonata, two string quartets, _Stabat_ _Mater_ (for soprano and string quartet), and the Second Symphony date from this period. In addition, shortly after completing _Four Saints_, he began a long series of "portraits" (140 as of early 1985), in which an individual "sits" for musical depiction. Among those who have been portrayed are: Aaron Copland, Eugene Ormandy, John Houseman, Gertude Stein and Pablo Picasso. Mostly conceived for piano, many of these pieces have been orchestrated or used as sections of larger works.

After the premiere of _Four Saints_ Thomson, much in demand, was asked by film maker Pare Lorentz to write music for a United States documentary about cattle raising, wheat growing, and dust storms on the Western plains. _The_ _Plow_ _That_ _Broke_ _the_ _Plains_ was so successful that the two collaborated again the following year (1937) on _The River_, which dealt with flooding along the Mississippi. For both scores Thomson drew on popular regional songs, and later he extracted orchestral suites which have been performed widely. Also at this time Thomson wrote incidental music for Federal Theater Project productions, including Orson Welles's _Macbeth_ with a black cast, and Broadway productions, including John Houseman's _Hamlet_. Finally, during this period Thomson was commissioned by Lincoln Kirstein's Ballet Caravan to provide music for _Filling_ _Station_. His creation consisted of waltzes, tangos, a fugue, a holdup, a chase, and a funeral, "all aimed to evoke roadside America as pop art."18 The first successful ballet by an American on an American subject, the work toured all over the United States and South America.

Although Thomson visited the United States often during the 1930's, he resided mainly in France. His home in a converted top story at 17 Quai Voltaire on the Left Bank became a meeting place for the artistic and intellectual elite of Paris. In addition to his composition and performing activities, he resumed writing about music in 1931, after a six-year self-imposed hiatus, with a series of articles in _Modern Music_. Perceptive, charming, and blunt, these essays increased the appeal of that journal 19 and attracted other composers to its pages.20 As Thomson's musical and critical reputation grew, several publishers asked him for a book. He accepted the highest bidder ($1,000), and in November of 1939 William Morrow published _The State of Music_. Witty and provocative, the book explained why and how the makers of music should and could also be the administrators of music.

Thomson left Paris during the next year, just a few days before the German invasion. He arrived in New York that fall with little money and no prospects. However, _The State of Music_ had impressed Geoffrey Parsons of the _Herald Tribune_, and Thomson was engaged as music critic to replace the late Lawrence Gilman. For the next fourteen years he held this post, establishing himself as one of the major critical writers of the day. No little controversy surrounded his critical style, which Donal Henahan has observed mixed "elegant and blunt talk, gravity and levity, objectivity and passion, all in exquisitely right proportions." 21

Thomson also founded the New York Music Critics' Circle, which, from 1941 to 1965, gave annual awards for excellence to one or more works that received New York premieres.

Budgeting his time carefully, Thomson continued to compose steadily. His works at this time include the "Three Pictures for Orchestra" (The Seine at Night, Wheatfield at Noon, and Sea Piece with Birds), concertos for cello and harp, two books of piano etudes, Five Songs from William Blake, Four Songs to Poems of Thomas Campion, film scores for "Tuesday in November" and "Louisiana Story" (the latter a Pulitzer Prize winner in 1949), incidental music for several plays, and numerous portraits.

The most famous work, however, was a second opera on a Gertrude Stein text, The Mother of Us All. Completed in March 1946 (four months before Stein's death), both the text and the music are less abstract than Four Saints. In fact, the work has a familiar and nostalgic quality to it, due to Thomson's evocations of marches, bugle calls, parlor songs, waltzes, and hymn tunes, even when he subjects these to polyphonic or bimodal treatment and abrupt, distant modulation for expressive purposes. The only preexisting tune he quotes is "London Bridge is Falling Down." Nevertheless, as John Cage has written,

> The Mother of Us All is everything an American remembers, if he remembers how it was at home of an evening when friends and relatives played and sang, how it was to hear a band playing in the park, a Salvation Army band on a corner, a soldiers' band going down Main Street, an organ when somebody was married or had died.22

In 1954 Thomson decided to resign from the Herald Tribune. For several years he had been earning more from his music and public appearances than from the paper. Moreoever, not yet tired of the job, he recalls seeing boredom on the horizon. "I had reviewed most of the artists that there were and all of the kinds of music...As my mother had said of visiting, one should leave while both you and the others are enjoying it."23

The composing of music did not immediately occupy all his time. Indeed, for a period he seemed to write less music than before. He traveled a great deal -- to South America, conducting and lecturing (in Spanish), to Venice for two festivals, to Berlin for another, and even to Japan. He wrote songs to old English texts, to Spanish texts, and to Shakespeare. And he continued to write incidental music (including five Shakespearean plays), film scores (The Goddess, Power Among Men, and Journey to America), and a ballet for Agnes de Mille, The Harvest According (which consisted of selections from his earlier works with continuity added). Vaguely discontent with merely traveling and composing short works, Thomson eventually began Missa pro defunctis. Complex and powerful, with overlapping lines and clashing chords, even the use of a 12-tone row in the Kyrie, the work, which is for double chorus and large orchestra, reflects the composer's life-long interest in liturgical music. It also reveals Thomson's fondness for popular forms and rhythms, employing even waltzes, tangos, and boogie-woogie for reverential duties. A year after its premiere in 1960, Thomson began his third opera.

Lord Byron tells the story of the Dean of Westminster Abbey's refusal to bury Byron. Framed by a choral elegy upon the return of the poet's body to England from Greece and a semichorus of welcoming Poets' Corner shades, the opera presents a series of flashback scenes covering Lord Byron's life. Thomson's setting of Jack Larson's libretto exhibits his usual sensitivity to prosody as well as his simplicity and playfulness, but the rhythmic interplay is more intricate and the harmonic palette richer than in Four Saints and The Mother of Us All. Reviewing the work for The New Yorker, Andrew Porter observed that

> Thomson has the gift to be simple; his notes come down where
> they ought to be, in the place just right. But his simplici-
> ty is that of a master, not a naïf.24

Lord Byron was premiered at the Juilliard School in 1972, and has yet to be performed by the Metropolitan Opera, for which it was commissioned by the Koussevitzky and Ford Foundations.

The 1970's and early 1980's have seen some slackening of Thomson's activity but a bountiful harvest of awards and honors. Following the premiere of Lord Byron, he wrote a Cantata on Poems of Edward Lear, five settings for two sopranos, baritone, chorus, piano, and chamber orchestra. Thomson adds a humorous dimension to Lear's whimsical texts by setting them in strongly contrasting musical styles. Another work during this period continued his long series of musical portraits. Family Portrait (1972-74) is a suite of five pieces written for the American Brass Quintet. Then in 1975 Thomson wrote his fifth ballet, Parson Weems and the Cherry Tree, for chamber orchestra, with choreography by Eric Hawkins. Commissioned by the Foundation for the Modern Dance and the National Endowment for the Arts, the work tells the "true" story of young George Washington and the cherry tree.

Also during this period Thomson frequently served as a lecturer or composer-in-residence. In 1966, he was appointed Andrew Mellon Professor of Music at the Carnegie Institute of Technology. Later, he served as composer-in-residence at the University of Bridgeport, Connecticut (1972), at Trinity College in Hartford, Connecticut (1973), at Claremont College in California (1974), at Dominican College in California (1974), at Otterbein College in Ohio (1974), at California State University at Fullerton (1975), and at the University of California at Los Angeles (1976). In addition, he has received sixteen honorary doctorates, including those from Columbia University (1978), Johns Hopkins University (1978), and Harvard University (1982).

Thomson has been given numerous prizes and awards in the course of his long and distinguished career. His Pulitzer Prize in 1949 for Louisiana Story has been mentioned previously. During that same year he was elected a member of the National Institute of Arts and Letters (he won the Institute's Gold Medal in 1966 and was named to its board in 1977), and the year before he was made an officer in the French Legion d'Honneur. Among his other awards are: the Creative Arts Award from Brandeis University (1968), the Handel Medallion of the City of New York (1971), the Henry Hadley Medal of the National Association for American Composers and Conductors (1972), the Edward MacDowell Medallion (1977), and a Guggenheim Fellowship. On the occasion of donating a huge collection of his autograph scores and letters to Yale University, a two-day

Thomson Festival was celebrated in New Haven on April 22 and 24, 1979. And, in October of the following year, Kansas City celebrated her native son's 84th birthday with a week-long festival of his music and the preview of a PBS television documentary on his life.   The program was broadcast to the rest of the nation a few weeks later.

In his Chelsea Hotel suite overlooking Manhattan, Virgil Thomson resides these days in active retirement. He continues most of his life-long activities, although on a moderate scale. Full of rich memories and himself richly memorable, he has become something of a national institution.   His aristocratic status was brought to the attention of the nation in 1983 when he was honored for lifetime achievement at the Kennedy Center.   On that occasion Edward Albee observed that Thomson is a precious paradox, "a man whose wisdom is offhand but whose wit is serious,"25 while John Houseman confessed to having been ever "awed by his wisdom, his clarity of vision, and his profound sense."26 Indeed, the qualities of wit, wisdom, and profound sense which Thomson has expressed both through his music and his writings have awed many and deeply influenced the artistic course of the twentieth century.

Notes

1   More detail and amplification of these and other aspects of Thom-
        son's life can be found in Virgil Thomson: His Life and Music
        by Kathleen Hoover and John Cage (New York: Thomas Yoseloff,
        1959) and Virgil Thomson by Virgil Thomson (New York: Knopf,
        1966).
2   Thomson, Thomson, p. 11.
3   Thomson, Thomson, p. 26.
4   Thomson, Thomson, p. 27.
5   Thomson, Thomson, p. 30.
6   Thomson, Thomson, p. 33.
7   Thomson, Thomson, p. 44.
8   Hoover and Cage, Virgil Thomson, p. 36.
9   Thomson, Thomson, p. 54.
10   "Jazz," August, 1924, pp. 465-67.
11   Nearly one a month for a year, beginning with "How Modern Music Gets
        That Way," April, 1925, pp. 46+.
12   Thomson, Thomson, p. 73.
13   Thomson, Thomson, p. 74.
14   Gertrude Stein, The Autobiography of Alice B. Toklas (New York:
        Harcourt-Brace, 1933), p. 279.
15   Thomson, Thomson, p. 89.
16   February 18, 1934, Sect. 9, p. 2.
17   Lucius Beebe, Snoot If You Must (New York: Appleton-Century, 1943),
        p. 168.
18   Thomson, Thomson, p. 275.
19   Minna Lederman, The Life and Death of a Small Magazine ("Modern
        Music," 1924-46) (New York: Institute for Studies in American
        Music, 1983), p. 22.
20   Michael Meckna, The Rise of the American Composer-Critic: Aaron
        Copland, Elliott Carter, Roger Sessions, and Virgil Thomson in
        the Periodical "Modern Music," 1924-1946 (Diss., University of

California at Santa Barbara, 1984), p. 211f.
21 "The Brow that Broke the Mold," Parnassus: Poetry in Review 5 (Spring/Summer, 1977), p. 481.
22 Hoover and Cage, Thomson, p. 203.
23 Thomson, Thomson, pp. 410-11.
24 "Musical Events," The New Yorker 52 (Jan 17, 1977), p. 108
25 Washington Post, December 5, 1983, p. B6.
26 Ibid., p. B15.

Works and Performances

The compositions listed here are classified by genre and arranged chronologically by date of composition. The "See" references identify manuscripts in "Appendix I," e.g., See: A12, and citations in the "Bibliography" sections, e.g., See: B123 or See: T45. Citations following the heading "Brief Mention" indicate short articles or even parts of articles which may be of interest but which did not warrant full annotation. The instrumentation of a given work follows the customary pattern of listing woodwinds first, followed by brasses, timpani, percussion, and strings. For example, 2.2.2.2./4.3.3.1./timp./3 perc./strings means that a work calls for 2 flutes, 2 oboes, 2 clarinets, and 2 bassoons; 4 horns, 3 trumpets, 3 trombones, and 1 tuba; timpani; 3 percussion players; and a full string section of violins, violas, 'cellos, and double basses. Other abbreviations are explained in the Preface, in which may also be found publishers' addresses.

OPERAS AND BALLETS

W1. Four Saints in Three Acts (1928; G. Schirmer; 90 min.) See: A5 & A11 and B7, B17, B26, B31, B36, B45, B60, B67, B75, B84, B88, B97, B103, B110, B115, B116, B125, B128, B131, B132, B134, B137, B138, B140, B141, B145, B146, B147, B148, B149, B150, B154, B156, B157, B158, B160, B164, B171, B177, B181, B188, B189, B190, B192, & B260 and T2 & T147.

Opera in four acts with two prologues
1.1.2.1./2.1.1.0./2 perc./accordion/harmonium/strings
Also published with pf. accompaniment (G. Schirmer)
Also available in abridged (45 min.) version (G. Schirmer)
Mixed chorus (SATB)/ballet/four stage sets
Main soloists: soprano, mezzo-soprano, contralto, tenor, baritone, bass
Minor soloists: 2 sopranos, 2 contraltos, 2 tenors, baritone, bass
Libretto by Gertrude Stein; scenario by Maurice Grosser
Excerpts: "Saints' Procession" (from Act III) for chorus (SATB) and pf. with solos for mezzo-soprano and bass (1928; G. Schirmer), or for men's chorus (TTBB) (ms.; See W72); "Pigeons on

the Grass Alas" (from Act III) for baritone and pf. (1934; G. Schirmer; See W124)

Arranged by Paul Reuter as Four Saints: an Olio for Chamber Orchestra, rev. version by Thomson (1984; G. Schirmer; See W59)

Brief Mention: NYT (Dec 31, 1933): sect. 9, p. 8; NYT (Jan 21, 1934): sec. 10, p. 6; MA 54:7 & 17 (Feb 1934); Literary Digest 117:21 (Feb 3, 1934);Newsweek 3:37-38 (Feb 17, 1934); NYT (Feb 9,1934): 22; NYT (Feb 21, 1934): 22; Commonweal 19:453 (Feb 23, 1934); NYT (Feb 23, 1934): 22; NYT (Feb 25, 1934): sec. 9, pp. 6 & 8; NYHT (Feb 25, 1934); NYT (Feb 27, 1934): 18;Na 138:256+ (Feb 28, 1934); NYT (March 1, 1934): 22;SR 10:519 (March 3, 1934); NYT (March 4, 1934): sec. 9, p. 18; Commonweal 19:525 (March 9, 1934);Literary Digest 117:22 (March 10, 1934); SR 10:572 (March 24, 1934); MM 11:146 (March-April 1934); American Magazine of the Arts 27:211+ (April 1934); Catholic World 139:87+ (April 1934); Theatre Arts 18:246+ (April 1934); NYT (April 3, 1934): 27; Na 138:396+ (April 4, 1934); NRe 78:246 (April 11, 1934); NYT (April 11, 1934): 24; American Mercury 32:104+ (May 1934); MA 54:12 (Aug 1934); NYT (Nov 9, 1934): 24; MM 12:193 (May-June 1935); MM 13:19 & 56 (March-April 1936); MM 13:5 (May-June 1936); MM 17:56 (Nov-Dec 1939); MM 18:4+ (Nov-Dec 1940); NYT (May 28, 1941): 32; MM 18:259 & 266 (May-June 1941); NYer 17:67 (June 7, 1941); Time 37:65+ (June 9, 1941); MM 19:197 (March-April 1942); MM 20:101, 104 & 107 (Jan-Feb 1943); MM 20:231 (May-June 1943); MM 21:118 (Jan-Feb 1944); MM 21:259 (May-June 1944); MM 23:4 & 94 (Winter 1946); NYT (May 25, 1947): sec. 2, p. 9; Gr 26:125 (Jan 1949); MC 139:23 (March 1, 1949); MA 69:36 (May 1949); Music & Letters 30:290+ (July 1949); MQ 35:210 & 217 (1949); MR 10:314 (Nov 1949); NYer 28:121+ (April 26, 1952); Time 59:42 (April 28, 1952); Newsweek 39:52 (April 28, 1952); Na 174:437+ (May 3, 1952); SR 35:33 (May 3, 1952); New Leader 35:27 (May 5, 1952); International Musician 50:37 (May 1952); Commonweal 56:117 (May 9, 1952); MA 72:7 (May 1952); NYT (May 31, 1952): 13; Catholic World 175:228 (June 1952); Theatre Arts 36:19 (June 1952); School & Society 75:393+ (June 21, 1952); Op 3:398 (July 1952); HF 4:50 (July 1954); NYT (July 27, 1954): 16; MA 74:14 (Aug 1954); Bucknell Review 5:1 (No. 1., Dec 1954); AM 199:53+ (March 1957); MA 80:29 (Jan 15, 1960); ARG 31:518+ & 521+ (Feb 1965); HF 15:70 (Feb 1965); HSR 14:64-67 (March 1965); ON 29:34 (April 3, 1965); Music & Musicians 13:29 (Aug 1965); NYT (April 26, 1970): 19; ON 35:23 (Oct 10, 1970); NYT (Oct 24, 1971): sect. 2, p. 9; NYT (Jan 16, 1972): 65; NYT (Dec 15, 1972): 60; NYT (Dec 22, 1972): 17; ON 36:32 (Feb 19, 1972); HF 22:MA31 (April 1972); HF 22:MA20 (June 1972); NYT (Feb 15, 1973): 50; NYT (Feb 18, 1973): sect. 2, p. 17; NYT (Feb 24, 1973): 17; ON 37:10+ (Feb 17, 1973); NYer 49:102+ (March 3, 1973); SR of the Sciences 1:105 (March 24, 1973); ON 37:22+ (April 7, 1973); MJ 31:55 (April 1973); Music & Musicians 21:56 (May 1973); Opernwelt 5:22+ (May 1973); HF 23:MA13 (June 1973); Tonfallet 8:1 (April 20, 1979); Opera Canada 21:39 (No. 2, 1980); New York Magazine 14:77 (Nov 30, 1981); Village Voice 26:94 (Dec 2-8, 1981); St 46:112 (Dec 1981); Op 33:154+ (Feb 1982); ON 46:30+ (Feb 27, 1982); HF 32:MA21+ (April 1982); Op 34:918+ (Aug 1983); Symphony 34:34 (Oct-Nov 1983). Also: What to

Listen For in Music by Aaron Copland.   New York: McGraw-Hill, 1939; rev. ed. 1957. (Mentor paperback, 1964), p241.   The Opera: A History of its Creation and Performances, 1600-1941 by Wallace Brockway & Herbert Weinstock.   New York: Simon & Schuster, 1941, p. 482.   Twentieth-Century Harmony by Vincent Persichetti.   New York: W.W. Norton, 1961, pp. 42 & 210.   A Short History of Opera by Donald Jay Grout.   2nd ed.   New York: Columbia University Press, 1965, p. 579.   The New Book of Modern Composers by David Ewen.   3rd ed., revised and enlarged.   New York: Alfred Knopf, 1969, p. 48.   Composers of Tomorrow's Music by David Ewen.   New York: Dodd, Mead, & Co., 1971, p. 148.   Last Operas & Plays by Gertrude Stein.   Edited by Carl van Vechten.   New York: Vantage, 1975, pp. ix-xii.

Premiere: Feb 8, 1934; Hartford, CT; a Friends and Enemies of Modern Music production; Avery Memorial Hall; John Houseman, director; Alexander Smallens, cond.; Florine Stettheimer, scenery & costumes; Frederick Ashton, staging & choreography; Abner Dorsey as Compère; Altonell Hines as Commere; Edward Matthews as St. Ignatius; Beatrice Robinson-Wayne as St. Teresa I; Bruce Howard as St. Teresa II; Embry Bonner as St. Chavez

W2.   Filling Station (1937; Boosey & Hawkes; 24 min.) See: B128, B166, B177, B181, B192, & B260

Ballet in twelve scenes
2.2.2.2./4.3.3.1. (or 2.2.3.0.)/timp./2 perc./harp/pf./ strings
Choreography by Lew Christensen
Also arranged for pf. (1937; Boosey & Hawkes; See W179)
Also arranged as orchestral suite (1937; Boosey & Hawkes; See W15)
No. 6, "Family Life," from the pf. portrait of John Mosher (1935; Boosey & Hawkes; See W224)
Scenario by Lincoln Kirstein
Commissioned by Lincoln Kirstein for Ballet Caravan
1.   Introduction
2.   Mac's Dance (Pas Seul)
3.   Scene (Mac and Motorist)
4.   Acrobatics (Mac and Truck Drivers)
5.   Scene (State Trooper and Truck Drivers)
6.   Family Life (Motorist's Family and Trucker Drivers)
7.   Tango (Rich Girl and Boy)
8.   Valse à trois (Rich Girl, Boy, Mac)
9.   Big Apple (Ensemble)
10. Hold Up (Ensemble)
11. Chase (Ensemble)
12. Finale (Ensemble)

Brief Mention: MM 15:100-01 & 122 (Jan-Feb 1938); NYT (Feb 19, 1938): 18; MM 15:186 (March-April 1938); MM 17:188 (March-April 1940); MM 20:128 (Jan-Feb 1943); MM 20:199 & 211 (March-April 1943); MM 23:38 (Nov-Dec 1944); MM 23:36 & 216 (Winter 1946); MQ 34:8 (1948)

Premieres:
With pf.: Jan 6, 1938; Hartford, CT; Avery Memorial Theater;

Ballet Caravan
With orchestra: Feb 18, 1938; New York City; Work   Projects
Administration-Federal Music Theatre; Ballet Caravan; The
Greenwich Orchestra

W3.   The Mother of Us All (1947; G. Schirmer; 103 min.) See: B7, B31,
B33, B37, B43, B67, B75, B77, B89, B97, B116, B128, B138, B146,
B149, B152, B157, B158, B160, B164, B168, B177, & B190 and T67

Opera in two acts
1.1.2.1/2.2.1.0./2 perc./harp/celesta/pf./strings
25 singers; 6 silent actors; 5 stage sets
Main soloists: 2 sopranos, contralto, 2 tenors, baritone, bass
Published with pf. accompaniment (G. Schirmer)
Also arranged as orchestral suite (1949; G. Schirmer; See W35)
Libretto by Gertrude Stein; scenario by Maurice Grosser
Commissioned by the Alice M. Ditson Fund

Brief Mention: NYT (June 9, 1946): sect. 2, p. 4; NYT (April 17,
1947): 34; NYT (May 8, 1947): 30; Newsweek 29:94 (May 19, 1947);
Time 49:47 (May 19, 1947); Commonweal 46:167+ (May 30, 1947); Na
164:667 (May 31, 1947); NRe 116:33 (June 2, 1947); Theatre Arts
31:17 (July 1947); School & Society 66:67 (July 12, 1947); MR
10:70+ (Feb 1949); MQ 35:210 & 219 (1949); New York Philharmonic
Program Notes (April 2, 1950); SR 33:56 (April 15, 1950); NYT
(April 15, 1956): sect. 2, p. 7; NYT (April 17, 1956): 27; SR
39:34 (May 5, 1956); Na 182:438 (May 19, 1956); MC 153:35 (June
1956); Op 7:423 (July 1956); Commonweal 64:634 (Sept 28, 1956);
NYT (Dec 7, 1961): 53; Op 14:396 (June 1963); NYT (April 1,
1964): 42; ON 28:27 (May 2, 1964); MA 84:29 (May 1964); NYT (Jan
29, 1967): 67; ON 31:32 (March 25, 1967); ON 35:4 (April 10,
1971); NYT (Aug 2, 1971): 12; ON 36:23 (Sept 1971); NYT (Nov 28,
1971): 82; HF 21:MA 10+ (Nov 1971); NYT (July 3, 1972): 7; NYT
(Nov 27, 1972): 43; ON 37:25 (Jan 20, 1973); HF 23:MA28 (March
1973); HF 23:MA18 (Dec 1973); ON 38:32 (June 1974); NYT (Dec 14,
1975): 73; ON 40:41 (May 1976); Wall Street Journal (Aug 13,
1976): 6; Time 108:37 (Aug 23, 1976); HF 26:MA26+ (Sept 1976);
ON 41:67 (Sept 1976); Op 27:848 (Sept 1976); Opernwelt 17:37
(Oct 1976); Op 27:1137+ (Dec 1976); St 38:89+ (June 1977); HF
27:92+ (July 1977); ARG 40:30 (Aug 1977); ON 42:72 (April 8,
1978); Op 3:818 (Aug 1979); Op 31:696+ (July 1980); Village
Voice 28:83 (April 5, 1983); NYer 59:115+ (April 11, 1983);
Village Voice 28:91 (April 19, 1983); ON 47:45+ (June 1983); Ms.
Magazine 12:31+ (July 1983); MT 124:444 (July 1983); Op 34:744
(July 1983); HF 33:MA27 (Aug 1983); Opera Canada 25:32 (No. 2,
1984); NYer 60:98+ (June 18, 1984); Ch 33:24+ (July 1984). See
also: A Short History of Opera by Donald Jay Grout. 2nd ed. New
York: Columbia Unversity Press, 1965, p. 579. Last Operas and
Plays by Gertrude Stein. Edited by Carl van Vechten. New York:
Vantage, 1975, pp. ix-xii. Music and Ballet, 1973-1983 by
Bernard Haggin. New York: Horizon Press, 1984, pp. 13 & 162.

Premiere: May 7, 1947; New York City; Brander Matthews Hall,
Columbia University; Columbia Theatre Associates Orchestra; Otto
Luening, cond.; John Taras, sets; Paul Dupont, costumes; Dorothy

Dow as Susan B. Anthony; Bertram Rowe as Daniel Webster; Robert
Grooters as Virgil Thomson; Belva Kibler as Anne; Hazel Gravell
as Gertrude Stein; Ruth King as Indiana Elliot; Alice Howland as
Constance Fletcher; William Horne as Jo the Loiterer; Carlton
Sunday as Chris; Robert Sprecher as John Adams

W4. Bayou (staged 1952; G. Schirmer; 14 min.)

Ballet with music from "Acadian Songs and Dances" from the film
Louisiana Story (1948; See W320)
2.2.2.2./2.2.2.0./2 perc./harp/accordion (or pf.)/strings
Choreography by George Balanchine; second version by Ruthanna
Boris

Brief Mention: NYT (Feb 22, 1952): 14

Premiere: Feb 21, 1952; New York City; New York Center for Music
and Drama; New York City Ballet

W5. The Harvest According (arranged 1952; ms.; 40 min.)

Ballet with music from Symphony on a Hymn Tune (1928; Southern;
See W10), Concerto for Violoncello and Orchestra (1950; Ricor-
di/Belwin Mills; See W36), and Suite from The Mother of Us All
(1949; G. Schirmer; See W35)
2.2.2.2./4.2.3.1./timp./2 perc./harp/strings
Choreography by Agnes de Mille

Brief Mention: NYT (Oct 2, 1952): 32; MA 72:6 (Nov 1, 1952)

Premiere: Oct 1, 1952; New York City; Metropolitan Opera House;
Ballet Theater Co.; Ballet Theatre Orchestra; Virgil Thomson,
cond.

W6. Lord Byron (1966-68; Southern; 99 min.) See: B7, B61,B67, B69,
B74, B75, B77, B78, B83, B91, B92, B143 & B229

Opera in three acts
2.2.2.2./4.2.3.1./timp./perc. (including xyl., marimba, vib.)/harp/
organ/strings
16 soloists: 4 sopranos, 2 mezzo-sopranos, 1 contralto, 2 tenors,
5 baritones, 1 bass-baritone, 1 bass; 6 male madrigalists: 2
tenors, 2 baritones, 2 basses; mixed chorus; SATB; boy choir.
5 stage sets
Libretto by Jack Larson
Published with pf. accompaniment and German trans. by John Gutman
(Southern)
Excerpts: Ballet from Act III, Scene 2 of the original production
is not included in the published score but is published
separately as the Third Symphony (1972; Boosey & Hawkes; See
W56) and is also arranged for pf. solo. (1966-68; ms.; See W197)
Commissioned by The Ford Foundation and The Koussevitzky Founda-
tion

Brief Mention: NYT (Nov 28, 1965): sect. 2, p. 13; NYT (April 8,

1966): 26; HF 16:112 (June 1966); NYT (Oct 21, 1968): 59; NYT (Nov 7, 1969): 39; SR 52:58 (Nov 22, 1969); HF 20:MA12 (Jan 1970); Boletin Interamericano de Musica 75-76:64 (Jan-March 1970); Nuova Rivista Musicale Italiana 6:256+ (No. 2, 1972); NYT (March 14, 1972): 50; NYT (April 9, 1972): sec. 2, p. 17; Vg 159:86+ (April 15, 1972); NYT (April 16, 1972): sect. 8, p. 1; NYT (April 22, 1972): 38; NYer 48:106 (April 29, 1972); Time 99:67 (May 1, 1972); Variety 266:81 (May 10, 1972); SR 55:20+ (May 20, 1972); Opernwelt 7:22 (July 1972); ASCAP Today 6:32 (July 1972); MT 113:689 (July 1972); PP 65:24+ (No. 2, 1973); NYT (Dec 17, 1975): 67.

Premiere: April 20, 1972; New York City; Juilliard American Opera Theatre; The Juilliard Orchestra and Opera Chorus; The Trinity Parish Choir of Southport, CT; John Houseman, Director; Gerhard Samuel, cond; Alvin Ailey, choreography; David Mitchell, set design; Patricia Zipprodt, costumes; Grayson Hurst as Lord Byron; Lenus Carlson as Thomas Moore; Walter Hook as John Hobhouse; Frederick Choepflin as John Murray; Frederick Burchinal as Count Gamba; David Wilder as John Ireland; Carolyn Val-Schmidt as The Hon. Mrs. Leigh; Lynne Wickenden as Lady Byron; Hari Katz as Contessa Guiccioli; Barrie Smith as Lady Melbourne; Barbara Henricks as Lady Charlotte; Jean Fuerstenau as Lady Jane; Ann Farr as Miss Rawdon; Diane Schwartz as Lady Caroline

W7.   Hurray!   (staged 1975; Leeds/Belwin-Mills; 15 min.)

Ballet to Symphony No. 2 in C Major (1931; Leeds/Belwin Mills; See W12)
3.3.3.3./4.2.3.1./timp./2 perc./strings
Originally entitled Fourth of July, 1900
Choreography by Erick Hawkins

Brief Mention: Symphony News 26:9+ (Feb 1975); NYT (Sept 11, 1975): 36; NYT (Sept 13, 1975): 14; Dance 49:21+ (Nov 1975); HF 25:MA15 (Dec 1975)

Premiere: July 5, 1975; Cleveland, OH; Blossom Music Center; The Erick Hawkins Dance Co.; The Cleveland Orchestra; Erick Kunzel, cond.

W8.   Parson Weems and the Cherry Tree (Oct 1975; Boosey & Hawkes; 25 min.)

Ballet
1 fl.-pic./1 cl.-bass cl./1 tpt.-flügelhorn/1 tbn./1 perc./1 vn./ 1 contrabass.
Choreography and scenario by Erick Hawkins
Commissioned by The Foundation for Modern Dance Inc.
Also arranged for pf. (1975; Boosey & Hawkes; See W199)

Premiere: Nov 1, 1975; Amherst, MA; Fine Arts Center Concert Hall; University of Massachusetts; The Erick Hawkins Dance Co.

ORCHESTRAL AND BAND WORKS

W9.   Two Sentimental Tangos (1923; ms.; 5 min.) See: A10 & A21

      Arranged for orchestra from the pf. original (1923; ms.; See W159)
      2.2.2.2./4.2.3.1./2 perc./harp/strings
      1. Slow and Smooth
      2. Not Fast

W10. Symphony on a Hymn Tune (1928; Southern; 19 min.)See: B128, B141,
         B146, B160, B177, B181, B192, B229, & B260

      2.2.2.2./4.2.3.1./timp./3 perc./strings
      Four movements to be played without pause
      1. Introduction and Allegro   3. Allegretto
      2. Andante cantabile   4. Allegro
      Also arranged for pf. 4 hands by John Kirkpatrick (1928; ms.)
      Portions used for the ballet The Harvest According (1952; ms.; See
         W5)

      Brief Mention: MQ 18:12 (1932); NYT (Feb 23, 1945): 20; Time 45:73
         (March 5, 1945); MM 22:182 & 200 (March-April 1945); MM 23:115
         (Spring 1946); MQ 35:214 (1949); Notes 13:130 (Dec 1955); MA
         76:24 (Nov 1, 1956); San Francisco Symphony Program Notes (Feb
         12, 1958): 365; ARG 32:596 (March 1966); American Ensemble 3:3
         (No. 1, 1980). See also: The Concert Companion by Robert Bogar
         and Louis Biancolli. New York: McGraw-Hill, 1947, pp. 740-1.

      Premiere: Feb 22, 1945; New York City; Carnegie Hall; The Philhar-
         monic Society of New York; Virgil Thomson, cond.

W11. Stabat Mater (1931; Boosey & Hawkes; 5 min.)

      Text in French by Max Jacob
      Arranged for voice and string orchestra from the original for
         voice and string quartet (1931; Boosey & Hawkes; See W121)

W12. Symphony No. 2 in C Major (1931; rev. 1941; Leeds/Belwin Mills; 15
         min.) See: B26, B44, & B177

      Originally Piano Sonata No. 1 (1929; MCA/Belwin Mills; See W169)
      3.3.3.3./4.2.3.1./timp./2 perc./strings
      Three movements to be played without pause
      1. Allegro con brio
      2. Andante
      3. Allegro
      Also arranged for piano 4 hands (1932; Leeds/Belwin Mills; See
         W177)
      Symphony No. 2 also used for the ballet Hurray! (1975; Leeds/Bel-
         win Mills; See W7)

      Brief Mention: MM 19:187 (March-April 1942); MM 20:125
         (Jan-Feb 1943); MQ 35:215 (1949); New York Philharmonic Program
         Notes (Nov 30, 1950); MA 70:32 (Dec 15, 1950); Notes 13:130 (Dec
         1955)

Premiere: Nov 17, 1941; Seattle, WA; The Music Hall; Seattle Symphony Orchestra; Sir Thomas Beecham, cond.

W13. Suite from "The Plow That Broke the Plains" (Feb 1936; G. Schirmer; 15 min.) See: B42 & B128

From the film by Pare Lorentz (1936; See W316)
1.1.3.1./2.2.2.0./2 perc. (including timp.)/banjo/guitar (or pf., harp)/strings
1. Prelude   4. Blues (Speculation)
2. Pastorale (Grass)   5. Drought
3. Cattle   6. Devastation
Also arranged for pf. (1936; G. Schirmer; See W178)

Brief Mention: MM 20:51 (Nov-Dec 1942); MM 20:179 (March-April 1943); MM 22:126 (Nov-Dec 1944); MM 22:200 (March-April 1945); MM 22:264 (May-June 1945); MQ 39:308+ (1952); ARG 28:704 (May 1962). See also: A Modern Guide to Symphonic Music by Alfred Frankenstein. New York: Merideth Press, 1966.

Premiere: Jan 2, 1943; Philadelphia, PA; The Academy of Music; Philadelphia Orchestra; Virgil Thomson, cond.

W14. Suite from "The River" (1937; Southern; 24 min.)See: B42

From the film by Pare Lorentz (1937; See W317)
1.2.2.1./2.2.2.0./2 perc.(including timp.)/banjo/strings
1. The Old South
2. Industrial Expansion in the Mississippi Valley
3. Soil Erosion and Flood
4. Finale
5-6 minutes from the first movement used in the ABC Circle film The Day After (1983) by Nicholas Meyer
Second movement used in the ABC News Film Suddenly an Eagle (1975; See W325)

Brief Mention: MM 18:246 (May-June 1941); NYT (Jan 6, 1943): 18; MM 22:200 (March-April 1945); ARG 28:704 (May 1962)

Premiere: Jan 12, 1943; New York City; The Brooklyn Academy of Music; Brooklyn Philharmonic Symphony Orchestra; Sir Thomas Beecham, cond.

W15. Suite from "Filling Station" (Nov 1937; Boosey & Hawkes; 15 min.)

Arranged from the ballet score (1937; Boosey & Hawkes; See W2)
2.2.2.2./4.2.3.1. (or 2.2.3.0.)/timp./2 or 3 perc./pf./strings
1. Prelude   5. Tango
2. Mac's Dance   6. Big Apple
3. Scene   7. Finale
4. Acrobatics

Brief Mention: MM 18:201 (March-April 1941); MM 19:110 & 136 (Jan-Feb 1942). See also: The Concert Companion by Robert Bogar and Louis Biancolli. New York: McGraw-Hill, 1947, pp. 741-2.

Premieres:
   On radio: Feb 2, 1941; New York City;Station WNYC; National
   Youth Administration Symphony Orchestra; Fritz Mahler, cond.
   In concert: Dec 14, 1941; New York City; Carnegie Hall; Phila-
   delphia Orchestra; Artur Rodzinski, cond.

W16. The John Mosher Waltzes (1937; Boosey & Hawkes; 2 min. 10 sec.)

   Arranged from the pf. portrait of John Mosher (1935; Boosey &
   Hawkes; See W224); also published as No. 6, "Family Life," from
   ballet Filling Station (1937; Boosey & Hawkes; See W2)
   2.2.2.2./4.3.3.1. (or 2.2.3.0.)/timp./2 perc./pf./harp/strings

W17. The Mayor LaGuardia Waltzes (1942; G. Schirmer; 7 min.) See: B177

   Portrait for orchestra
   2.2.2.2./4.2.3.0./4 perc./strings
   Commissioned by Andre Kostelanetz

   Brief Mention: Time 39:53 (May 11, 1942); NYT (July 24, 1942): 22;
   MM 20:31-2 & 39 (Nov-Dec 1942)

   Premiere: May 14, 1942; Cincinnati, OH; Music Hall; Cincinnati
   Symphony Orchestra; Andre Kostelanetz, cond.

W18. Canons for Dorothy Thompson (1942; G. Schirmer; 3 min.)

   Portrait for orchestra
   2.2.2.2./4.2.3.0/3 perc./strings
   Commissioned by Andre Kostelanetz for the New York Philharmonic
   Orchestra

   Brief Mention: Time 39:53 (May 11, 1952); NYT (July 24, 1942): 22;
   MM 20:31-2 & 39 (Nov-Dec 1942)

   Premiere: July 23, 1942; New York City; Lewisohn Stadium; New York
   Philharmonic Orchestra; Andre Kostelanetz, cond.

W19. Barcarolle for Woodwinds (1944; G. Schirmer; 1 min. 30 sec.)

   Arranged from the pf. portrait of Georges Hugnet (1940; G. Schirmer; See W238)
   Fl./ob./Eng. hn./cl./bass cl./bn.

   Brief Mention: MC 143:29 (May 15, 1951); Notes 9:166 (Dec 1951)

   Premiere: Nov 29, 1946; Pittsburgh, PA; Syria Mosque; Pittsburgh
   Symphony Orchestra; Virgil Thomson, cond.

W20. Bugles and Birds (1944; G. Schirmer; 2 min. 15 sec.)

   Arranged from the pf. portrait of Pablo Picasso (1940; G. Schirmer; See W243)
   2.2.2.2./4.2.3.0./no perc./strings

Brief Mention: MM 22:108 (Jan-Feb 1945); MM 23:66+ (Winter 1946); Time 52:63 (Dec 20, 1948); MC 139:16 (Jan 15, 1949); HF 32:MA27 (Aug 1982)

Premiere: Nov 17, 1944; Philadelphia, PA; Academy of Music; Philadelphia Orchestra; Virgil Thomson, cond.

W21.   Cantabile for Strings (1944; G. Schirmer; 4 min. 30 sec.) See: B75

Arranged from the pf. portrait of Nicholas de Chatelain (1940; G. Schirmer; See W253)

Brief Mention: MM 22:108 (Jan-Feb 1945); MM 23:66+ (Winter 1946)

Premiere: Nov 17, 1944; Philadelphia, PA; Academy of Music; Philadelphia Orchestra; Virgil Thomson, cond.

W22.   Fanfare for France (1944; Boosey & Hawkes; 3 min.) See: B177

Arranged from the pf. portrait of Max Kahn (1940; G. Schirmer; See W237)
4 hn./3 tpt./3 tbn./side drum/field drum
Commissioned by the Cincinnati Symphony Orchestra

Brief Mention: MM 20:190 (March-April 1943); NYT (June 30, 1967): 29

Premiere: Jan 15, 1943; Cincinnati, OH; Music Hall; Cincinnati Symphony Orchestra; Eugene Goossens, cond.

W23.   Fugue (1944; G. Schirmer; 2 min. 30 sec.)

Arranged from the pf. portrait of Alexander Smallens (1940; G. Schirmer; See W257)
2.2.2.2./4.2.3.0./snare drum/strings

Brief Mention: MM 22:108 (Jan-Feb 1945); MM 23:66+ (Winter 1946)

Premiere: Nov 17, 1944; Philadelphia, PA; Music Academy; Philadelphia Orchestra; Virgil Thomson, cond.

W24.   Meditation (1944; G. Schirmer; 1 min. 30 sec.)

Arranged from the pf. portrait of Jere Abbott (1935; G. Schirmer; See W227)
2.2.2.2./2.2.2.0./strings
Commissioned by the San Antonio Symphony Orchestra

Brief Mention: HF 32:MA27 (Aug 1982)

Premiere: Nov 21, 1948; Vancouver, British Columbia, Canada; Orpheum Theatre; Vancouver Symphony Orchestra; Jacques Singer, cond.

W25.   Pastorale (1944; G. Schirmer; 3 min. 15 sec.)

Arranged from the pf. portrait of Aaron Copland entitled
  Persistently Pastoral (1942; Boosey & Hawkes; See W266)
2.2.2.2./4.2.3.1./strings
Featured in film "Tuesday in November" (1945; See W319)

Brief Mention: HF 32:MA27 (Aug 1982)

Premiere: March 15, 1945; New York City; New York Center for Music
  and Dance; New York City Symphony Orchestra; Virgil Thomson,
  cond.

W26. Percussion Piece (1944; G. Schirmer; 2 min. 30 sec.)

Arranged from the pf. portrait of Jessie K. Lasell (1941; ms.; See
  W260)
2.2.2.2./4.2.3.0./perc./strings

Brief Mention: MM 22:108 (Jan-Feb 1945); MM 23:66+ (Winter 1946)

Premiere: Nov 17, 1944; Philadelphia, PA; Academy of Music; Philadelphia Orchestra; Virgil Thomson, cond.

W27. Tango Lullaby (1944; G. Schirmer; 3 min. 30 sec.)

Arranged from the pf. portrait of Flavie Alvarez de Toledo (1940;
  G. Schirmer; See W241)
Fl./pic./Eng. hn./cl./bn./bells/strings

Brief Mention: MM 23:66+ (Winter 1946); NYT (Oct 14, 1971): 54

Premiere: Nov 17, 1944; Philadelphia, PA; Academy of Music; Philadelphia Orchestra; Virgil Thomson, cond.

W28. Fugue and Chorale on "Yankee Doodle" (1945; G. Schirmer; 4 min.)

From film "Tuesday in November" by John Houseman (1945; See W319)
1.1.2.1./2.2.2.0./2 perc./harp/strings

Premiere: April 16, 1969; Atlanta, GA; Glenn Memorial Auditorium,
  Emory University; The Emory Chamber Orchestra; William Lemonds,
  cond.

W29. The Seine at Night (Dec 1947; G. Schirmer; 9 min.) See: A2 and
  B18, B64, B177, & B229

One of the "Pictures for Orchestra" with Wheat Field at Noon
  (1948; G. Schirmer; See W32) and Sea Piece with Birds (1952; G.
  Schirmer; See W38)
3.3.3.3./4.3.3.1./2 perc./2 harps/strings
Commissioned by the Kansas City Philharmonic

Brief Mention: MQ 35:220 (1949); MC 141:28 (May 1, 1950);
  Cincinnati Symphony Orchestra Program Notes (Jan 8, 1954): 329+;
  Philadelphia Orchestra Program Notes (Jan 22, 1954): 401; NYT
  (Feb 3, 1954): 20; NYT (Nov 18, 1971): 57; HF 22:MA23 (Feb

1972). See also: The New York Philharmonic Guide to the Symphony by Edward Downes. New York: Walker & Co., 1976, pp. 979-81.

Premiere: Feb 24, 1948; Kansas City, MO; Music Hall; Kansas City Philharmonic; Efrem Kurtz, cond.

W30. Suite from "Louisiana Story" (1948; G. Schirmer; 18 min.) See: B177

From the film by Robert Flaherty (1948; See W320)
2.2.2.2./4.2.3.1./timp./2 perc./harp/strings
1. Pastoral (The Bayou and the Marsh Buggy)
2. Chorale (The Derrick Arrives)
3. Passacaglia (Robbing the Alligator's Nest)
4. Fugue (Boy Fights Alligator)
Second movement also arranged for woodwinds by Frank Erickson (1967; G. Schirmer)
Fourth movement available separately from G. Schirmer

Brief Mention: MA 68:28 (Dec 15, 1948); New York Philharmonic Program Notes (Jan 29, 1949); Proceedings of the Music Teachers National Association, Series 43:40 (1940); Variety 174:2 (May 2, 1949); Music Clubs Magazine 29:16 (Dec 1949); Boston Symphony Concert Bulletin 23:1260 (April 21, 1950); Notes 8:130+ (Dec 1950); Philadelphia Orchestra Program Notes (Jan 11, 1952): 334+; NYT (July 27, 1954): 16; MA 74:14 (Aug 1954); San Francisco Symphony Program Notes (April 25, 1957): 831+; Philadelphia Orchestra Program Notes (March 28-29, 1975): 19+. See also: A Modern Guide to Symphonic Music by Alfred Frankenstein. New York: Merideth Press, 1966.

Premiere: Nov 26, 1948; Philadelphia, PA; Academy of Music; Philadelphia Orchestra; Eugene Ormandy, cond.

W31. Acadian Songs and Dances from "Louisiana Story" (1948; G. Schirmer; 14 min.)

From the film by Robert Flaherty (1948; See W320)
2.2.2.2./2.2.2.0./2 perc./harp/accordion (or pf.)/strings
1. Sadness   5. Super-Sadness
2. Papa's Tune   6. Walking Song
3. A Narrative   7. The Squeeze-Box
4. The Alligator and the 'Coon

Brief Mention: Philadelphia Orchestra Program Notes (Jan 11, 1952): 334+; Music and Musicians 14:44 (Sept 1965)

Premiere: Jan 11, 1951; Philadelphia, PA; Academy of Music; Philadelphia Orchestra; Eugene Ormandy, cond.

W32. Wheat Field at Noon (1948; G. Schirmer; 7 min.)See: B26, B177, & B229

One of the "Pictures for Orchestra" with The Seine at Night (1947; G. Schirmer; See W29) and Sea Piece with Birds (1952; G. Schir-

mer; See W38)
3.3.3.3./4.3.3.0./2 perc./xyl./harp/strings
Commissioned by the Louisville Philharmonic Society

Brief Mention: Time 52:63 (Dec 20, 1948); MC 139:16 (Jan 15,
1949); MA 69:367 (Feb 1949); New York Philharmonic Program Notes
(March 24, 1949); MQ 37:255 (1951); Cincinnati Symphony Orchestra Program Notes (Jan 8, 1954): 329+; Philadelphia Orchestra
Program Notes (Jan 22, 1954): 401+; NYT (Feb 3, 1954): 20;
Musical Opinion 78:351 (March 1955); MQ 41:77 (1955); Notes
13:130 (Dec 1955); NYT (Nov 18, 1971): 57; HF 22:MA23 (Feb 1972)

Premiere: Dec 7, 1948; Louisville, KY; Columbia Auditorium; Louisville Philharmonic Orchestra; Virgil Thomson, cond.

W33. At the Beach: Concert Waltz for Trumpet and Band (Jan 15, 1949;
Carl Fischer; 4 min. 40 sec.)

Originally Le Bains-Bar for vn. and pf. (1929; ms.;See W168)
2 pic./fl./2 ob./all cl./2 bn./4 sax./4 cornet/tpt./4 hn./3 tbn./
2 bar./2 tubas/timp./2 perc.
Commissioned by the Goldman Band

Brief Mention: Notes 22:1102 (March 1966); NYT (June 30, 1967): 29

Premiere: July 21, 1951; New York City; Band Shell, Central Park;
Guggenheim Memorial Concert; The Goldman Band, Richard Franko
Goldman, cond.; Edna White, cornet

W34. A Solemn Music (May 1949; G. Schirmer; 7 min.) See: B19, B165, &
B229

2 pic./2 fl./2 ob./2 bn./all cl./4 sax./3 cornet/2 tpt./4 hn./3
tbn./2 bar./2 tuba/timp./2 perc.
Also arranged for orchestra (1961; G. Schirmer; See W45)

Brief Mention: Boletin Interamericano de Musica 48:15 (July 1949);
MQ 36:594 (1950); Notes 7:44 (June 1950); MQ 41:407 (1955); NYT
(June 30, 1967): 29. See also: Twentieth-Century Harmony by
Vincent Persichetti. New York: W.W. Norton, 1961, p. 74.

Premiere: June 17, 1949; New York City; Band Shell, Central Park;
Guggenheim Memorial Concert; The Goldman Band; Richard Franko
Goldman, cond.

W35. Suite from "The Mother of Us All" (1949; G. Schirmer; 18 min.)

Arranged from the opera (1947; G. Schirmer; See W3)
1.1.2.1./2.2.1.0./2 perc.(including timp.)/harp/pf./strings
1. Prelude   3. Wedding Hymn and Finale
2. Cold Weather   4. A Political Meeting
Portions used for the ballet The Harvest According (1952; ms.; See
W5)

Brief Mention: New York Philharmonic Program Notes (April 2, 1950)

Premiere: Jan 17, 1950; Knoxville, TN; Bijou Theatre; Knoxville Symphony Orchestra; Virgil Thomson, cond.

W36. Concerto for Violoncello and Orchestra (1950; Ricordi/Belwin Mills; 21 min.) See: B22, B39, B64, B128, B146, B177, & B229

2.2.2.3./4.2.0.0./3 perc./harp/celeste/strings
1. Rider on the Plains
2. Variations on a Southern Hymn
3. Children's Games
Also arranged for vc. and pf. (1950; Ricordi/Belwin Mills; See W186)
Portions used for the ballet The Harvest According (1952; ms.; See W5)

Brief Mention: MC 141:3 (April 15, 1950); Chesterian 25:49 (Oct 1950); MA 73:24 (Jan 1, 1953); Stradivarius 84:225 (Aug 1973)

Premiere: March 24, 1950; Philadelphia, PA; Academy of Music; Philadelphia Orchestra; Paul Olefsky, vc.; Eugene Ormandy, cond.

W37. Five Songs from William Blake (1951; Southern; 18 min.)

Arranged for baritone and orchestra (2.2.2.2./4.2.3.1. (or 2.1.1.0.)/2 perc./harp/strings) from the original for baritone and pf. (1951; Southern; See W130)

Brief Mention: MC 145:14 (March 15, 1952); Philadelphia Orchestra Program Notes (Oct 10, 1952); Notes 12:154 (Dec 1954); MQ 41:77 (1955); MA 81:44 (Dec 1961); National Association of Teachers of Singing Bulletin 23:16+ (No. 3, 1967)

Premiere: Feb 5, 1952; Louisville, KY; Louisville Orchestra; Mack Harrell, baritone

W38. Sea Piece with Birds (Nov 1952; G. Schirmer; 5 min.) See: B64, B177, & B229

One of the"Pictures for Orchestra" with The Seine at Night (1947; G. Schirmer; See W29) and Wheat Field at Noon (1948; G. Schirmer; See W32)
3.3.3.3./4.3.3.0./2 perc./harp/strings
Commissioned by the Dallas Symphony Orchestra

Brief Mention: Cincinnati Symphony Orchestra Program Notes (Jan 8, 1954): 329+; Philadelphia Orchestra Program Notes (Jan 22, 1954): 401; NYT (Feb 3, 1954):20; Musical Opinion 78:351 (March 1955); Notes 13:130+ (Dec 1955); Buffalo Philharmonic Program Notes (March 19, 1967): 12; HF 22:MA23 (Feb 1972); NYT (Nov 18, 1971): 57

Premiere: Dec 10, 1952; Dallas, TX; McFarlin Memorial Auditorium; The Dallas Symphony Orchestra; Walter Hendl, cond.

W39. Concerto for Flute, Strings, Harp, and Percussion (1954;

Ricordi/Belwin Mills; 13 min. 30 sec.) See: B20, B128, & B177

Portrait of Roger Baker
1 or 2 harps/celesta/1 perc./strings
1. Rapsodico (unaccompanied)
2. Lento
3. Ritmico
Also arranged for fl. and pf. (1954; Ricordi/Belwin Mills; See W191)
Commissioned by Efrem Kurtz for flautist Elaine Shaffer

Brief Mention: Philadelphia Orchestra Program Notes (Feb 10, 1956): 471; SR 39:34 (May 5, 1956); San Francisco Symphony Program Notes (Feb 12, 1958): 363; MC 157:45 (April 1958); Louisville Orchestra Program Notes (Feb 1, 1966); ARG 33:221 (Nov 1966)

Premiere: Sept 17, 1954; Venice, Italy; 17th International Festival of Contemporary Music; La Biennale de Venezia; Orchestra del Teatro La Fenice; Elaine Shaffer, fl.; Nicanor Zabaleta, harp; Nino Sanzogno, cond.

W40. Eleven Chorale Preludes for Organ, Op. 122, by Johannes Brahms (Dec 1956; Boosey & Hawkes; 25 min. 30 sec.)

Arranged by Virgil Thomson
3.3.3.3./4.2.3.1./1 perc./strings
Commissioned by Edward B. Benjamin for the New Orleans Philharmonic-Symphony Society
1. My Jesus Calls To Me (Mein Jesu, der du mich)
2. O Blessed Jesus (Herzliebster Jesu) (2 orchestral versions)
3. O World, I Now Must Leave Thee (O Welt, ich muss dich lassen; Brahms's first setting)
4. My Faithful Heart Rejoices (Herzlich tut mich erfreuen)
5. Deck Thyself, My Soul (Schmücke dich, O Liebe Seele)
6. Blessed Are Ye Faithful Souls (O wie selig seid ihr doch, ihr Frommen)
7. O God, Thou Faithful God (O Gott du frommer Got)
8. Behold, a Rose Is Blooming (Es ist ein' Rose' entsprungen)
9. My Heart Is Filled with Longing (Herzlich tut mich verlangen; Brahms's first setting)
10. My Heart Is Filled with Longing (Herzlich tut mich verlangen; Brahams's second setting)
11. O World, I Now Must Leave Thee (O Welt, ich muss dich lassen; Brahms's second setting)

Brief Mention: NYT (Oct 30, 1957): 25

Premiere: March 25, 1957; New Orleans, LA; Municipal Auditorium; The New Orleans Philharmonic-Symphony; Virgil Thomson, cond.

W41. The Lively Arts Fugue (Sept 13, 1957; ms.; 1 min. 40 sec.)

Ob./cl./hr./tbn./1 perc./strings

W42. Fugues and Cantilenas (Feb 1959; Boosey & Hawkes; 15 min. 30 sec.)

From the United Nations film "Power Among Men" (1958; See W322)
2.2.2.2./4.2.3.1./2 perc./harp/strings
1. Prelude with Fugal Exposition
2. Fugue No. 1
3. Ruins and Jungles
4. Fugue No. 2
5. Joyous Pastoral
6. Finale

Premiere: May 2, 1959; Ann Arbor, MI; Hill Auditorium; The Philadelphia Orchestra; Virgil Thomson, cond.

W43. Collected Poems (May, 1959; Southern; 7 min.)

Text by Kenneth Koch
Arranged for soprano, baritone, and orchestra (1.1.1.1./tpt./1
perc./pf./string quintet) from the original for soprano, baritone, and pf. (1959; Southern, See W143)

[Missa pro defunctis, for choruses and orchestra; 1960; Gray/Belwin
Mills; See W87]

W44. Crossing Brooklyn Ferry (Nov 11, 1961; Boosey & Hawkes)

Text by Walt Whitman
Arranged for mixed chorus (SSATB) and orchestra
(2.2.2.2./4.3.3.0./timp./2 perc./harp/strings) from the original
for chorus and pf. (1958; Boosey & Hawkes; See W86)

W45. A Solemn Music and a Joyful Fugue (1961-62; G. Schirmer; 12 min.)
See: B128

3.3.3.3./4.3.3.1./timp./2 perc./strings
A Solemn Music only originally for band (1949; G. Schirmer; See
W34)
Commissioned by Edward B. Benjamin of New Orleans

Brief Mention: MA 83:19+ (April 1963)

Premieres:
A Solemn Music: Feb 15, 1962; New York City; New York
Philharmonic; Nadia Boulanger, cond.
A Joyful Fugue: Feb 1, 1963; Philadelphia, PA; Academy of Music;
Philadelphia Orchestra; Eugene Ormandy, cond.

[Dance in Praise, for mixed chorus (SATB) and orchestra; 1962; Boosey &
Hawkes; See W89]

W46. Mass for Solo Voice (1962; G. Schirmer)

In Latin
Vocal range: b flat-f
Arranged for solo voice (or unison choir) and orchestra

(2.2.2.2./2.2.1.0./perc./harp/strings) from the original for
solo voice and pf. (Sept 1960; G. Schirmer; See W144)

Premiere: May 20, 1974; York, England; York Arts Centre; York
University Ensemble

W47. Pilgrims and Pioneers (March 1964; G. Schirmer; 10 min.)

From the film "Journey to America" by John Houseman (1964; See
W323)
1.1.2.1./4.2.0.0./1 perc./strings

Brief Mention: International Musician 69:29 (Feb 1971)

Premiere: Feb 27, 1971; New York City; Town Hall; The Mozart
Festival Orchestra; Baird Hastings, cond.

W48. The Feast of Love (July-Aug, 1964; G. Schirmer; 8 min.) See: B73
and T174

From the Pervigilium Veneris (See T41), translated by Virgil
Thomson
Arranged for baritone (vocal range: d-g) and orchestra
(1.1.2.1./perc./harp/strings) from the original for baritone and
pf. (1964; ms.; See W148)
Commissioned by The Elizabeth Sprague Coolidge Foundation

Brief Mention: MA 84:64 (Dec 1964); Philadelphia Orchestra Program
Notes (Dec 6, 1968): 19-25; NYT (Dec 11, 1968): 50; HF 19:30
(March 1969); Music and Artist 2:36 (No. 1, 1969); Boletin
Interamericano de Musica 72:70 (July 1969)

Premiere: Nov 1, 1964; Washington, DC; The Coolidge Auditorium,
Library of Congress; David Clatworthy, baritone; members of the
National Symphony; Walter Hendl, cond.

W49. Autumn: Concertino for Harp, Strings, and Percussion (1964; G.
Schirmer; 9 min.) See: T174

Scored from the pf. portrait Homage to Marya Freund and to the
Harp (1956; Boosey & Hawkes; See W270) and from Piano Sonata No.
2 (1929; MCA/Belwin Mills; See W170)
Commissioned by the Northern California Harpists' Association for
Nicanor Zabaleta
1. Salute to the Wind   3. Love Scene
2. Dialogue   4. Promenade

Brief Mention: Harp News 3:2 (No. 10, 1964); Boletin Interamericano de Musica (English ed.) 45:2 (Jan 1965)

Premiere: Oct 19, 1964; Madrid, Spain; First Festival of American
and Spanish Music; Municipal Orchestra of Valencia; Nicanor
Zabaleta, harp; Enrique Jorda, cond.

W50. Ode to the Wonders of Nature (Aug 1965; G. Schirmer; 3 min.)

3 tpt./2 hn./3 tbn./timp./snare drum/field drum
Commissioned by the Smithsonian Institute for the bicentennial
celebration of the birth of James Smithson

Premiere: Sept 16, 1965; Washington, DC; The Smithsonian
Institute; The Smithsonian Tower Musicians

W51.   Fantasy in Homage to an Earlier England (Feb 1966; Boosey &
       Hawkes; 12 min.)

2.2.2.2./4.2.3.0./timp./2 perc./strings
Commissioned by the Performing Arts Foundation of Kansas City, MO
1. Fanfare for a Victory at Sea
2. The Unfaithful: His Complaint
3. Royal Hunt of the Faerie Queen
4. The Court's Pavane

Brief Mention: Musical Leader 98:23 (June 1966); MT 107:618
(July 1966); HF 16:MA9 (Aug 1966); Pittsburgh Symphony Program
Notes (Sept 30, 1966): 67; Musical Leader 98:22 (Dec 1966)

Premiere: May 27, 1966; Kansas City, MO; Music Hall; Kansas City
Symphony; Nicola Rescigno, cond.

[The Nativity As Sung By the Shepherds, for mixed chorus, soloists, and
       orchestra; 1966-67; G. Schirmer; See W94]

W52.   From Byron's "Don Juan" (July 17-Aug 13, 1967; Southern; 14 min.)

For orchestra and tenor
Commissioned by the New York Philharmonic for its 125th anniversary
1. Shipwreck (4.4.4.4./4.4.4.1./timp./2 perc./harp/pf./strings)
2. Juan and Haidee (Tenor with 3.3.4.2./4.4.0.0./2 perc./harp/pf./
       strings); Also arranged by Paul Turok for tenor and pf.
       (1967; ms.)

Brief Mention: New York Philharmonic Program Notes (April 11,
1968); NYT (April 12, 1968): 42

Premiere: April 11, 1968; New York City; Avery Fisher Hall; New
York Philharmonic Orchestra; Richard Kness, tenor; Leopold Stokowski, cond.

W53.   Metropolitan Museum Fanfare: Portrait of An American Artist
       (1969; G. Schirmer; 1 min. 45 sec.)

Arranged from the pf. portrait of Florine Stettheimer (1941;
Boosey & Hawkes; See W261)
3 cornet/2 tpt./4 hn./3 tbn./tuba/timp./3 perc.
Commissioned by the New York Metropolitan Museum of Art in connec-
tion with its centennial festivities

Brief Mention: NYT (Oct 17, 1969): 37; NYT (Nov 2, 1969): sect. 21,
p. 19

Premiere: Oct 16, 1969; New York City; Metropolitan Museum of Art; Virgil Thomson, cond.

W54. Edges: A Portrait of Robert Indiana (1969; G. Schirmer; 2 min.)

Arranged from the pf. portrait (1966; G. Schirmer; See W271)
Pic./2 fl./2 ob./all cl./2 bn./4 sax./3 cornet/2 tpt./4 hn./3 tbn./ 2 bar./tuba/timp./2 perc.
Commissioned by the Harvard University Band for its 50th anniversary celebration

Premiere: Spring, 1970; Cambridge, MA; Harvard University Band

W55. Study Piece: Portrait of a Lady (1969; G. Schirmer; 2 min. 30 sec.)

Freely arranged from the pf. portrait of Louise Crane entitled Insistences (1941; G. Schirmer; See W259)
Pic./2 fl./2 ob./all cl./2 bn./4 sax./3 cornet/2 tpt./4 hn./3 tbn./2 bar./tuba/timp./3 perc.
Commissioned by the Harvard University Band

Premiere: Spring 1970; Cambridge, MA; Harvard University Band

W56. Symphony No. 3 (1972; Boosey & Hawkes; 21 min.)

Scored for orchestra from String Quartet No. 2 (1932; Boosey & Hawkes; See W176)
2.2.2.2./4.2.3.1./timp./4 perc./harp/strings
1. Swinging   3. Adagio sostenuto
2. Tempo di Valzer   4. Allegretto

Premiere: Dec 26, 1976; New York City; Carnegie Hall; The American Symphony Orchestra; Kazuyoshi Akiyama, cond.

[Cantata on Poems of Edward Lear, for chorus, soloists, and orchestra; 1973-74; G. Schirmer; See W97]

W57. Thoughts for Strings (Aug 1-2, 1981; Boosey & Hawkes; 3 min. 40 sec.)

For string orchestra

W58. Eleven Portraits for Orchestra (July-Aug 1982; Boosey & Hawkes)

Those orchestrated by Virgil Thomson:
A Love Scene
From the pf. portrait Dead Pan: Mrs. Betty Freeman (1981; Boosey & Hawkes; See W284)
2.2.2.2./4.2.3.0./2 perc./strings

Intensely Two: Karen Brown Waltuck
From the pf. portrait (1981; Boosey & Hawkes; See W288)
2.2.2.2. (including Eng. hn. and bass cl.)/2 hn./1 tpt./harp/ strings

Loyal, Steady, Persistent: Noah Creshevsky
From the pf. portrait (1981; Boosey & Hawkes; See W279)
2.2.2.3./4.2.3.0./strings

Something of a Beauty: Anne-Marie Soullière
From the pf. portrait (1981; Boosey & Hawkes; See W289)
2.2.2.2./4.2.3.0./2 perc./strings

David Dubal in Flight
From the pf. portrait (1982; G. Schirmer; See W298)
2.2.2.2./4.2.3.0./xyl./marimba/strings

Those orchestrated by Scott Wheeler:
Scott Wheeler: Free-wheeling
From the pf. portrait (1981; Boosey & Hawkes; See W277)
2.2.2.2./2 hn./strings

Dennis Russell Davies: In a Hammock
From the pf. portrait (1982; G. Schirmer; See W294)
2.2.2.2./2.2.0.0./1 perc./harp/strings

Richard Flender: Solid, Not Stolid
From the pf. portrait (1981; Boosey & Hawkes; See W276)
2.2.2.2./2.2.0.0./1 perc./strings

Those orchestrated by Rodney Lister:
Bill Katz: Wide Awake
From the pf. portrait (1981; Boosey & Hawkes; See W274)
2.2.2.2./2.2.3.0./2 perc./marimba/glock./sidedrum/cymbals/large
  gong/strings

Sam Byers: With Joy
From the pf. portrait (1981; Boosey & Hawkes; See W280)
2.2.2.2./strings

Christopher Cox: Singing a Song
From the pf. portrait (1981; Boosey & Hawkes; See W282)
2.2.2.2./2hn./strings

W59. Four Saints: An Olio for Chamber Orchestra (1984; ms.)

Arranged by Paul Reuter from the opera Four Saints in Three Acts
(1928; G. Schirmer; See W1)
Rev. version by Virgil Thomson (1984; G. Schirmer.)
2.2.2.2./2.1.1.0./2+ perc./accordion/strings

W60. A Pair of Portraits: "A Double Take" and "Major Chords" (Dec 11,
1984; ms.)

Arranged respectively from the pf. portraits of John Houseman, No
Changes (1984; ms.; See W310) and Anthony Tommasini, A Study in
Chords (1984; ms.; See W313)
2.2.2.2./4.2.3.1./2 perc./strings

CHORAL WORKS

W61. De Profundis (July 1920; rev. 1951; Weintraub; 2 min. 30   sec.)

       In English for mixed chorus (SATB)

       Brief Mention: Notes 9:494 (June 1952)

W62. O My Deir Hert (1921; rev. 1978; Heritage; 2 min.)

       Text by Martin Luther
       In English for mixed chorus (SATB)

W63. Sanctus (Dec 1921; ms.; 1 min. 30 sec.)

       In English for men's chorus (TTBB)

W64. Tribulationes Civitatum (Aug 1922; Weintraub; 3 min.)

       In Latin for mixed chorus (SATB)
       Also for men's chorus (TTBB)

       Brief Mention: Notes 9:494 (June 1952)

       Premiere: 1922; Boston, MA; The Harvard Glee Club; Virgil Thomson,
         cond.

W65. Three Antiphonal Psalms (1922-24; G.Schirmer; 5 min.)

       In English for 2-part chorus (SA or TB)
       Commissioned by the University Women's Chorus of New York
       1. Psalm 123: Unto Thee Lift I Up Mine Eyes
       2. Psalm 133: Behold How Good and Pleasant It Is, Brethren
       3. Psalm 136: O, Give Thanks to the Lord, For He Is Gracious

       Brief Mention: MM 3:18 (March-April 1926)

       Premiere: 1923; New York City; Engineer's Hall; University Women's
         Chorus of New York; Gerald Reynolds, cond.

W66. Agnus Dei (1924; Presser; 2 min.) See: A20

       In Latin
       Canon for three equal voices
       Published in Modern Canons: 38 Contemporary Canons for 2-5 Voices,
         edited by Herman Reichenbach (1946; Music Press, Inc.)

       Brief Mention: Music News 43:25 (April 1951)

W67. Missa Brevis (Jan 1924; ms.; 14 min.)

       In Latin for men's chorus (TTBB)

       Brief Mention: MM 3:18 (March-April 1926)

W68. Fête Polonaise (Jan 1924; ms.; 7 min.)

Arranged from Chabrier's Le Roi malgré lui for men's chorus (TTBB) and pf.

Premiere: 1925; Boston, MA; Symphony Hall; Harvard Glee Club; Virgil Thomson, cond.

W69. Agnus Dei (March 1925; ms.; 1 min.)

In Latin for men's chorus (TTBB)

W70. Benedictus (1926; ms.; 1 min.)

In Latin for men's chorus (TTBB)

W71. Sanctus (Aug 1926; ms.; 1 min. 30 sec.)

In Latin for men's chorus (TTBB) with children's chorus (SS or SA).

[Capital Capitals, for four male voices; 1927; Boosey & Hawkes; See W109]

W72. Saints' Procession (Aug 1928; G. Schirmer; 4 min. 30 sec.)

From the opera Four Saints in Three Acts (1928; G. Schirmer; See W1)
For mixed chorus (SATB) and pf. with solos for mezzo-soprano and bass; also published in The Choral Repertory for Mixed Voices, red book (G. Schirmer)
Also arranged for men's chorus (TTBB) (ms.)

W73. Seven Choruses from the "Medea" of Euripides (Aug 1934; G. Schirmer; 9 min. 30 sec.)See: B186

English translation by Countee Cullen
For women's chorus (SSAA) and perc., ad lib.
Also arranged for mixed chorus (SATB) by Daniel Pinkham (1967; G. Schirmer)
Commissioned by John Houseman
1. O Gentle Heart
2. Love, Like a Leaf
3. O, Happy Were Our Fathers
4. Weep for the Little Lambs
5. Go Down, O Sun
6. Behold, O Earth
7. Immortal Zeus Controls the Fate of Man

Brief Mention: MM 20:204 (March-April 1943); MM 20:259 (May-June 1943)

Premiere:
For Women's Chorus: Dec 16, 1942; New York City; Hotel Plaza Ballroom; the St. Cecelia Club; Hugh Ross, cond.; David Gusi-

koff, perc.
For Mixed Chorus: June 13, 1967; Cambridge, MA; Isabella Stewart Gardner Museum; the Choir of King's Chapel; Daniel Pinkham, cond.; Frederick Buda, perc.

W74. Mass for Two-Part Chorus and Percussion (Sept 1934; MCA/Belwin
Mills; 14 min.) See: B186

In Latin with English translation by Virgil Thomson (SA or TB or
ST/AB)
Commissioned by the League of Composers for the Adesdi Chorus of
the Dessoff Choir

Brief Mention: MM 12:192+ (May-June 1935); MA 71:18 (Aug 1951); MA
80:29 (Jan 15, 1960)

Premiere: April 10, 1935; New York City; Town Hall; Adesdi Chorus
of the Dessoff Choir; Margarete Dessoff, cond.

W75. My Shepherd Will Supply My Need (Oct 1937; Gray/Belwin Mills; 3
min.)

Isaac Watts's paraphrase of Psalm 23
For mixed chorus (SATB or SAB)
Also for men's chorus (TTBB) and for women's chorus (SSAA, SSA, or
SA)
Also arranged for voice and pf. or organ (1959; Gray/Belwin Mills;
See W141)

Brief Mention: Choir Guide 2:39 (May-June 1949); Notes 11:439
(June 1959)

W76. Scenes from the Holy Infancy According to Saint Matthew (Nov 6-21,
1937; G. Schirmer; 9 min. 30 sec.)

For mixed chorus (SATB) with solos for tenor, baritone, and bass
1. Joseph and the Angel
2. The Wise Men
3. The Flight into Egypt

Brief Mention: MM 15:99 (Jan-Feb 1938); MM 21:240 & 259 (May-June
1944)

Premiere: Dec 12, 1937; New York City; 46th Street Theatre; The
Madrigal Singers; Lehman Engel, cond.

W77. The Bugle Song (Sept 1941; Holt, Rinehart, and Winston; 1 min. 30
sec.)

Text by Tennyson
Arranged for unison children's chorus and pf. from the solo vocal
original (1941; ms.; See W128)
Published in Exploring Music 5 by E. Boardman and B. Landis, 1966
and 1975
Also arranged for two-part children's chorus (SS or SA) (ms.)

W78. Surrey Apple-Howler's Song (Sept 1941; Holt, Rinehart, and Winston; 1 min.)

Traditional words
A round for children's chorus
Published also in Exploring Music 5 by E. Boardman and B. Landis, 1966 and 1975

W79. Welcome to the New Year (Sept 1941; Holt, Rinehart, and Winston; 1 min.)

Text by Eleanor Farjeon
For two-part children's chorus (SS or SA) and pf.
Published in Exploring Music: The Junior Book by B. Landis and L. Hoggard, 1968
Also for mixed chorus (SATB) (ms.)

W80. Hymns from the Old South (June 1949; Gray/Belwin Mills; each published separately)

For mixed chorus (SATB)
1. Death, 'Tis a Melancholy Day (Isaac Watts) (3 min)
2. Green Fields (John Newton) (2 min. 30 sec.)
3. The Morning Star (Anon.) (Also for women's chorus (SSA) (Gray/Belwin Mills; 1 min. 20 sec.)

W81. Kyrie Eleison (Aug 1953; Gray/Belwin Mills; 3 min.)

In Greek
For mixed chorus (SATB)
Published in the Missa pro defunctis (1960; Gray/Belwin Mills; See W87)

W82. Never Another (Dec 28, 1955; Columbia; 2 min. 30 sec.)

Text by Mark Van Doren
Hymn for mixed chorus (SATB)
Published with the title "Praise Him Who Makes Us Happy" in American Hymns Old and New by Albert Christ-Janer (p. 808)

W83. Song for the Stable (Dec 28, 1955; Columbia; 2 min. 30 sec.)

Text by Amanda Benjamin Hall
Hymn for mixed chorus (SATB)
Published with the title "It Seems that God Bestowed Somehow" in American Hymns Old and New by Albert Christ-Janer (p. 807)

W84. Four Songs to Poems of Thomas Campion (1955; Southern; each published separately)

Arranged for mixed chorus (SATB) and pf. from the solo vocal original (1951; Southern; See W129)

Brief Mention MC 155:38 (March 1, 1957)

Premieres:
"Follow Your Saint," and "There is a Garden in Her Face": Feb
   24, 1956; Cambridge, MA; Sanders Theatre; The Harvard Glee
   Club and Radcliffe Choral Society; G. Wallace Woodworth, cond.
"Rose Cheek'd Laura, Come," and "Follow They Fair Sun": Dec 9,
   1963; New York City; Plaza Hotel; Choral Group of the Oratorio
   Society of New York; Dr. T. Charles Lee, cond.

W85. Tiger! Tiger! (1955; Southern; 4 min.)

Arranged for mixed chorus (SATB) and pf. or men's chorus (TTBB)
   and pf. from Five Songs from William Blake for baritone and pf.
   (1951; Southern; See W130)

W86. Crossing Brooklyn Ferry (March 1958; Boosey & Hawkes; 7 min.)

Text by Walt Whitman
For mixed chorus (SSATB) and pf.
Also arranged for chorus and orchestra (1961; Boosey & Hawkes; See
   W44)
Commissioned by the Brooklyn Academy of Music

Premiere: April 26, 1958; Brooklyn, NY; The Randolph Singers; Carl
   Mosbacher, pf.

W87. Missa pro defunctis (1960; Gray/Belwin Mills; 45 min.) See: B50,
   B109, B128, B160, B177, B190, & B229

Requiem mass in Latin
For men's chorus, women's chorus, and orchestra:
   3.3.3.3./4.3.3.1./timp./3 perc./celesta/harp/strings
Also published with pf. accompaniment (Gray/Belwin Mills)
Kyrie Eleison for mixed chorus (SATB) published separately (1953;
   Gray/Belwin Mills; See W81)
Commissioned by the State University College of New York at Pots-
   dam for the Crane Chorus

Brief Mention: Le Guide de Concert 305:808 (March 10, 1961); World
   of Music 3:40 (April 1961); NYer 38:183+ (May 19, 1962); SR
   45:39 (May 26, 1962); MA 82:24 (July 1962)

Premiere: May 14, 1960; Potsdam, New York; State University College of Education; Crane Chorus and Symphony; Virgil Thomson,
   cond.

W88. Mass for Solo Voice (Sept 1960; G. Schirmer; 10 min.)

In Latin
Vocal range: b flat-f
Arranged for unison choir and pf. from the solo voice original
   (1960; G. Schirmer; See W144)
Also arranged for solo voice (or unison choir) and orchestra
   (1962; G. Schirmer; See W46)

W89. Dance in Praise (1962; Boosey & Hawkes; 9 min.)

"Gaudeamus Igitur" translated by John A. Symonds as "Let Us Live Then and Be Glad"
Text in Latin and English
For mixed chorus (SATB) and orchestra: 2.2.2.2./2.2.0.0./3 perc./ pf./strings
Commissioned by the Henry and Ruth Blaustein Rosenberg Foundation for the dedication of the College Center, Goucher College

Brief Mention: MA 83:16 (Feb 1963)

Premiere: Jan 13, 1963; Baltimore, MD;College Center, Goucher College; The Princeton University Glee Club; The Goucher College Glee Club; The Baltimore Chamber Orchestra; Elliott Galkin, cond.

W90.   The Holly and the Ivy (Dec 10, 1963; G. Schirmer; 3 min.)

A carol of Nativity and Lent (Anon., 1557)
For mixed chorus (SATB) and pf. from the solo vocal original (1955; ms.; See W132)

W91.   My Master Hath a Garden (Dec 15, 1963; G. Schirmer; 2 min.)

Anonymous text
Arranged for mixed chorus (SATB) or women's chorus (SSA) and pf. from the solo vocal original in Praises and Prayers (March 1963; G. Schirmer; See W146)
Also published in 20th Century Choral Music for Mixed Voices, complied by Karl Bradley (G.Schirmer)

W92.   Five Auvergnat Folk Songs (1962 and 1964; Presser; 16 min.)

Arranged from Joseph Canteloube's solo version with pf. or orchestra (unchanged) for mixed chorus (SATB)
Commissioned by Hugh Ross
1. La Pastoura als camps (La Bergère aux champs), Vol. 1, #1
2. Bailèro (Chant de bergers de Haute-Auvergne), Vol 1, #2
3. Pastourelle, Vol. 2, #1
4. La Fiolairé (La Fileuse), Vol. 3, #1, for women only
5. Passo pel prat (Viens par le pré), Vol 3, #2

Premiere: April 16, 1964; New York City; Philharmonic Hall; Schola Cantorum of New York; Members of the New York Philharmonic; Hugh Ross, cond.

W93.   When I Survey the Bright Celestial Sphere (Sept 19-22, 1964; Peters; 5 min.)

Text by William Habbingdon
For unison chorus and organ (or pf.)
Also arranged with brass accompaniment (2 tpt./2 hn./tbn.) by Scott Wheeler (1981; Peters)

W94.   The Nativity As Sung by the Shepherds (Nov 1966-April 1967; G.

Schirmer; 7 min. 10 sec.) See: B63

Text by Richard Crashaw
For mixed chorus (SATB), soloists (alto, tenor, bass), and orches-
tra: 2.2.2.1./2.2.0.0./2 perc./pf./organ ad lib./ strings
Also with one or two pf. accompaniment (G.Schirmer)
Commissioned by the Women's Board of the University of Chicago for
the 75th anniversary of the university

Brief Mention: <u>American</u> <u>Choral</u> <u>Review</u> 9:53 (No. 4, 1967); <u>NYT</u> (11-
18-71): 59; <u>NYer</u> 47:97+ (Nov 27, 1971)

Premiere: May 7, 1967; Chicago, IL; Rockefeller Chapel; University
of Chicago; Rockefeller Chapel Choir; Members of the Chicago
Symphony; Charlotte Brent, mezzo-soprano; Walter Carringer,
tenor; Henri Noel, bass; Richard Vikstrom, cond.

W95. <u>How</u> <u>Will</u> <u>Ye</u> <u>Have</u> <u>Your</u> <u>Partridge</u> <u>Today?</u> (Oct 29, 1967; ms.; 1 min.
30 sec.)

Text by Nicholas Brown
Round for four voices

W96. <u>A</u> <u>Hymn</u> <u>for</u> <u>Pratt</u> <u>Institute</u> (Sept 3, 1968; ms.;1 min 30
sec.) See: A20

Text by Rolf Fjelde
For mixed chorus (SATB)

W97. <u>Cantata</u> <u>on</u> <u>Poems</u> <u>of</u> <u>Edward</u> <u>Lear</u> (1973-74; G. Schirmer; 21 min. 20
sec.)

For mixed chorus (SATB), soprano (d-g) and baritone (c-g) soloists, with pf. accompaniment
Also with orchestral accompaniment (G. Schirmer)
Commissioned by Towson State University, Baltimore, MD
1. The Owl and the Pussycat, for soprano and baritone (originally
   for 2 sopranos)
2. The Jumblies, for soprano and chorus (also published separate-
      ly; G. Schirmer) (originally for 2 sopranos, perc., pf.,
      vn., vc., and bass)
3. The Pelican Chorus, for soprano, baritone, and chorus (orch:
   1.0.1.1./2.1.1.0./perc./pf./vn./vc./bass)
4. Half an Alphabet, for chorus (also published separately; G.
   Schirmer) (orch:2.2.2.2./4.2.3.0./perc./strings)
5. The Akond of Swat, for baritone and chorus (also published
   separately; G. Schirmer) (orch: 2.2.2.2./4.2.3.0./perc./strings)

Brief Mention: <u>NYT</u> (April 30, 1975): 24

Premiere: Nov 18, 1973; Towson, MD; Fine Arts Building Concert
Hall, Towson State University; Esther Coulange, soprano; Ruth
Drucker, soprano; Gerald Phillips, baritone; the Towson State
University Community Orchestra; The Towson State University
Madrigal Singers; Virgil Thomson, cond.

W98. The Peace Place (July-Aug 1979; Heritage)

Text by Jack Larson
For mixed chorus (SATB) and pf.
Rev. with title Fanfare for Peace, for mixed chorus and pf. or
    brass and perc. (1983; Southern; See W101)

Brief Mention: Music Educators' Journal 67:11 (Jan 1981)

Premiere: Sept 30, 1980; New York City

W99. A Prayer to Venus (Aug 12-22 1981; G. Schirmer)

Text by John Fletcher
For mixed choir and pf.

W100. Cantantes Eamus (July-Aug 1982; G. Schirmer)

Text by Virgil
For men's chorus (TTBB) and pf.
Also arranged with brass accompaniment (3 tpt./3 tbn./2 perc./
    timp.) (1982; G. Schirmer)

W101. Fanfare for Peace (1983; Southern; 1 min 30 sec.)

Arranged for chorus (SATB) and pf. or brass (2 tpt. in C/3
    tbn./snare drum/timp.) from The Peace Place for mixed chorus and
    pf. (1979; Heritage; See W98)

W102. Southern Hymns (Jan 1984; Southern; 7 min. 5 sec.)

For mixed choir (SATB) and pf.
1. "How Bright Is the Day!" (Text by Rev. S.B. Sawyer, 1859)
2. Mississippi ("When Gabriel's Awful Trump Shall Sound" from
    Kentucky Harmony, 1820)
3. Death of General Washington (Text by Stephen Jenks, 1799)
4. Convention ("How Firm a Foundation" from Caldwell's
    Union Harmony, 1837)

VOCAL WORKS

W103. Vernal Equinox (July 1920; ms.; 1 min.)

Text by Amy Lowell
Vocal range: e flat-f sharp
With pf. accompaniment

W104. The Sunflower (Sept 1920; ms.; 1 min.)

Text by William Blake
Vocal range: e flat-a flat
With pf. accompaniment

W105. Three Sentences from the "Song of Solomon" (Aug 1924; ms. 3 min.)

With pf. accompaniment
1. Thou That Dwellest in the Gardens (vocal range: e flat-a)
2. Return, O Shulamite (vocal range: e-g)
3. I Am My Beloved's (vocal range: f-a)

W106. <u>Susie Asado</u> (April 1926; Boosey & Hawkes; 1 min. 30 sec.) See: A20

Text by Gertrude Stein
Two vocal versions: d-g (in <u>Cos Cob Song Volume</u>) and b-e (ms.)
With pf. accompaniment

Premiere: June 17, 1929; Paris, France; Salle Chopin; Marthe-
Marthine, soprano; Virgil Thomson, pf.

W107. <u>Five Phrases from "The Song of Solomon"</u> (April-May 1926; American
Music Edition/Presser; 6 min.) See: B76

For soprano and 1 perc.
1. Thou That Dwellest in the Gardens (vocal range: e   flat-a)
2. Return, O Shulamite (vocal range:e-g)
3. O, My Dove (vocal range: e-flat-a)
4. I Am My Beloved's (vocal range: f-a)
5. By Night (vocal range: g-g)

Brief Mention: <u>MQ</u> 38:596 (1952); <u>Notes</u> 12:333 (March 1955)

Premieres:
   Private: July 2, 1926; Paris, France; the home of Mrs. Christian
      Gross; Alice Mock, soprano; Jean Morel, perc.
   Public: April 22, 1928; New York City; Edythe Totten   Theatre;
      Radiana Pazmor, mezzo-soprano; Aaron Copland, perc.

W108. <u>The Tiger</u> (Sept 1926; G. Schirmer; 3 min.)

Text by William Blake
Vocal range: d-g
With pf. accompaniment
Also published in <u>Contemporary Art Songs: 28 Songs by American and
British Composers</u> (1970; G. Schirmer)

W109. <u>Capital Capitals</u> (April 1927; rev. 1968; Boosey & Hawkes; 16 min.)
   See: B76 & B160
Text by Gertrude Stein
For four male voices (TTBB) and pf.

Brief Mention: <u>MM</u> 6: 18 & 24 (May-June 1929); <u>MM</u> 9:93 (Nov-Dec
1931); <u>MM</u> 18:247 (May-June 1941); <u>MQ</u> 40:471+ (July   1954)

Premieres:
   Private: June 1927; Paris, France; the home of the Duchesse de
      Clermont-Tonnerre; unidentified quartet; Virgil Thomson, pf.
   Public: May 30, 1928; Paris, France; Nouveau Salle d'Orgue du
      Conservatoire; Parker Steward and O.S. Walker, tenors; Victor
      Prahl, baritone; Emory Foster, bass; Edmond Pendleton, pf.

W110. <u>Preciosilla</u> (Feb 4, 1927; G. Schirmer; 5 min.) See: B161

    Text by Gertrude Stein
    With pf. accompaniment
    Two vocal versions: c-f sharp (in <u>Songs by 22 Americans: High or
    Low Voice</u>, compiled by Bernard Taylor for G. Schirmer) and e
    flat-a (published separately by G. Schirmer and also in <u>Songs by
    22 Americans</u>)

    Brief Mention: <u>MC</u> 139:31 (Jan 1, 1949)

    Premiere: June 17, 1929; Paris, France; Salle Chopin; Marthe-
    Marthine, soprano; Virgil Thomson, pf.

W111. <u>La Valse Grégorienne</u> (Nov 30, 1927; Southern; 2 min. 20 sec.)

    Text by Georges Hugnet, translated by Donald Sutherland as
    "Gregorian Waltz"
    Vocal range: d-a
    With pf. accompaniment
    Rev. 1971 for medium voice (Southern)
    To be sung without pause:
    1. Les Ecrevisses (Crayfish)
    2. Grenadine (Pomegranate)
    3. La Rosée (Dew)
    4. Le Wagon Immobile (The Motionless Box-Car)

    Premiere: June 17, 1929; Paris, France; Salle Chopin; Marthe-
    Marthine, soprano; Virgil Thomson, pf.

W112. <u>Le Berceau de Gertrude Stein, ou Le Mystère de la Rue de Fleurus</u>
    (April 29, 1928; Southern; 4 min. 15 sec.)

    Eight poems (to be sung without pause) by Georges Hugnet, trans-
    lated by Donald Sutherland as "The Cradle of Gertrude Stein, or
    Mysteries in the rue de Fleurus"
    Music by Thomson entitled <u>Lady Godiva's Waltzes</u>
    Vocal range: e-f
    With pf. accompaniment

    Premiere: June 17, 1929; Paris, France; Salle Chopin; Marthe-
    Marthine, soprano; Virgil Thomson, pf.

W113. <u>Trois Poèmes de la Duchesse de Rohan</u> (May 17, 1928; 6 min. 30
    sec.) See: T78 & T158

    With pf. accompaniment
    1. A son Altesse le Princesse Antoinette Murat (vocal range:
        c-a; ms.)
    2. Jour de chaleur aux bains de mer (translated by Sherry Mangan
        as "Hot Day at the Seashore") (vocal range: c-g; Boosey &
        Hawkes.)
    3. La Seine (vocal range: c-b flat; in <u>Parnassus: Poetry in Review</u>
        5 (Spring/Summer 1977): 410+)

Premiere: Of "La Seine" only: June 17, 1929; Paris, France; Salle
Chopin; Martha-Marthine, soprano; Virgil Thomson, pf.

W114. Commentaire sur Saint Jérome (Oct 8, 1928; Southern; 1 min.)

Text by Marquis de Sade, translated by Donald Sutherland as "Com-
mentary on Saint Jerome"
Vocal range: d-f
With pf. accompaniment

W115. Les Soirées Bagnolaises (Oct 18 & Nov 5, 1928; ms. 6 min.)

Text by Georges Hugnet
Vocal range: d-b flat
With pf. accompaniment

W116. Portrait of F.B. [Frances Blood] (Sept 1929; G. Schirmer; 4 min.
30 sec.)

Text by Gertrude Stein
Vocal range: c-g
With pf. accompaniment

W117. Le Singe et le léopard (April 7, 1930; Southern; 4 min. 30 sec.)

Text by Jean de La Fontaine, translated by Donald Sutherland as
"The Monkey and the Leopard"
Vocal range: d-g
With pf. accompaniment

Brief Mention: MM 13:36 (Jan-Feb 1939); Notes 31:162 (Sept 1974)

W118. Oraison Funèbre de Henriette-Marie de France, Reine de la Grande-
Bretagne (April-May 1930; rev. 1934; ms. 14 min.)

Text by Jacques Bossuet, translated by Donald Sutherland
Two vocal versions: c-a and bar. a-g
With pf. accompaniment

W119. Air de Phèdre (Aug 1-15, 1930; Southern; 6 min.)

Words by Jean Racine, translated by Donald Sutherland as
"Phaedra's Farewell"
Two vocal versions: d-b (Southern) and b-g (ms.)
With pf. accompaniment

Brief Mention: MM 20:114 (Jan-Feb 1943); NYT (Feb 5, 1969): 38

W120. Film: Deux Soeurs qui ne sont pas soeurs (Sept 1-2, 1930; Southern; 4 min. 45 sec.)

Text by Gertrude Stein originally written for an unproduced film;
translated by Donald Sutherland as "Two Sisters Not Sisters"
Vocal range: d-g
The pf. accompaniment is a portrait of Stein's dog, Basket I

W121. Stabat Mater (March 1931; rev. 1981; Boosey & Hawkes; 5 min.) See:
       B47, B55, B171, B176, B185, & B229

       Text in French by Max Jacob
       For soprano and string quartet
       Vocal range: d-b flat
       Also arranged for voice and string orchestra (1931; Boosey &
       Hawkes; See W11)
       Also arranged for voice and pf. (1960; Boosey & Hawkes; See W145)

       Brief Mention: MM 9:173-4 (May-June 1932); MM 10:162+ (March-
       April 1933); MM 19:38 (Nov-Dec 1941); MM 21:243+ (May-June
       1944); MM 22:180 (March-April 1945); MQ 40: 471 & 475 (1954); MA
       74:26 (Dec 1, 1954)

       Premiere: June 15, 1931; Paris, France; Salle Chopin; Madeleyne
       Leymo, soprano; The Krettly Quartet: Robert Krettly and René
       Costard, vn.; Roger Météhen, va.; André Navarra, vc.

W122. Chamber Music March 16, 1931; ms.; 2 min.)

       Text by Alfred Kreymbord
       Vocal range: c-g
       With pf. accompaniment

W123. La Belle en dormant (Aug 20 & Oct 1, 1931; G. Schirmer (o.p.);
       Boosey & Hawkes; 4 min. 30 sec.)

       Text by Georges Hugnet, translated by Elaine de Sirçay as "Beauty
       Sleeping"
       With pf. accompaniment
       1. Pour chercher sur la carte des mers ("Scanning Booklets from
           Ocean Resorts") (vocal range: d-e)
       2. La Première de toutes ("My True Love Sang Me No Song") (vocal
           range: c-g.)
       3. Mon Amour es bon à dire ("Yes, My Love is Good To Tell of")
           (vocal range: c-f.)
       4. Partis les vaisseaux ("All Gone Are the Ships") (vocal range:
           c-f.)

       Brief Mention: MM 21:164 (March-April 1944); MA 71:30 (July 1951);
       Notes 8:580+ (June 1951)

W124. Pigeons on the Grass Alas (1934; G. Schirmer; 3 min.)

       Text by Gertrude Stein
       Arranged for baritone and pf. from the opera Four Saints in Three
       Acts (1928; G. Schirmer; See W1)

W125. Go to Sleep, Alexander Smallens, Jr. (Dec 1935; ms.; 1 min.)

       Vocal range: b-d
       For voice unaccompanied

W126. Go to Sleep, Pare McTaggett Lorentz (June 1937; ms.; 1 min.)

Vocal range: d-d sharp
For voice unaccompanied

W127. <u>Dirge</u> (July 19, 1939; G. Schirmer; 1 min. 30 sec.) See: A20

Text by John Webster
Vocal range: d-f
With pf. accompaniment

W128. The <u>Bugle Song</u> (Sept 1941; ms; 1 min. 30 sec.)

Text by Tennyson
For mezzo-soprano or baritone and pf.
Also arranged for union children's chorus and pf. (1961; Holt, Rinehart, & Winston; See W77)
Also arranged for two-part children's chorus (SS or SA) (ms.)

W129. <u>Four Songs to Poems of Thomas Campion</u> (July 10-13, 1951; Southern; 9 min.) See: B55 & B161

For mezzo-soprano and pf.
Also arranged for mezzo-soprano with cl., va., and harp (1951; Southern; See W187)
Also arranged for mixed chorus (SATB) and pf. (1955; Southern; See W84)
1. Follow Your Saint (vocal range: c sharp-f)
2. There is a Garden in Her Face (vocal range:d-e)
3. Rose Cheek'd Laura, Come (vocal range: d flat-f)
4. Follow Thy Fair Sun (vocal range: c (a flat)-f(a flat))

Brief Mention: <u>NYT</u> (Feb 12, 1952): 22; <u>Notes</u> 12:154 (Dec 1954); <u>MA</u> 74:26 (Dec 1, 1954); <u>Na</u> 188:415 (May 2, 1959); <u>NYT</u> (Nov 5, 1963): 24; <u>Notes</u> 31:162 (Sept 1974)

W130. <u>Five Songs from William Blake</u> (1951; Southern; 18 min.) See: B146, B160, B161, B167, & B180

For baritone and pf.
Also arranged for baritone and orchestra (1951; Southern; See W37)
1. The Divine Image (vocal range: a flat-e flat)
2. Tiger! Tiger! (vocal range: a-g.) Also arranged for mixed chorus (SATB) and pf. or men's chorus (TTBB) and pf. (1955; Southern; See W85)
3. The Land of Dreams (vocal range one version: c-f sharp; (Southern Music); Second version (for baritone and pf. only): b flat-e (ms.))
4. The Little Black Boy (vocal range one version: a flat- f; (Southern); Second version(for baritone and pf. only): g-e (ms.))
5. "And Did Those Feet" (vocal range: a-g)
Commissioned by the Louisville Philharmonic Society

Brief Mention: <u>MC</u> 145:14 (March 15, 1952); <u>Notes</u> 12:154 (Dec 1954); <u>MQ</u> 41:77 (1955); <u>MA</u> 81:44 (Dec 1961); <u>National Associa-</u>

tion of Teachers of Singing Bulletin 23:16+ (No. 3; 1967); Notes 31:162 (Sept 1974)

Premiere: Feb 6, 1952; Louisville, KY; Columbia Auditorium; Mack Harrell, baritone; Louisville Orchestra; Virgil Thomson, cond.

W131. Consider, Lord (Aug 25, 1955; Southern; 1 min.)

Text by John Donne
Vocal range: b flat-d
With pf. accompaniment

W132. The Holly and the Ivy (Aug 25, 1955; ms.; 2 min. 15 sec.)

A carol of Nativity and Lent (Anonymous text, 1557)
Two vocal versions: b flat-f and c-g
Also arranged for mixed chorus (SATB) (1963; G. Schirmer; See W90)

Brief Mention: MA 79:23 (Dec 15, 1959)

Premiere: Nov 16, 1959; New York City; Carnegie Recital Hall; Phyllis Curtin, soprano; Virgil Thomson, pf.

W133. Remember Adam's Fall (Aug 1955; Gray/Belwin Mills; 2 min. 30 sec.)

Anonymous text (15th century)
4 vocal versions: c-g (Gray/Belwin Mills); a-e (Gray/Belwin Mills); b (d)-f sharp (ms.); bar. a-e (ms.)
With pf. accompaniment

Brief Mention: MA 79:23 (Dec 15, 1959)

Premiere: Nov 16, 1959; New York City; Carnegie Recital Hall; Phyllis Curtin, soprano; Virgil Thomson, cond.

W134. At the Spring (August 1955; Gray/Belwin Mills; 1 min.)

Text by Jasper Fisher
Vocal range: d-g
With pf. accompaniment

Brief Mention: MA 79:23 (Dec 15, 1959)

Premiere: Nov 16, 1959; New York City; Carnegie Recital Hall; Phyllis Curtin, soprano; Virgil Thomson, pf.

W135. The Bell Doth Toll (Aug 1955; Southern; 1 min. 40 sec.)

Text by Thomas Heywood
Vocal range: b-e
With pf. accompaniment

W136. Look, How the Floor of Heaven (Aug 1955; Gray/Belwin Mills; 1 min.)

Text by Shakespeare
Vocal range: c sharp-g flat
With pf. accompaniment

Brief Mention: MA 79:23 (Dec 15, 1959)

Premiere: Nov 16, 1959; New York City; Carnegie Recital Hall;
    Phyllis Curtin, soprano; Virgil Thomson, pf.

W137. If Thou A Reason Dost Desire to Know (Begun Sept 4, 1955; com-
    pleted 1958; Southern; 2 min.)

Text by Sir Francis Kynaston
Two vocal versions: c-f (Southern) and bar. b-e (ms.)
With pf. accompaniment

W138. John Peel (Sept 1955; Southern; 3 min.)

Text by John Woodcock Graves
Two vocal versions: Bar. b-e (Southern) and bar. a-d (ms.)
With pf. accompaniment

W139. Shakespeare Songs (1956-57; Southern; 4 min.)

With pf. accompaniment
1. Was This Fair Face the Cause? (from All's Well That Ends
    Well), vocal range: f-f
2. Take, O Take Those Lips Away (from incidental music to Measure
    for Measure; 1956; See W341), vocal range: e-f
3. Tell Me Where is Fancy Bred (from incidental music to The
    Merchant of Venice; 1957; See W343), vocal range: f-g
4. Pardon, Goddess of the Night (from incidental music to Much
    Ado About Nothing; 1957; See 344), vocal range: d-e flat
    (Published individually but o.p.)
5. Sigh No More, Ladies (from incidental music to Much Ado About
    Nothing; 1957; See W344), vocal range: d-a(f)

W140. Tres Estampas de Niñez (1957; Southern; 6 min.)

Text by Reyna Rivas, translated by Sherry Mangan as "Three
    Sketches from Childhood"
1. Todas las horas ("All Through the Long Day"), vocal range: e-f
2. Son amigos de todos ("They Are Everyone's Friends"), vocal
    range: e-f sharp
3. Nadie lo oye como ellos ("No One Can Hear Him The Way They
    Can"), vocal range: d-g

Brief Mention: MA 79:23 (Dec 15, 1959); NYT (Nov 5, 1963): 24

W141. My Shepherd Will Supply My Need (Feb 21, 1959; Gray/Belwin Mills;
    3 min.)

Isaac Watts's paraphrase of Psalm 23
Arranged for voice and pf. (or organ) from the choral original
    (1937; Gray/Belwin Mills; See W75)

Vocal range: d-f sharp
Also published in: <u>Folk</u> <u>Songs</u> <u>in</u> <u>Settings</u> <u>by</u> <u>Master</u> <u>Composers</u>
edited by Herbert Haufrecht. New York: Funk & Wagnalls,1970.
Rpt. New York: Da Capo Press, 1977. See: T138

W142. <u>Mostly</u> <u>About</u> <u>Love</u> (April & October 1959; G. Schirmer) See: B4

Text by Kenneth Koch
With pf. accompaniment
Originally titled <u>Songs</u> <u>for</u> <u>Alice</u> <u>Esty</u>
Each published separately
1. Love Song (vocal range: c-g; 3 min.)
2. Down at the Docks (vocal range: d-g; 3 min.)
3. Let's Take a Walk (vocal range: d-g; 3 min.)
4. A Prayer to St. Catherine (vocal range: e flat-f; 4 min.)

Premiere: April 3, 1960; New York City; Carnegie Recital Hall;
Alice Esty, soprano; David Stimer, pf.

W143. <u>Collected</u> <u>Poems</u> (April 1959; Southern; 7 min.)

Text by Kenneth Koch
For soprano, baritone, and pf.
Vocal range: d-g and bar. c-f
Also arranged for soprano, baritone, and orchestra (1959; Sou-
thern; See W43)
Commissioned by the Festival of Two Worlds (Spoleto, Italy)

Brief Mention: <u>MA</u> 82:42+ (Feb 1962)

Premiere: Dec 14, 1961; New York City; Carnegie Recital Hall;
Marten Sameth, baritone; Dorothy Renzi, soprano; David Garvey,
pf.

W144. <u>Mass</u> <u>for</u> <u>Solo</u> <u>Voice</u> (Sept 1960; G. Schirmer; 10 min.)

In Latin
Vocal range: b flat-f
With pf. accompaniment
Also arranged for unison choir and pf. (Sept 1960; G. Schirmer;
See W88)
Also arranged for voice (or unison choir) and orchestra (1962; G.
Schirmer; See W46)

Brief Mention: <u>MA</u> 80:63 (Nov 1960); <u>MC</u> 162:34 (Dec 1960); <u>NYT</u> (Dec
19, 1961): 37; <u>MA</u> 82:44 (Feb 1962); <u>NYT</u> (Nov 5, 1963):24

Premiere: Oct 3, 1960; New York City; Town Hall; Betty Allen,
mezzo-soprano; Paul Ulanovsky, pf.

W145. <u>Stabat</u> <u>Mater</u> (1960; rev. 1981; Boosey & Hawkes; 5 min.)

Text in French by Max Jacob
Arranged for voice and pf. from the original for soprano and
string quartet (1931; Boosey & Hawkes; See W121)

W146. Praises and Prayers (March 1963; G. Schirmer; 20 min.)

Each published separately
1. From "The Canticle of the Sun," by St. Francis of   Assisi,
    translated by Matthew Arnold (vocal range: c sharp-e (f
    sharp))
2. My Master Hath a Garden (Anon.) (vocal range: f-e flat) Also
    arranged for mixed chorus (SATB) or women's chorus (SSA) and
    pf.(Dec 15, 1963; G. Schirmer; See W91)
3. Sung by the Shepherds (from "Hymn to the Nativity" by Richard
    Crashaw) (vocal range: d-g) (Also published in Contemporary
    American Sacred Songs (G. Schirmer), 1985)
4. Before Sleeping (Anon.) (Two vocal versions: d-d (G. Schir-
    mer) and b flat-b flat (ms.))
5. Jerusalem, My Happy Home (from The Meditations of St.
    Augustine, Chapter XXV) (vocal range: d-f sharp)

Brief Mention: MA 83:40 (Nov 1963); NYT (Nov 5, 1963):24; Listen
(Metropolitan Museum of Art Notes) (Dec 1963): 23

Premiere: Oct 24, 1963; New York City; Grace Rainey Rogers Auditorium; Metropolitan Museum of Art; Betty Allen, mezzo-soprano;
Virgil Thomson, pf.

W147. Two by Marianne Moore (Aug 8, 1963; G. Schirmer; 4 min. 30 sec.)

Each published separately
1. English Usage (vocal range: d-e) Also published in
    Contemporary Art Songs: 28 Songs by American and British
    Composers (1970; G. Schirmer)
2. My Crow Pluto (vocal range: d-f)

Brief Mention: MA 84:34 (Feb 1964)

Premiere: Of "My Crow Pluto": Jan 13, 1964; New York City;
Carnegie Recital Hall; Alice Esty, soprano; David Stimer, pf.

W148. The Feast of Love (July-Aug 1964; ms.; 8 min.) See: B177

From the Pervigilium Veneris (see T41), translated by Virgil
Thomson
For baritone and pf. (vocal range: d-g)
Also arranged for baritone and orchestra (vocal range d-g) (1964;
G. Schirmer; See W48)

Brief Mention: MA 84:64 (Dec 1964); HF 19:30 (March 1969); Musicians and Artists 2:36 (No. 1, 1969); Boletin Interamericano de
Musica 72:70 (July 1969)

[From Byron's "Don Juan" for orchestra and tenor; 1967; Southern; See
W52]

W149. From "Sneden's Landing Variations" (April 6, 1972; Lingua Press; 2
min)

Text by Frank O'Hara
Vocal range: e-e flat
With pf. accompaniment

Brief Mention: NYT (April 28, 1972): 34; HF 22:MA13 (Aug 1972)

Premiere: April 26, 1972; New York City; Whitney Museum; Composers' Showcase Concert; Phyllis Curtin, soprano

W150. The Courtship of Yongly Bongly Bo (1973-74; G. Schirmer; 6 min. 16 sec.)

Text by Edward Lear
Originally a portion of the Cantata on Poems of Edward Lear (1973-4; G. Schirmer; See W97)
Vocal range: e flat-f
With pf. accompaniment

Brief Mention: NYT (April 30, 1975): 24

Premiere: April 28, 1975; New York City; Fifth Avenue Presbyterian Church Chapel; Emily Derr, soprano; John Ryan, pf.

W151. Go to Sleep, Gabriel Liebowitz (Nov 17. 1979; ms.; 1 min.)

For voice unaccompanied

W152. What Is It? (Dec 1979; Presser)

Text by Thomas Campion
With pf. accompaniment
Also arranged with guitar accompaniment by David Leisner (Presser)

W153. The Cat (June and July 1980; G. Schirmer)

Text by Jack Larson
For soprano and baritone with pf.

CHAMBER AND INSTRUMENTAL WORKS

W154. Prelude (Nov 25, 1921; McAfee Music; 2 min.)

For pf.
Also arranged for organ by Calvin Hampton (1979; McAfee Music)

W155. Pastorale on a Christmas Plainsong (Jan 3, 1922; Gray/Belwin Mills; 3 min.)

For organ
Also appears in collection Contemporary Organ Series (14; 1942)
1. Divinium Mysterium
2. God Rest Ye Merry
3. Picardy

W156. Fanfare (Jan 4, 1922; H.W.Gray/Belwin Mills; 2 min.)

For organ

W157. Prelude (Feb 10, 1922; G. Schirmer; 2 min.)

For organ

W158. Passacaglia (June 1922; rev. 1974; G. Schirmer; 6 min. 30 sec.)

For organ

W159. Two Sentimental Tangos (1923; ms.; 5 min.) See: A10 & A21

For pf.
Originally Three Sentimental Tangos
Also arranged for orchestra (1923; ms.; See W9)
1. Slow and Smooth
2. Not Fast

W160. Five Chorale-Preludes (1924; G. Schirmer; 7 min.)

For organ
1. O,Sacred Head Now Wounded!   (O,   Haupt   von   Blut   und
   Wunden!)
2. The   New-Born   Babe   (1st   version)   (Das   neugeborne   Kinde-
   lein)
3. The New-Born Babe (2nd version)
4. The New-Born Babe (3rd version)
5. Praise God, ye Christians Ev'rywhere (Lobt Gott ihr   Christen
   allzugleich)

W161. Synthetic Waltzes (1925; Presser; 6 min.) See: A21

For 2 pf., 4 hands
Also for 1 pf., 4 hands (Presser)

Brief Mention: MM 20:201 (March-April 1942); Music Clubs Magazine
28:15 (Jan-Feb 1949); MA 69:293 (Feb 1949); Musicology 2:317
(April 1949); NYT (Nov 18, 1971):59; NYer 47:97+ (Nov 27,   1971)

W162. Sonata da Chiesa (Feb 1926; rev. 1973; Boosey & Hawkes; 15 min.)
       See: B44, B141, B160, & B176

For cl. in E flat, tpt. in D, va., hn., and tbn.
1. Chorale
2. Tango
3. Fugue

Brief Mention: MM   4:35 (Nov-Dec 1926); MM 21:243+ (May-June
1944); MM 22:200 (Jan-Feb 1945); MM 22:258+ (May-June 1945); MQ
35:211 (1949); Na 188:415 (May 2, 1959); NYT (Dec 19, 1961): 37;
MA 82:44 (Feb 1962)

Premiere: May 5, 1926; Paris, France; Salle des Concerts, Maison
Gaveau; Chester Mackee, cond.

W163. <u>Five</u> <u>Two-Part</u> <u>Inventions</u> (1926; Presser; 6 min. 15 sec.)

    For pf.
    1. With Marked Rhythm   4. Rhythmically
    2. Freely   5. Firmly
    3. Flowing
    Also four of the five inventions arranged for guitar by David
        Leisner (1981; Presser)
    Also arranged for two pf. by Arthur Gold and Robert Fizdale (ms.)

    Brief Mention: <u>MM</u> 23:123 (Winter 1946)

W164. <u>Ten</u> <u>Easy</u> <u>Pieces</u> <u>and</u> <u>a</u> <u>Coda</u> (Dec 1926; Southern; 6 min.) See: A20

    For pf.
    To be played without pause
    1. A Plain Song   7. Two People
    2. Light Fingers   8. Improvising
    3. Pathos   9. The Night Before
    4. Counting   Christmas
    5. Marching   10.Assembly
    6. Two-Part Invention   Coda

W165. <u>Variations</u> on <u>Sunday</u> <u>School</u> <u>Tunes</u> (1926-27; Gray/Belwin Mills; 24
    min.) See: B139, B141, & B160

    For organ
    Originally published separately; now collected as <u>Variations</u> <u>on</u>
    <u>Four</u> <u>Sunday</u> <u>School</u> <u>Themes</u>
    1. Come, Ye Disconsolate (Dec 8-9, 1926)
    2. There's Not a Friend Like the Lowly Jesus (Dec 1926)
    3. Will There Be Any Stars in My Crown? (Jan & May, 1927)
    4. Shall We Gather at the River? (Nov 7, 1927)

    Brief Mention: <u>Diapason</u> 45:34 (Nov 1, 1954)

W166. <u>Portraits</u> <u>for</u> <u>Violin</u> <u>Alone</u> (1928-1940; Boosey & Hawkes)

    Published together
    1. Señorita Juanita de Medina Accompanied by Her Mother (July 21,
        1928; 1 min. 30 sec.)
    2. Madame Marthe-Marthine (Aug 31, 1928; 1 min.)
    3. Georges Hugnet, Poet and Man of Letters (Oct 1928; 1 min.)
    4. Miss Gertrude Stein as a Young Girl (Oct 14, 1928; 1 min.)
    5. Cliquet-Pleyel in F (Oct 14, 1928; 2 min.)
    6. Mrs. C.W.L. [i.e.,Chester Whitin Lasell] (Oct 18, 1928; 1 min.
        30 sec.)
    7. Sauguet, From Life (Nov 5, 1928; 1 min.)
    8. Ruth Smallens (Sept 15, 1940; 2 min.)

    Brief Mention: <u>MM</u> 23:124 (Spring 1946)

    Premiere: Nov 14, 1928; Paris, France; Salle Majestic; Lucien
        Schwartz, vn.

W167. Five Portraits for Four Clarinets (1929; G. Schirmer; 9 min.)

For 2 cl., alto cl. in E flat, bass cl.
Commissioned by Georges Hugnet
1. Portrait of Ladies: A Conversation (Jan 16, 1929)
2. Portrait of a Young Man in Good Health: Maurice Grosser with a
     Cold (July 7, 1929)
3. Christian Bérard, Prisoner (May 4 & 8, 1929)
4. Christian Bérard as a Soldier (July 9, 1929)
5. Christian Bérard in Person (July 11, 1929)

Premiere: 1929; Boston, MA; The Boston Flute Players Club

W168. Le Bains-Bar (1929; ms.; 4 min. 40 sec.)

Waltz for vn. and pf.
Also arranged for two vn., vc., bass, and pf. (ms.)
Also arranged with the title At the Beach for tpt. and pf.
  (1949; Carl Fischer; See W185) or for tpt. and band (1949; Carl
  Fischer; See W33)

W169. Piano Sonata No. 1 (Nov 1929; MCA/Belwin Mills; 15 min.) See: B112
  & B175

1. Allegro
2. Uguale
3. Finale
Also scored for orchestra as Symphony No. 2 in C Major (1931; rev.
  1941; Leeds/Belwin Mills; See W12)

W170. Piano Sonata No. 2 (Dec 10-16, 1929; MCA/Belwin Mills; 7 min.)
  See: B112 & B175

1. Cantabile
2. Sostenuto
3. Leggiero e brillante
Also scored for harp and orchestra and published as last three
  movements of Autumn: Concertino for Harp, Strings, and Percussion (1964-65; G.Schirmer; See W49)

W171. Sonata for Violin and Piano(July 26, 1930; Boosey & Hawkes; 14
  min.) See: B47

1. Allegro
2. Andante Nobile
3. Tempo di Valzer
4. Andante: Doppio movimento

Brief Mention: MM 19:175 & 205 (March-April 1942); MM 19:271 (May-
  June 1942); MM 23:144 (Spring 1946); MA 75:27 (Dec 15, 1955); Na
  188:415 (May 2, 1959); NYT (Dec 19, 1961): 37; MA 82:44 (Feb
  1962)

Premiere: Jan 24, 1931; Paris, France; Salle des Conferences du
  Parthénon; Lucien Schwartz, vn.; Virgil Thomson, pf.

W172. Portraits for Violin and Piano (1930-40; G. Schirmer)

Published in 1983 together with another portrait (Cynthia Kemper, A Fanfare; 1983; See W204) with the title Five Ladies
1. Alice Toklas (March 27, 1930; 3 min.)
2. Mary Reynolds (April 15, 1930; 1 min.)
3. Anne Miracle (April 21, 1930; 1 min.)
4. Yvonne de Casa Fuerte (April 17, 1940; 2 min.)

W173. Piano Sonata No. 3, "on white keys" (July 17-18, 1930; Southern; 5 min.) See: B112 & B175

For Gertrude Stein
Four movements to be played without pause
1. Bold
2. Softer
3. Very Soft and Without Accent; Gay and Getting Gradually Louder and Gayer
4. Sustained

Brief Mention: MM 21:183 (March-April 1944)

W174. String Quartet No. 1 (March 1931; rev. 1957; Boosey & Hawkes; 19 min.) See: B176

1. Allegro moderato   3. Tempo di Valzer
2. Adagio   4. Lento; presto

Brief Mention: MM 18:245 & 259 (May-June 1941); MM 19:110 (Jan-Feb 1942); MM 21:259 (May-June 1944); MA 80:29 (Jan 15, 1960)

Premiere: June 15, 1931; Paris, France; Salle Chopin; The Krettly Quartet: Robert Krettly & René Costard, vn.; Roger Météhen, va.; André Navarra, vc.

[Stabat Mater, March, 1931, for soprano and string quartet; See W121]

W175. Serenade for Flute and Violin (Nov 1931; Southern; 5 min.) See: B12

1. March   4. Flourish
2. Aria   5. Hymn
3. Fanfare

Brief Mention: MM 13:36 (Jan-Feb 1936); MM 20:259 (May-June 1943); MA 72:26 (Nov 15, 1952); MC 146:31 (Nov 15, 1952); Notes 10:144 (Dec 1952); HF 23:96 (Sept 1973)

Premiere: Nov 13, 1935; New York City; Midtown Community Music Center; The WPA-Federal Music Project Concerts; Dr. Carleton Sprague Smith, fl.; Ruth Kemper, vn.

W176. String Quartet No. 2 (1932; rev. 1957; Boosey & Hawkes; 21 min.) See: B152 & B176

1. Allegro moderato   3. Adagio sostenuto
2. Tempo di valzer   4. Allegretto
Also arranged for use in the ballet in Act III, Scene 2 of the
  opera Lord Byron (1966-68; Southern; See W6); also arranged for
  pf. solo (1966-68; ms.; See W197)
Also scored for orchestra with the title Symphony No. 3 (1972;
  Boosey & Hawkes; See W56)

Brief Mention: MM 18 245+ & 259 (May-June 1941); MM 19:110 (Jan-
  Feb 1942); MM 23:67 (Winter 1946); MQ 41:551+ (1955); Music &
  Musicians 25:64+ (Nov 1976)

Premieres:
  Private: April 14, 1933; New York City; the home of Philip
    Johnson; The Philharmonic String Quartet: Joseph Reilich &
    Ralph Hersh, vn.; David Dawson, va.; Martin Siecholz, vc.
  Public: Dec 15, 1934; Hartford, CT; Avery Auditorium; The Wads-
    worth Atheneum; The Friends and Enemies of Modern Music con-
    certs; The Philharmonic String Quartet (see private premiere
    above)

W177. Symphony No. 2 in C Major (1932; Leeds/Belwin Mills; 15 min.)

      Arranged for 1 pf., 4 hands from the orchestral original (1931;
      Leeds/Belwin Mills; See W12)

W178. Suite from "The Plow That Broke the Plains" (Feb 1936; G. Schir-
      mer; 9 min. 40 sec.)

      Arranged for pf. from the orchestral original (1936; G. Schirmer;
      See W13)
      1. Prelude   3. Blues
      2. Cowboy Songs   4. Finale
      "Prelude" also published in Keyboard Classics, March/April 1981,
      pp. 30-31.

W179. Filling Station (Nov 1937; Boosey & Hawkes; 21 min.)

      Arranged for pf. from the original ballet score (1937; Boosey &
      Hawkes; See W2)

W180. Church Organ Wedding Music (1940; rev. 1978; Randall M. Eagan and
      Associates, 2 min.)

      1. To Go In
      2. To Come Out

[Piano Sonata No. 4: Guggenheim jeune (Portrait of Peggy Guggenheim);
      1940; Southern; See W244]

W181. Ten Etudes for Piano (1943-44; Carl Fischer; 17 min.) See: A1 and
      B130, B172, & B229

      1. Repeating Tremolo (Fanfare) (July 12, 1943)
      2. Tenor Lead (Madrigal) (July 9, 1943; also published

separately by Carl Fischer)
3. Fingered Fifths (Canon) (July 14, 1943)
4. Fingered Glissando (Aeolian Harp) (Sept 29, 1944)
5. Double Glissando (Waltz) (July 11, 194)
6. For the Weaker Fingers (Music Box Lullaby) (Aug 12, 1943)
7. Oscillating Arm (Spinning Song) (Aug 11, 1943)
8. Five-Finger Exercise (Portrait of Briggs Buchanan; Aug 15, 1943; See W267)
9. Parallel Chords (Tango) (Aug 16, 1943)
10. Ragtime Bass (Aug 12, 1943; also published separately in two versions, one simplified, both by Carl Fischer)

Brief Mention: NYT (Nov 28, 1945): 21; MM 23:50 & 136 (Winter 1946); Notes 12:329+ (March 1955); MQ 40:629 (1954)

Premiere: Nov 27, 1945; New York City; Carnegie Hall; E. Robert Schmitz, pf.

W182. Sonata for Flute Alone (Sept 1943; Presser; 10 min.)

1. Adagio; Allegro
2. Adagio
3. Vivace

Premiere: Autumn, 1943; Rene LeRoy, fl.

W183. Barcarolle for Woodwinds (1944; G. Schirmer; 1 min. 30 sec.)

Arranged from the pf. portrait of Georges Hugnet (1940; G. Schirmer; See W238)   Fl./ob./Eng. hn./hn./cl./bass cl./bn.

Brief Mention: MC 143:29 (May 15, 1951); Notes 9:166 (Dec 1951)

Premiere: Nov 29, 1946; Pittsburgh, PA; Syria Mosque; Pittsburgh Symphony Orchestra; Virgil Thomson, cond.

W184. Sonorous and Exquisite Corpses (1944-47; Peters)

20 short pieces composed collaboratively by John Cage, Henry Cowell, Lou Harrison, and Virgil Thomson
Also arranged by Robert Hughes for fl., cl., bn., hn., and pf., and published with the title Party Pieces (1982; Peters)

W185. At the Beach (Jan 1949; Carl Fischer; 4 min. 40 sec.)

Concert waltz for tpt. and pf. from the original for vn. and pf. entitled Le Bains-Bar (1929; ms.; See W168)
Commissioned by Edna White

Premiere: Feb 19, 1949; New York City; Carnegie Hall; Edna White, tpt.

W186. Concerto for Violoncello and Orchestra (1950; Ricordi/Belwin Mills; 21 min.)

Arranged for vc. and pf. (1950; Ricordi/Belwin Mills; See W36)
1. Rider on the Plains
2. Variations on a Southern Hymn
3. Children's Games

W187. Four Songs to Poems of Thomas Campion (1951; Southern)

Arranged for mezzo-soprano with cl., va., and harp from the original for mezzo-soprano and pf. (1951; Southern; See W129)

Brief Mention: NYT (Feb 12, 1952): 22; Notes 12:154 (Dec 1954); MA 74:26 (Dec 1, 1954); Na 188:415 (May 2, 1959); NYT (Nov 5, 1963): 24; Notes 31:162 (Sept 1974)

Premiere: Feb 1, 1952; New York City; Town Hall; Musicians' Guild Concert; Herta Glaz, mezzo-soprano; Lillian Fuchs, va.; Carlos Salzedo, harp; Napoleon Cerminara, cl.

W188. Nine Etudes for Piano (1940 and 1951; G. Schirmer; 15 min.) See: B23 & B172

1. With Trumpet and Horn (Portrait of Louise Ardant; April 11, 1940; G. Schirmer; See W235)
2. Pivoting on the Thumb (June 23, 1951)
3. Alternating Octaves (June 26, 1951)
4. Double Sevenths (July 7, 1951)
5. The Harp (June 22, 1951)
6. Chromatic Major Seconds (The Wind) (June 20, 1951)
7. Chromatic Double Harmonies (Portrait of Sylvia Marlowe; June 17,1951; See W269) (Also published by G. Schirmer in Etudes, Vol. 2, 1985)
8. Broken Arpeggios (The Waltzing Waters) (July 10,1951)
9. Guitar and Mandolin (June 18,1951)

Brief Mention: MA 82:44 (Feb 1962)

W189. Walking Song (1951; ms.; 2 min.)

Arranged for pf. from the score for the film "Tuesday in November" (1945; See W319)
Also arranged for two pf. by Arthur Gold and Robert Fizdale (between 1945 and 1950; G. Schirmer)

Brief Mention: Musical Opinion 76:353 (March 1953)

W190. For a Happy Occasion (June 23, 1951; Peters; 20 sec.)

Originally entitled "Happy Birthday, Mrs. Zimbalist"
Published in Waltzes by 25 Contemporary Composers (1978; Peters)

W191. Concerto for Flute, Strings, Harp, and Percussion (1954; Ricordi/Belwin Mills; 13 min.)

Portrait of Roger Baker
Arranged for fl. and pf. (1954; Ricordi/Belwin Mills; See W39)

1. Rapsodico (unacc.)
2. Lento
3. Ritmico

W192. A Study in Stacked-Up Thirds (Aug 18, 1958; Southern; 1 min.)

For pf. solo
Rev. 1969 and published in Nine Portraits for Piano with the title
For Eugene Ormandy's Birthday, 18 November 1969: A Study in
Stacked-Up Thirds (Southern; See W272)

W193. Lamentations: Etude for Accordion (May 1959; Santee Music; 5 min.)
See: B8

Commissioned by the American Accordionists' Association for
publication, not performance

Brief Mention: NYT (Dec 19, 1961): 37; NYT (Nov 29, 1964): 14

W194. Variations for Koto (Oct 1961; ms.; 2 min. 50 sec.)

W195. Pange Lingua (March 1962; G. Schirmer; 9 min.) See: B21

For organ

Brief Mention: American Organist 46:14 (Feb 1963); MA 83:22+ (Feb
1963); MJ 21:98 (Feb 1963)

Premiere: Dec 15, 1962; New York City; Philharmonic Hall; E.
Power Biggs, organ

W196. Etude for Cello and Piano: A Portrait of Frederic James (Dec 18,
1966; ms. 1 min. 30 sec.)

W197. Ballet Music from Act III, Scene 2 of "Lord Byron" (1966-68; ms.)

Arranged for pf. solo from the opera Lord Byron (1966-68; Southern; See W6)

W198. Family Portrait (1974; G. Schirmer; 10 min. 15 sec.)

For brass quintet (2 tpt./hn./2 tbn.)
1. A Fanfare: Robin Smith
2. At Fourteen: Anne Barnard
3. Digging: A Portrait of Howard Rea
4. A Scherzo: Priscilla Rea
5. Man of Iron: Willy Eisenhart (from the pf. portrait; 1972; G.
     Schirmer; See W273)
Commissioned by the American Brass Quintet

Premiere: March 24, 1975; New York City; Carnegie Recital Hall;
The American Brass Quintet: Raymond Mase & Louis Ranger, tpt.;
Edward Birdwell, hn.; Herbert Ranklin, tenor tbn.; Robert Bid-
dlecome, bass tbn.

W199. Parson Weems and the Cherry Tree (Oct 1975; Boosey & Hawkes; 25 min.)

Arranged for pf. from the ballet (1975; Boosey & Hawkes; See W8)

W200. Theme for Improvisation (Aug 1-2, 1981; ms.)

For organist McNeil Robinson of St. Mary the Virgin

W201. For Lou Harrison and His Jolly Games 16 Measures (Count'em) (Oct 13, 1981; ms.) See: B34

Theme without instrumentation
Also arranged for gamelan and speaking voice by Lou Harrison and Jody Diamond with the title Gending Chelsea (1981; ms.)

Premiere: Of Gending Chelsea: May 10, 1982; Oakland, CA: Mills College; at a birthday celebratory concert for Lou Harrison

W202. A Short Fanfare (Oct 25, 1981; ms.)

For 2 or 3 trumpets, or 3 trumpets and 2 drums

W203. Bell Piece (April 9-10, 1983; G. Schirmer)

Written for the Yale Carillon
For 2 or 4 players

W204. Cynthia Kemper: A Fanfare (May 8, 1983; G. Schirmer)

Portrait for vn. and pf.
Published in Five Ladies with the Portraits for Violin and Piano (1930-40; G. Schirmer; See W172)

W205. Lili Hastings (Oct 6, 1983; ms.)

Portrait for vn. and pf.

Premiere: Oct 9, 1983; Middletown, CT; Wesleyan University; Sharan Leventhal, vn.; Anthony Tommasini, pf.

W206. A Portrait of Two (April 18 & 19, 1984; G. Schirmer)

For ob., bn., and pf.
1. Tempo commodo
2. Andante
3. Alert

W207. Jay Rozen (April 24, 1984; ms.)

For bass tuba and pf.

W208. Stockton Fanfare (Jan 3, 1985; Gentry Publications)

For 3 tpt. and 2 side drums (1 snare and 1 field)

PIANO PORTRAITS

The following abbreviations have been used to indicate collective publication of the portraits:

> GS-1 = Portraits for Piano Solo, Album 1
> GS-2 = Portraits for Piano Solo, Album 2
> GS-3 = Portraits for Piano Solo, Album 3
> GS-4 = Portraits for Piano Solo, Album 4
> SOU = Nine Portraits for Piano
> B&H-1981 = Thirteen Portraits for Piano
> B&H-1983 = Nineteen Portraits for Piano
> GS-1984 = Seventeen Portraits for Piano

Portraits published separately are indicated as such. Also indicated is whether portraits or portions of portraits are used in other works.

The following are brief mentions about the portraits in general or the collections:

> GS-1: Music Clubs Magazine 28:15 (Jan-Feb 1949); MA 69:291 (Feb 1949)

> GS-2: Notes 8:137 (Dec 1950)

> GS-3: MC 142:29 (Nov 1, 1950); MA 70:30 (Nov 15, 1950); Music Clubs Magazine 30:19 (Feb 1951)

> GS-4: MA 73:24 (Dec 15, 1953); Canon 7:220 (Dec 1953-Jan 1954)

> In General: MM 13:51 (Nov-Dec 1935); MM 18:246 (May-June 1941); MM 20:31 (Nov-Dec 1942); Revue Musicale 212:16 (1952); MR 16:269 (Aug 1955). See also: B103, B183 & B229

Anthony Tommasini's Virgil Thomson's Musical Portraits discusses each of the works below. See B184.

W209. Travelling in Spain: Alice Woodfin Branliere (Oct 24, 1929; B&H-1981; 1 min. 30 sec.)

W210. Alternations: A Portrait of Maurice Grosser (Oct 28, 1929; GS-1; 1 min. 30 sec.)

W211. Catalan Waltz: A Portrait of Ramón Senabre (Nov 2, 1929; GS-2; 1 min. 30 sec.)

W212. Clair Leonard's Profile (Jan 22, 1930; B&H-1981; 1 min.)

W213. Madame Dubost chez elle (Feb 1, 1930; SOU; 1 min.)

> Also arranged by Y. Mikhashoff for tbn. with va. and vc. accompaniment (1979; ms.)

W214. Pastoral: A Portrait of Jean Ozenne (Feb 20, 1930; GS-3; 1 min. 20 sec.)

W215. Russell Hitchcock, Reading (May 29, 1930; SOU; 1 min.)

    Also arranged by Y. Mikhashoff for tbn. with va. and vc. accompaniment (1980; ms.)

W216. Sea Coast: A Portrait of Constance Askew (April 30, May 4 1935; GS-2; 1 min.)

W217. A Portrait of R. Kirk Askew [Jr.] (May 1, 1935; GS-2; 1 min. 30 sec.)

W218. Souvenir: A Portrait of Paul Bowles (May 2, 1935; GS-3; 1 min.)

W219. Ettie Stettheimer (May 5, 1935; SOU; 1 min.)

W220. An Old Song: A Portrait of Carrie Stettheimer (May 5-10, 1935; GS-1; 1 min. 30 sec.)

    Also arranged by Y. Mikhashoff for tbn. with va. and vc. accompaniment (1980; ms.)

W221. Tennis: A Portrait of Henry McBride (May 9, 1935; GS-4; 1 min. 20 sec.)

W222. The Hunt: A Portrait of A. Everett Austin, Jr. (May 21, 1935; GS-4; 1 min. 15 sec.)

W223. Hymn: A Portrait of Josiah Marvel (May 22, 1935; GS-4; 1 min. 30 sec.)

W224. The John Mosher Waltzes (May 1935; Boosey & Hawkes; 2 min. 10 sec.)

    Published as both The John Mosher Waltzes (1937; Boosey & Hawkes; See W16) and No. 6, "Family Life," of the ballet Filling Station (1937; Boosey & Hawkes; See W2)

W225. Prelude and Fugue: A Portrait of Miss Agnes Rindge (Sept 2, 1935; GS-3; 2 min.)

W226. Helen Austin at Home and Abroad (Sept 3, 1935; SOU; 1 min. 20 sec.)

W227. Meditation: A Portrait of Jere Abbott (Sept 6, 1935; GS-2; 2 min.)

    Also arranged for orchestra (1944; G. Schirmer; See W24)

W228. Connecticut Waltz: A Portrait of Harold Lewis Cook (Sept 16, 1935; B&H-1981; 1 min. 15 sec.)

W229. A Day Dream: Portrait of Herbert Whiting (Sept 17, 1935; 2 min.)

    Originally published separately by Carl Fischer
    Also appears in Masters of Our Day (Carl Fischer)

W230. Portrait of Claude Biais (Aug 15, 1938; ms.; 1 min.)

W231. A French Boy of Ten: Louis Lange (Aug 16, 1938; SOU; 1 min.)

W232. Maurice Bavoux: Young and Alone (Aug 17-18, 1938; B&H-1981; 2 min.)

W233. The Bard: A Portrait of Sherry Mangan (April 1, 1940; GS-3; 1 min. 30 sec.)

W234. In a Bird Cage: A Portrait of Lise Deharme (April 8, 1940; GS-2; 1 min. 30 sec.)

> Also arranged for vn. by Samuel Dushkin and published in Three Portraits for Violin and Piano (1946; G. Schirmer)
> Also arranged for vc. and pf. by Luigi Silva and published in Four Portraits for Cello and Piano (1942; G. Schirmer)
> Also arranged for vn. by Frances-Marie Vitti (1982; ms.)

> Brief Mention: MM 23:124 (Spring 1946); MC 143:66 (Feb 15, 1951)

> Premieres:
>> Of Arrangement for Vc. and Pf.: Jan 5, 1943; Rochester, NY; Kilbourn Hall, Eastman School of Music; Luigi Silva, vc.; Emmanuel Balaban, pf.
>> Of Arrangement for Vn. and Pf.: March 12, 1946; New York City; Town Hall; Samuel Dushkin, vn.; Erich Itor Kahn, pf.

W235. With Trumpet and Horn: A Portrait of Louise Ardant (April 11, 1940; G. Schirmer; 2 min. 30 sec.)

> Published in Nine Etudes for Piano (G. Schirmer; See W188)

W236. Poltergeist: A Portrait of Hans Arp (April 12, 1940; GS-4; 1 min.)

W237. Fanfare for France: A Portrait of Max Kahn (April 15, 1940; GS-2; 3 min.)

> Also arranged for brass and perc. (1944; Boosey & Hawkes; See W22)
> Also arranged for vc. and pf. by Luigi Silva and published in Four Portraits for Cello and Piano (1942; G. Schirmer)

> Premiere: Of Arrangement for Vc. and Pf.: Jan 5, 1943; Rochester, NY; Kilbourn Hall, Eastman School of Music; Luigi Silva, vc.; Emmuel Balaban, pf.

W238. Barcarolle: A Portrait of Georges Hugnet (April 17, 1940; GS-1; 1 min. 30 sec.)

> Also arranged as Barcarolle for Woodwinds (1944; G. Schirmer; See W19)
> Also arranged for vn. and pf. by Samuel Dushkin and published in Three Portraits for Violin and Piano (1946; G. Schirmer)

> Brief Mention: MM 23:124 (Spring 1946); MC 143:66 (Feb 15, 1951)

Premiere: Of Arrangement for Vn. and Pf.: March 12, 1946; New York City; Town hall; Samuel Dushkin, vn.; Erich Itor Kahn, pf.

W239. Swiss Waltz: A Portrait of Sophie Tauber-Arp (April 18, 1940; GS-4; 2 min. 20 sec.)

W240. Eccentric Dance: Portrait of Madame Kristians Tonny (April 22, 1940; published separately by Carl Fischer; 2 min.)

W241. Tango Lullaby: A Portrait of Mlle. [Flavie] Alvarez de Toledo (April 24, 1940; GS-1; 2 min. 25 sec.)

Also arranged for orchestra (1944; G. Schirmer; See W27)
Also arranged for vc.and pf. by Luigi Silva and published in Four Portraits for Cello and Piano (1942; G. Schirmer)
Also arranged for vn. and pf. by Samuel Dushkin and published in Three Portraits for Violin and Piano (1946; G. Schirmer)

Brief Mention: MM 23:124 (Spring 1946); MC 143:66 (Feb 15, 1951)

Premieres:
Of Arrangement for Vc. and Pf.: Jan 5, 1943; Rochester, NY; Kilbourn Hall, Eastman School of Music; Luigi Silva, vc., Emmanuel Balaban, pf.
Of Arrangement for Vn. and Pf.: March 12, 1946; New York City; Town Hall; Samuel Dushkin, vn.; Erich Itor Kahn, pf.

W242. Invention: Theodate Johnson Busy and Resting (April 29, 1940; B&H-1981; 1 min. 30 sec.)

W243. Bugles and Birds: A Portrait of Pablo Picasso (April 30, 1940; GS-1; 2 min. 15. sec.)

Also arranged for orchestra (1944; G. Schirmer; See W20)
Also arranged for vc. and pf. by Luigi Silva and published in Four Portraits for Cello and Piano (1942; G. Schirmer)

Premiere: Of Arrangement for Vc. and Pf.: Jan 5, 1943; Rochester, NY; Kilbourn Hall, Eastman School of Music; Luigi Silva, vc.; Emmanuel Balaban, pf.

W244. Piano Sonata No. 4: Guggenheim jeune (May 2, 1940; published separately by Southern; 7 min.) See: B112 & B175

Portrait of Peggy Guggenheim

Brief Mention: MM 20:201 (March-April 1944)

W245. Lullaby Which Is Also a Spinning Song: A Portrait of Howard Putzel (May 3, 1940; GS-4; 2 min. 50 sec.)

W246. Five-Finger Exercise: A Portrait of Léon Kochnitzky (May 4, 1940; GS-2; 1 min. 30 sec.)

W247. The Dream World of Peter Rose-Pulham (May 7, 1940; GS-3; 2 min. 20

sec.)

W248. Dora Maar or The Presence of Pablo Picasso (May 8, 1940; B&H-1981; 2 min.)

W249. Pastoral: A Portrait of Tristan Tzara (May 9, 1940; SOU; 2 min.)

W250. Aria: A Portrait of Germaine Hugnet (May 12, 1940; GS-2; 2 min. 40 sec.)

W251. Toccata: A Portrait of Mary Widney (May 13, 1940; GS-3; 1 min. 30 sec.)

W252. Awake or Asleep: Pierre Mabille (May 15, 1940; Southern; 1 min.)

W253. Cantabile: A Portrait of Nicolas de Chatelain (May 29, 1940; GS-3; 4 min. 30 sec.) See: A14

Also arranged for string orchestra (1944; G.Schirmer; See W21)

W254. Duet: A Portrait of Clarita, Comtesse de Forceville (July 2, 1940; B&H-1981; 1 min. 45 sec.)

W255. Stretching: A Portrait of Jamie Campbell (July 3, 1940; B&H-1981; 1 min. 15 sec.)

W256. Canons with Cadenza: A Portrait of André Ostier (July 9, 1940; GS-3; 1 min.)

W257. Fugue: A Portrait of Alexander Smallens (Sept 6, 1940; GS-1; 2 min. 40 sec.)

Also arranged for orchestra (1944; G. Schirmer; See W23)

W258. With Fife and Drums: A Portrait of Mina Curtiss (June 15, 1941; GS-1; 2 min.)

W259. Insistences: A Portrait of Louise Crane (July 6, 1941; GS-4; 1 min. 40 sec.)

Also freely arranged for band with the title Study Piece: Portrait of a Lady (1969; G. Schirmer; See W55)

W260. Percussion Piece: A Portrait of Jessie K. Lasell (Sept 27, 1941; ms.; 2 min. 30 sec.)

Also arranged for orchestra (1944; G. Schirmer; See W26)

W261. Parades: A Portrait of Florine Stettheimer (Oct 5, 1941; B&H-1; 2 min. 20 sec.)

Originally published in View Magazine (2nd series, no. 4, "Americana Fantastica," Jan 1943, pp. 49-52).
Also arranged for brass and perc. with the title Metropolitan Museum Fanfare: Portrait of an American Artist (1969; G. Schir-

mer; See W53)

W262. James Patrick Cannon, Professional Revolutionary (July 21, 1942; B&H-1981; 1 min. 45 sec.)

W263. Scottish Memories: Peter Monro Jack (July 29, 1942; B&H-1981; 2 min. 30 sec.)

W264. Prisoner of the Mind: Schuyler Watts (Sept 30, 1942; SOU; 1 min. 30 sec.)

W265. Wedding Music: A Portrait of Jean [Mrs. Schuyler] Watts (Oct 1, 1942; GS-4; 1 min. 30 sec.)

W266. Aaron Copland, Persistently Pastoral (Oct 16, 1942; B&H-1981; 3 min. 15 sec.)

  Also published in Keyboard Classics 2 (March/April 1982): 6-9 and in Perspectives in New Music 19 (Fall/Winter 1980; Spring/Summer 1981): 92-95.
  Also arranged for orchestra with title Pastorale (1944; G. Schirmer; See W25) and used in the film "Tuesday in November" (1945; See W319)

W267. Five-Finger Exercise: Portrait of Briggs Buchanan (Aug 15, 1943; Carl Fischer; 2 min.)

  Published in Ten Etudes for Piano (Carl Fischer; See W181)

W268. Solitude: A Portrait of Lou Harrison (Dec 5, 1945; GS-1; 1 min.)

W269. Chromatic Double Harmonies: Portrait of Sylvia Marlowe (June 17, 1951; G. Schirmer; 2 min. 30 sec.)

  Published in Nine Etudes for Piano (G. Schirmer;See W188) and also in Etudes, Vol. 2 (G. Schirmer; 1985)

W270. Homage to Marya Freund and to the Harp (July 25, 1956; B&H-1981; 1 min.)

  Also scored for harp and orchestra and published as the first movement of Autumn: Concertino for Harp, Strings, and Percussion (1965; G. Schirmer; See W49)

W271. Edges: A Portrait of Robert Indiana (Dec 24-25, 1966; published separately by G. Schirmer; 2 min.)

  Also arranged for band (1969; G. Schirmer; See W54)

W272. For Eugene Ormandy's Birthday, 18 November 1969: A Study in Stacked-Up Thirds (1969; Southern; 1 min.)

  Rev. from the original A Study in Stacked-Up Thirds for pf. (Aug 18, 1958; Southern; See W192)

W273. Man of Iron: A Portrait of Willy Eisenhart (Aug 23, 1972; G. Schirmer; 2 min. 25 sec.)

Also arranged for brass quintet and published as the last movement of Family Portrait (1974; G. Schirmer; See W198)

W274. Bill Katz: Wide Awake (June 15, 1981; B&H-1983)

Also arranged for orchestra and published in Eleven Portraits for Orchestra (1982; Boosey & Hawkes; See W58)

W275. Norma Flender: Thoughts about Flying (June 20, 1981; B&H-1983)

Premiere: Oct 4, 1981; Middletown, CT; Wesleyan University; Anthony Tommasini, pf.

W276. Richard Flender: Solid Not Stolid (June 21, 1981; B&H-1983)

Also arranged for orchestra and published in Eleven Portraits for Orchestra (1982; Boosey & Hawkes; See W58)

Premiere: Oct 4, 1981; Middletown, CT; Wesleyan University; Anthony Tommasini, pf.

W277. Scott Wheeler: Free-Wheeling (June 23, 1981; B&H-1983)

Also arranged for orchestra and published in Eleven Portraits for Orchestra (1982: Boosey & Hawkes; See W58)

Premiere: Oct 4, 1981; Middletown, CT; Wesleyan University; Anthony Tommasini, pf.

W278. Gerald Busby: Giving Full Attention (June 25, 1981; B&H-1983)

W279. Noah Creshevsky: Loyal, Steady, Persistent (June 26, 1981; B&H-1983)

Also arranged for orchestra and published in Eleven Portraits for Orchestra (1982: Boosey & Hawkes; See W58)

W280. Sam Byers: With Joy (June 28, 1981; B&H-1983)

Also arranged for orchestra and published in Eleven Portraits for Orchestra (1982; Boosey & Hawkes; See W58)

W281. Morris Golde: Showing Delight (June 29, 1981; B&H-1983)

W282. Christopher Cox: Singing a Song (July 1, 1981; B&H-1983)

Also arranged for orchestra and published in Eleven Portraits for Orchestra (1982; Boosey & Hawkes; See W58)

W283. Barbara Epstein: Untiring (July 2, 1981; B&H-1983)

W284. Dead Pan: Mrs. Betty Freeman (Aug 11, 1981; B&H-1983)

Also arranged for orchestra as A Love Scene and published in Eleven Portraits for Orchestra (1982: Boosey & Hawkes; See W58)

W285. John Wright, Drawing (Aug 15, 1981; B&H-1983)

W286. Franco Assetto, Drawing V.T. (Aug 23, 1981; B&H-1983)

W287. Round and Round: Dominique Nabokov (Oct 17, 1981; B&H-1983)

W288. Karen Brown Waltuck: Intensely Two (Oct 19, 1981; B&H-1983)

Also arranged for orchestra and published in Eleven Portraits for Orchestra (1982; Boosey & Hawkes; See W58)
Originally published on menu at Chanterelle Restaurant (New York City) for Thomson's 85th birthday (Nov 25, 1982)

W289. Anne-Marie Soullière: Something of a Beauty (Nov 14, 1981; B&H-1983)

Also arranged for orchestra and published in Eleven Portraits for Orchestra (1982; Boosey & Hawkes; See W58)

W290. Buffie Johnson: Drawing V.T. in Charcoal (Dec 30, 1981; B&H-1983)

W291. Craig Rutenberg: Swinging (Dec 31, 1981; B&H-1983)

W292. Paul Sanfacon: On the Ice (Jan 2, 1982; B&H-1983)

W293. Molly Davies: Terminations (Jan 8, 1982; GS-1984)

W294. Dennis Russell Davies: In a Hammock (Jan 9, 1982; GS-1984)

Also arranged for orchestra and published in Eleven Portraits for Orchestra (1982; Boosey & Hawkes; See W58)

W295. Rodney Lister: Music for a Merry-Go-Round (Jan 27, 1982; GS-1984)

W296. Doña Flor: Receiving (Feb 2, 1982; GS-1984)

W297. Dr. Marcel Roche: Making a Decision (Feb 6, 1982; GS-1984)

W298. David Dubal in Flight (March 3, 1982; GS-1984)

Also arranged for orchestra and published in Eleven Portraits for Orchestra (1982; Boosey & Hawkes; See W58)

W299. Peter McWilliams: Firmly Spontaneous (May 11, 1983; GS-1984)

W300. Vassilis Voglis: On the March (July 4, 1983; GS-1984)

W301. Power Boothe: With Pencil (July 12, 1983; GS-1984)

W302. Mark Beard: Never Alone (July 23, 1983; GS-1984)

W303. Louis Rispoli: In a Boat (Aug 5, 1983; GS-1984)

W304. Malitte Matta: In the Executive Style (Aug 20, 1983; GS-1984)

W305. Glynn Boyd Harte: Reaching (Sept 27, 1983; GS-1984)

W306. Senza Espressione: Bennett Lerner (Sept 29, 1983; GS-1984)

W307. Phillip Ramey: Thinking Hard (Oct 2, 1983; GS-1984)

W308. Charles Fussell: In Meditation (Nov 19, 1983; GS-1984)

W309. Brendan Lemon: A Study Piece for Piano (May 4, 1984: GS-1984)

W310. John Houseman: No Changes (June 25, 1984; ms.)

    Also arranged for orchestra with the title A Double Take in A Pair
        of Portraits for Orchestra (Dec 1984; ms.; See W60)

W311. Lines: for and about Ron Henggeler (June 28, 1984; ms.)

W312. Boris Baranovic: Whirling (July 21, 1984; ms.)

W313. Tony Tommasini: A Study in Chords (Aug 28, 1984; ms.)

    Also arranged for orchestra with the title Major Chords in A Pair
        of Portraits for Orchestra (Dec 1984; ms.; See W60)

W314. Christopher Beach Alone (Jan 1, 1985; ms.)

W315. Danyal Lawson: Playing (Jan 10, 1985; ms.)

FILM MUSIC

W316. The Plow That Broke the Plains (1936; ms.; 27 min.) See: B141,
        B152, B160, B181, & B192

    Film by Pare Lorentz
    Produced by the Works Progress Administration-Farm Security Admin-
        istration
    1.1.3.1./2.2.2.0./2 perc. (including timp.)/banjo/guitar (or pf.,
        harp), strings
    Also arranged as orchestral suite (1936; G. Schirmer; See W13)
    Filmtrack production: Alexander Smallens conducting members of the
        New York Metropolitan Opera and Philharmonic Orchestras

    Brief Mention: MM 13:46+ (May-June 1936); MM 14:83 (Jan-Feb 1937);
        MM 15:52 (Nov-Dec 1937); MM 17:185 (March-April 1940); MQ 27:163
        (1941); MM 22:200 (March-April 1945); MM 23:189 (Summer 1946);
        MQ 35:115, 116, 210 & 221 (1949); MQ 37:161 (1951); FM

    Premiere: May 25, 1936; New York City; 14th annual Women's Exposi-
        tion of Arts and Industries

W317. The River (1937; ms.) See: B44, B141, B160, & B192

Film by Pare Lorentz
Produced by the Works Projects Administration-Farm Security Admin-
istration
35 mm. version, 36 min.
16 mm. version, 27 min.
1.2.2.1./2.2.2.0./2 perc. (including timp.)/banjo/strings
Also arranged as orchestral suite (1937; Southern; See W14)
Filmtrack production: Alexander Smallens conducting members of the
New York Philharmonic Orchestra; musical supervision by Virgil
Thomson

Brief Mention: MM 15:52+ (Nov-Dec 1937); MM 17:185 (March-April
1940); MQ 27:163 (1941); MM 18:178 (March-April 1941); MM 22:20
(March-April 1945); MM 23:189 (Summer 1946); MQ 35:116, 210 &
222 (1949); MQ 37:161 (1951); FM

Premiere: Oct 29, 1937; New Orleans, LA; Strand Theatre

W318. The Spanish Earth (1937; 63 min.)

Film by Joris Ivens and Ernest Hemingway
A montage of recorded Spanish folk music made in collaboration
with Marc Blitzstein

Brief Mention: MM 15:253+ (May-June 1938); MQ 35:116 (1949); FM

W319. Tuesday in November (1945; ms.; 18 min.) See: B141 & B144

Film directed by John Berry
Produced by John Houseman for the U.S. Office of War Information
1.1.2.1./2.2.2.0./2 perc./harp/strings
Includes Pastorale for orchestra (1944; G. Schirmer; See W25)
Excerpts: Fugue and Chorale on "Yankee Doodle", for orchestra
(1945; G. Schirmer; See W28), and also arranged for band by
Frank Erickson (1970; G. Schirmer); and Walking Song, for pf.
(1951; ms.; See W189) and also for two pf. by Arthur Gold and
Robert Fizdale (1945-50; G. Schirmer)
Filmtrack production: Virgil Thomson conducting a pick-up orches-
tra in Los Angeles

Brief Mention: MQ 35:116 (1949); FM

W320. Louisiana Story (1948; ms.; 81 min.) See: B44, B68, B95, B96,
B128, B157, B158, B160, B229

Film produced and directed by Robert Flaherty
2.2.2.2./2.2.2.0./2 perc./harp/accordion/strings
Also arranged as orchestral suite (1948; G. Schirmer; See W30)
Excerpts: Acadian Songs and Dances for orchestra (1948; G. Schir-
mer; See W31); Bayou, ballet with music from Acadian Songs and
Dances (1952; G. Schirmer; See W4); Three pieces arranged for
pf. by Andor Foldes and published with the title Suite from
"Louisiana Story": Three Pieces for Piano (post-1948; G. Schir-
mer)
Filmtrack production: Eugene Ormandy conducting members of the

Philadelphia Orchestra; musical supervision by Virgil Thomson

Brief Mention: MA 69:37 (May 1949); Variety (May 4, 1949): 2; Film Quarterly 18:11 (Summer 1965); FM

Premiere: August 22, 1948; Edinburgh, Scotland; Cally Picture House; Second International Festival of Documentary Films

W321. The Goddess (Nov 1957; ms.; 100 min.) See: B229

Film written by Paddy Chayevsky and directed by John Cromwell
2.2.2.2./3 sax./2.2.3.0./2 perc./guitar/pf./strings
Filmtrack production: Virgil Thomson conducting members of the New York Philharmonic

Brief Mention: FM

Premiere: June 1958; Brussels, Belgium; Grand Auditorium; Third International Film Festival

W322. Power Among Men (Nov-Dec 1958; ms.)

Film directed by Thorold Dickinson and J.C. Sheers
Produced by Thorold Dickinson for the United Nations Film Unit (90 min)
TV version for Omnibus (NBC) (47 min. 10 sec.)
2.2.2.2./2.2.3.0./2 perc./harp/strings
Excerpt: Fugues and Cantilenas for orchestra (1959; Boosey & Hawkes; See W42)
Filmtrack production: Virgil Thomson conducting members of the New York Philharmonic

Brief Mention: MA 79:34 (April 1959); FM

Premiere: March 5, 1959; New York City; The Museum of Modern Art

W323. Journey to America (1964; ms.; 11 min.)

Film produced and directly by John Houseman film for U.S. Pavilion at New York World's Fair
1.1.2.1./4.1.1.0./1 perc./strings
Excerpt: Pilgrims and Pioneers for orchestra (1964; G. Schirmer; See W47)
Filmtrack production: Virgil Thomson conducting members of the New York Philharmonic

Premiere: July 1964; Queens, NY; Flushing Meadow Park; Opening celebrations of the New York World's Fair

W324. The Baby Maker (1970)

Film for James Bridges
Musical supervision by Virgil Thomson

W325. Suddenly an Eagle (Aug 1975; ms.)

ABC News film by William Peters.
A T.V. historical evocation of the American Revolution with
    musical supervision by Virgil Thomson
Includes 2nd movement of Suite from "The River" (1937;See W14)

[The Day After; 1983; See W14]

INCIDENTAL MUSIC

W326. Le Droit de Varech (April 16, 1930; ms.)

Accordion solo for unproduced play by Georges Hugnet

W327. A Bride for the Unicorn (1934; ms.)

Play by Denis Johnston
Directed by Joseph Losey for the Harvard Dramatic Club
Male chorus, 3 perc. players

W328. Macbeth (1936; ms.)

Play by Shakespeare
Directed by Orson Welles for the WPA-Federal Theatre
Fl./3 cl./3 tpt./perc./guitar/strings/4 African drums on stage/2
    tbn.

W329. Injunction Granted (1936; ms.)

Directed by Joseph Losey for the WPA-Federal Theater
Pic./3 tpt./tbn./16 perc. players

Brief Mention: MM 14:43-4 (Nov-Dec 1936); MM 15:52 (Nov-Dec 1937)

W330. Horse Eats Hat (Un Chapeau de paille d'Italie) (1936; ms.) See:
    T33

Play by Eugène Labiche, translated by Edwin Denby
Directed by Orson Welles for the WPA-Federal Theater
Music by Paul Bowles, orchestrated by Virgil Thomson
2.2.2.2./4.2.3.0./2 perc./2 solo pf./strings; also cornet soloist,
    small jazz band, gypsy waltz orchestra, player piano, bass vocal
    soloist (for song:"The Rubber Plant")

Brief Mention: MM 14:43 (Nov-Dec 1936)

W331. Hamlet (1936; ms.) See: B143

Play by Shakespeare
Directed by John Houseman for the WPA-Federal Theatre
Recorder/hn./2 tpt./2 bagpipes/3 perc.

Brief Mention: MM 15:32 (Nov-Dec 1937)

W332. <u>Antony</u> <u>and</u> <u>Cleopatra</u> (1937; ms.)

Play by Shakespeare
Directed by Reginald Bache (opened Nov 10, 1937)
Ob./2 tpt./2 perc.

Brief Mention: <u>MM</u> 15:52 (Nov-Dec 1937)

W333. <u>Androcles</u> <u>and</u> <u>the</u> <u>Lion</u> (1938; ms.)

Play by George Bernard Shaw
For the WPA-Federal Theater
(Music composed but not orchestrated by Virgil Thomson)

W334. <u>The</u> <u>Trojan</u> <u>Women</u> (1940; ms.)

Play by Eurpides; translated by Edith Hamilton
Directed by John Houseman for CBS Workshop
Fl./Eng. hn./cl./tpt./hn./perc./sound effects

Brief Mention: <u>MM</u> 18:132 (Jan-Feb 1941)

W335. <u>The</u> <u>Life</u> <u>of</u> <u>a</u> <u>Careful</u> <u>Man</u> (1941; ms.)

Soundtrack for CBS Workshop
2 cl./2 hn./2 perc./organ/strings/women's voices (SA)

W336. <u>Oedipus</u> <u>Tyrannos</u> (1941; ms.)

Play by Sophocles
Produced in Greek at Fordham University
Fl./2 hn./perc./male chorus

W337. <u>King</u> <u>Lear</u> (1952; ms.)

Play by Shakespeare
Directed by Peter Brook for TV-Radio Workshop of the Ford Foundation
2 tpt./2 hn./2 perc./2 va./2 vc.

W338. <u>The</u> <u>Grass</u> <u>Harp</u> (1952; Boosey & Hawkes)

Play by Truman Capote
Directed by Robert Lewis
Fl./harp/celesta/vn./va./vc.

W339. <u>Ondine</u> (1954; Originally Ricordi/Belwin Mills, now Boosey &
Hawkes)

Play by Jean Giraudoux, adapted by Maurice Valency
Directed by Alfred Lunt
Fl./1 perc./harp/celesta/string quartet

W340. <u>King</u> <u>John</u> (June 1956; ms.) See: B143

Play by Shakespeare
Directed by John Houseman for the American Shakespeare Festival
  Theater, Stratford, CT
2 hn./2 tpt./2 perc.

W341. Measure for Measure (June 1956; ms.)See: B143

Play by Shakespeare
Directed by John Houseman for the American Shakespeare Festival
  Theater, Stratford, CT
2 hn./2 tpt./2 perc./tack piano/boy soprano soloist
"Take, O Take Those Lips Away" published in Shakespeare Songs
  (Southern; See W139)

W342. Othello (June 1957; ms.) See: B143

Play by Shakespeare
Directed by John Houseman for the American Shakespeare Festival
  Theater, Stratford, CT
Fl./2 tpt./1 perc./lute/va./vc./bass

W343. The Merchant of Venice (June 1957; ms.)

Play by Shakespeare
Directed by Jack Landau for the American Shakespeare Festival
  Theater, Stratford, CT
Fl./2 tpt./1 perc./lute/va./vc./bass/tenor soloist
"Tell Me Where Is Fancy Bred" published in Shakespeare Songs
  (Southern; See W139)

W344. Much Ado About Nothing (July 1957; ms.) See: T108

Play by Shakespeare
Directed by John Houseman for the American Shakespeare Festival
  Theater, Stratford, CT
Fl./pic./cl.-sax./2 tpt./lute/va./vc./bass/tenor soloist
"Pardon, Goddess of the Night" and "Sigh No More, Ladies" publish-
  ed in Shakespeare Songs (Southern; See W139)

W345. Bertha (Dec 1959; ms.)

Play by Kenneth Koch
Performed at The Living Theater (1959) and the Cherry Lane Thea-
  ter (1961)
Trumpet solo

Discography

This list includes all comercially-produced discs, whether or not currently available. "See" references, e.g. See: B123, identify citations in the "Bibliography" section.

D1. Acadian Songs and Dances (from film score Louisiana Story)

Cleveland Pops Orchestra; Louis Lane, cond.
Epic LC-3809/BC-1147. 1961.

Little Orchestra Society; Thomas Scherman, cond.
Decca DL-9616. 1952. See: B208
Brunswick AXTL-1022. Pre-1956.
Decca DCM-3207. 1962.
Reviews: ARG 7-52, p335; CR 8-52, p35;Gr 10-53, p133; GS 7-52, p3; HF 9 & 10-52, p52; NR 9-52, p4; SR 8-16-52, p 41.

The Oshkosh Symphony Orchestra; Henri B. Pensis, cond.
Privately recorded. 1983.

D2. (Three) Antiphonal Psalms: (No. 1) Psalm 123 and (No. 3) Psalm 136.

Yale Divinity School Choir; James I. Borden, cond.
Overtone LP-2. 1954. See: B208
Reviews: ARG 2-54, p188; HF 7-54, p52; NYT 5-9-54, pX8.

D3. At The Beach

Gerard Schwarz, cornet; William Bolcom, pf.
Nonesuch H-71298/HQ-1298. 1974. See: B209
Reviews: CU 5-76, p301. CR 1-75, p36; Gr 3-75, p1710; HF 11-74, p129; NR 7-74, p14; SFCh 7-21-74, p25; St 8-74, p112.

D4. Autumn

Ann Mason Stockton, harp; Los Angeles Chamber Symphony; Neville Marriner, cond.

Angel SQ-37300. 1976.
Reviews: HF 9-76, p98; NR 5-76, p4; NYT 5-7-76, pC15; St 7-76,
    p83.

D5.   Cantata on Poems of Edward Lear: Half an Alphabet

Gregg Smith Singers; Gregg Smith, cond.
Grenadilla Records GS-1041. 1977.
Reviews: FF 1 & 2-80, p163; NR 10-79, p8.

D6.   Capital Capitals

Joseph   Crawford,   tenor;   Clyde S.   Turner,   tenor;   Joseph
    James,   baritone; William C. Smith, bass; Virgil Thomson,
    pf.
Columbia ML-4491. 1952. See: B208
Reviews: ARG 3-53, p211; CR 4-53, p35; GS 2-53, p9; HF 7 & 8-53, p
    46; MA 4-15-53, p17; MQ 7-54, p471; Na 4-11-53, p314; NR 3-53,
    p5; NYT 2-15-53, pX9; SR 2-28-53, pp60, 75.

D7.   Chorale Preludes for Organ, Op. 122, by Johannes Brahms, tran-
    scribed for orchestra by Virgil Thomson. (Nos. 3,6,8,10, and 11)

Crane Department of Music, chorus and orchestra, State University
    College of Education, Potsdam, New York; Virgil Thomson, cond.
Private Recording (mono) L80P-6613 and 6614. 1980.

D8.   Concerto for Flute, Strings, Harp and Percussion

Francis Fuge, fl.; Louisville Orchestra; Robert Whitney, cond.
LOU-66-3/LS-66-3 (Louisville Orchestra First Edition Records 1966,
    No. 3). 1966. See: B209
Reviews: ARG 11-66, p221; HF 10-66, p158; HSR 11-66, p104; SR 8-
    27-66, p54.

D9.   Concerto for Violoncello and Orchestra

Luigi Silva, vc.; Janssen Symphony Orchestra of Los Angeles;
    Werner Janssen, cond.
Columbia ML-4468. 1952. See: B208
Columbia CML-4468. 1968.
Columbia AML-4468. 1974.
Reviews: ARG 1-53, p158; CU 3-53, p134; GS 2-53, p6; HF 3 & 4-53,
    p56; LJ 4-1-53, p587; Na 2-28-53, p195; NR 1-53, p5; NYT 1-11-
    53, pX9; SR 1-31-53, p56.

D10.   (Nine) Etudes for Piano

Arthur Tollefson, pf.
Finnadar SR-9027. 1980.
Reviews: ARG 2-81, p34; Contemporary Keyboard 9-80, p 71;
    FF 11 & 12-80, p188; HF 10-80, pp91-2; NR 12-80, p10; St 1-81,
    p87.

D11. (Ten) Etudes for Piano

      Maxim Schapiro, pf.
      Decca DL-4083. 1954.
      Brunswick AXL-2009. Pre-1956.
      Reviews: ARG 2-54, p208; CR 5-54, p128; Gr 5-54, p482; ML 5-54,
        p11; MQ 9-54, p629; NYT 1-3-54, pX9; SR 7-31-54, p63.

      Arthur Tollefson, pf.
      Finnadar SR-9027. 1980.
      Reviews: ARG 2-81, p34; Contemporary Keyboard 9-80, p71; FF 11 &
        12-80, p188; HF 10-80, pp91-2;MQ 10-54, pp629-30; NR 12-80,
        p10; St 1-81, p87.

D12. (Ten) Etudes for Piano: (No. 7) "Oscillating Arm" (Spinning
      Song) and (No. 10) "Ragtime Bass"

      Andor Foldes, pf.
      Vox 16068-71 (in set 174); 78 rpm; 4-10" discs. 1947.
      Polydor/Deutsche Grammophon 46002; 78 rpm.   Pre-1953. (Excerpt:
        "Ragtime Bass")
      Polydor/Deutsche Grammophon 36104; 78 rpm.   Pre-1956. (Excerpt:
        "Ragtime Bass")

D13. (Ten) Etudes for Piano: (No. 9) "Parallel Chords" (Tango) and (No.
      10) "Ragtime Bass"

      Grant Johannesen, pf.
      Golden Crest CR-4065/CRS-4065.   1963/1966.   (Excerpt: "Ragtime
        Bass") See: B209
      Golden Crest CRS-4132. 1975.
      Reviews: NR 9-63, p13; NYT 8-18-63, pX10; St 2-75, p115.

      Roger Shields,pf.
      Vox SVBX-5303. 3 discs. 1977.
      Reviews: ARG 5-77, p9; NYT 7-3-77, pD14.

D14. (Ten) Etudes for Piano: (No. 6) "For the Weaker Fingers"
      (Music Box Lullaby)

      Maryla Jonas, pf.
      Columbia ML-4624. 1953.

D15. (Ten) Etudes for Piano: (No. 10) "Ragtime Bass"

      David Dubal, pf.
      Musical Heritage Society MHS-3808. 1978.
      Review: FF 3 & 4-79, p140.

D16. (Ten) Etudes for Piano: (No. 10) "Ragtime Bass" arranged for four
      pianos

      First Piano Quartet
      Victor 12-0588-90 (in set MO-1263); 78 rpm; 3 discs.
      Pre-1956.

D17. A Family Portrait for Brass Quintet

The American Brass Quintet.
Nonesuch D-79024. With liner notes by the composer. 1982.
Reviews: ARG 7 & 8-82, p40; FF 5 & 6-82, p223; NR 3-82,
p6; NYT 4-25-82, pD21; St 5-82, p66.

D18. Fanfare

Richard Ellsasser, organ
MGM E-3005. 1953. See: B208
Review: NR 3-53, p14.

Rollin Smith, organ
Repertoire Recording Society RRS-12. 1974.
Reviews: HF 7-74, p108; ARG 3-78, p47.

D19. Fanfare for France

London Philharmonic Orchestra; Jorge Mester, cond.
Varèse/Sarabande VCDM-1000.240. 1982.
Reviews: ARG 7 & 8-82, p47; FF 5 & 6-82, p 291; NR 9-82, p3; St 7-
82, p73.

D20. The Feast of Love

David Clatworthy, baritone; Eastman-Rochester Symphony Orchestra;
Howard Hanson, cond.
Mercury MG-50429/SR-90429. 1965.
Mercury SRI-75063. 1976.
Reviews: ARG 3-66, p596; HF 3-66, p 92; HSR 5-66, p89; NR
3-66, p2; NYT 1-30-66, pX22; SR 2-26-66, p51.

D21. Filling Station

New York City Ballet Orchestra; Leon Barzin, cond.
Vox PLP-9050. 1955. See: B208
Reviews: ARG 2-55, p197; HF 2-55, p68; MA 2-15-55, p218; Na
1-29-55, p107; NR 3-55, p7; NYT 3-27-55, pX11.

D22. For A Happy Occasion (originally titled Happy Birthday for
Mrs. Zimbalist)

Yvar Mikhashoff, pf.
Nonesuch D-79011. 1981.
Reviews: FF 9 & 10-81, p241; HF 9-81, p81; NR 7-81, p13; NYT 6-7-
81, pD26.

D23. Four Saints in Three Acts (abridged)

Beatrice Robinson-Wayne as St. Teresa I; Inez Matthews as St.
Settlement; Altonell Hines as Commère; Ruby Greene as St. Teresa
II; Charles Holland as St. Chavez; David Bethea as St. Stephen;
Edward Matthews as St. Ignatius; Randolph Robinson as St. Plan;
Abner Dorsey as Compère; double chorus; orchestra; Virgil Thom-

son, cond.
Victor 12-0451 (in set M-1244); 78 rpm; 5 discs; 1948.
RCA LCT-1139. 1954. See: T147
RCA LM-2756. 1964.
Reviews: ARG 12-48, p124; Gr 1-49, p125; GS 1-49, p7;HSR 3-65,
pp64-67; JR 1 & 2-49, p21; LJ 6-1-49, p902; MA 5-49, p36; Music
& Musicians 8-65, p29; Na 12-11-48, p676; NR 12-48, p7; SR 12-4-
48, p67 & 12-25-48, p41. ARG 7-54, p354; HF 7-54, p50; NYT 7-4-
54, pX6; SR 7-31-54, p63. ARG 2-65, p518+; Au 2-65, p50; Gr 4-
65, p490; HF 2-65, p70; HSR 3-65, p64+; LJ 5-15-65, p2247; ML 5-
65, p14; Music & Musicians 8-65, p29; NR 1-65, p11; NRe 3-27-65,
p34; ON 4-3-65, p34; SR 12-26-64, p52.

D24. Four Saints in Three Acts (complete opera)

Betty Allen as Commère; Benjamin Matthews as Compère; Arthur
Thompson as St. Ignatius; Clamma Dale as St. Teresa I; Florence
Quivar as St. Teresa II; William Brown as St. Chavez; Gwendolyn
Bradley as St. Settlement; The Chorus and Orchestra of our Time;
Joel Thome, cond.
Nonesuch NON 79035X. With liner notes by the composer. 1982.
Reviews: ARG 2-83, p57; Cal 1-83, p103; Ch 1-83, p104; CR
8-83, p43; FF 11 & 12-82, p241; Gr 1-83, p859; HF 1-83, p74; H&G
12-82, p12; NR 11-82, p9; NYT 10-3-82, pH21; ON 2-26-83, p44; OQ
Summer 83, p187-8; St 12-82, p78; Vg 12-82, p65.

D25. Fugue and Chorale on "Yankee Doodle" (from film score for "A Tuesday in November")

Amerigo Marino, cond. Bowmar Orchestral Library: Music, U.S.A.
Bowmar Records BOL #65. 1963.

D26. (Three) Hymns from the Old South

Peabody Conservatory Concert Singers; Gregg Smith, cond.
Vox SVBX-5353. 1979.
Reviews: NR 12-79, p8; NYT 7-1-79, pD22.

D27. (Three) Hymns from the Old South: (No. 1) "The Morning Star" and
(No. 2) "Death, 'Tis a Melancholy Day"

Vienna Academy Chamber Chorus; Ferdinand Grossman, cond.
VOX PLP-7750. 1952.
Reviews: CU 4-53, p174; GS 1-53, p10; HF 3 & 4-53, p57; LJ
6-1-53, p 984; NYT 12-28-52, pX8.

D28. Let's Take a Walk

Nancy Tatum, soprano; Geoffrey Parsons, pf.
London OS-26053. 1968.

D29. Louisiana Story (Suite)

Philadelphia Orchestra; Eugene Ormandy, cond.
Columbia 13049-50D (in set MX-329); 78 rpm; 2 discs. Pre-1952.

Columbia LX-8802-03; 78 rpm; 2 discs. Pre-1952.

Philadelphia Orchestra; Virgil Thomson, cond.
Columbia ML-2087; 33 rpm; 10" disc. 1950.
Reviews: ARG 2-50, p194; Gr 7-51, p31; JR 3 & 4-50, p30; LJ 4-15-
   50, p715; ML 7-51, p5; MR 2-52, p81; Na 2-18-50, p162; NR 3-50,
   p4; SR 2-25-50, p58 & 3-4-50, p46.

Westphalian Symphony Orchestra; Siegfried Landau, cond.
Turnabout TVS-34534. 1973. See: B209
Reviews: NR 8-73, p2; St 10-73, p139.

D30. Metropolitan Museum Fanfare: Portrait of an American Artist
      (Portrait of Florine Stettheimer)

Brass and percussion ensemble; Frederik Prausnitz, cond.
Metropolitan Museum of Art AKS-10001. 1970.

D31. Missa brevis

King's Chapel Choir, Boston; Lloyd S. McCausland, perc.;   Virgil
   Thomson, cond.
Cambridge CRM-412. 1962.

D32. Missa pro defunctis

Crane Department of Music, chorus and orchestra; State University
   College of Education, Potsdam, New York; Virgil Thomson, cond.
Private Recording (mono) L80P-6613 and 6614. 1980.

D33. Mostly About Love: "A Prayer to St. Catherine"

Frederica von Stade, soprano; Martin Katz, pf.
CBS Masterworks IM 37231. 1981.
Reviews: FF 9 & 10, p413; Gr 6-82, p 72; MG 9-82, p24; NR 6-82,
   p12; NYT 9-26-82, pH21; St 11-82, p99.

D34. The Mother of Us All

Mignon Dunn as Susan B. Anthony; James Atherton as Jo the Loiter-
   er; Joseph McKee as Chris; Philip Booth as Daniel Webster; Helen
   Vanni as Constance Fletcher; Ashley Putnam as Angel More; Linn
   Maxwell as Indiana Elliot; William Lewis as John Adams; Santa Fe
   Opera Chorus and Orchestra; Raymond Leppard, cond.
New World NW-288-89; 2 discs. 1977. See: B209
Reviews: HF 7-77, p92; ARG 8-77, pp30+; NYT 2-13-72, pD16; NYer 3-
   27-78, p108+; ON 3-19-77, p40; St 6-77, p89+.

D35. The Mother of Us All (Suite)

Janssen Symphony Orchestra of Los Angeles; Werner Janssen,   cond.
Columbia ML-4468. 1952. See: B208
Columbia CML-4468. 1968.
Columbia AML-4468. 1974.
Reviews: ARG 1-53, p158; CU 3-53, p134; GS 2-53, p6; HF 3 & 4-53,

p56; <u>LJ</u> 4-1-53, p587; <u>Na</u> 2-28-53, p195; <u>NR</u> 1-53, p5; <u>NYT</u> 1-11-53, pX9; <u>SR</u> 1-31-53, p56.

D36. <u>My Shepherd Will Supply My Need</u>

Heinz Chapel Choir; Theodore Finney, cond.
ASCAP CB-162; Pittsburgh International Contemporary Music Festival. 1954.

Peabody Conservatory Concert Singers; Gregg Smith, cond.
Vox SVBX-5353; 3 discs. 1979.
Reviews: <u>NR</u> 12-77, p8; <u>NYT</u> 7-1-79, pD22.

The Shadyside Presbyterian Church Choir; Russell G. Wichmann, cond.
Image Recordings LP 113. 1962.

Stanford University Chorus; Harold C. Schmidt, cond.
Music Library MLR-7022. 1955. See: B208

D37. <u>Ondine</u> (Incidental Music)

Performance details unknown.
Available for rental on 2-reel tape set from Thomas J. Valentino, Inc., 151 W. 46th Street, New York, NY 10036. A copy of the play with music cues indicated is available from Samuel French, 45 West 25th Street, New York, NY 10010.

D38. <u>Party Pieces</u>

The Brooklyn Philharmonic Symphony Orchestra; Lukas Foss, cond.
Gramavision Inc. Records, GR-7006. 1983.
Review: <u>HF</u> 6-84, p75.

D39. <u>Pastorale on a Christmas Plainsong</u>

Richard Ellsasser, organ.
MGM E-3064. 1953. See: B208
Review: <u>NR</u> 3-53, p14.

D40. <u>The Plow That Broke the Plains</u> (motion picture soundtrack)

Members of the New York Philharmonic; Alexander Smallens, cond.
AEI Records, Benchmark Series; mono; ABM 3501. 1982.

D41. <u>The Plow That Broke the Plains</u> (Suite)

Hollywood Bowl Symphony Orchestra; Leopold Stokowski, cond.
Victor 11-9520-21 (in set M-1116); 78 rpm; 2 discs. Pre-1948.

Little Orchestra Society; Thomas Scherman, cond.
Decca DL-7527; 10" disc. 1952.
Brunswick AXL-2006. Pre-1956.
Reviews: <u>ARG</u> 7-52, p335; <u>CR</u> 7-53, p11; <u>Gr</u> 7-53, p40; <u>GS</u> 7-

52, p3; HF 9 & 10-52, p52; ML 7-53, p3; MQ 4-53, p307+; NR   9-
52, p4; SR 8-16-52, p41.

Los Angeles Chamber Orchestra; Neville Marriner, cond.
Angel SQ-37300. 1976.
Reviews: HF 9-76, p98; NR 5-76, p4; NYT 5-7-76, pC15; St 7-76,
p83.

Symphony of the Air; Leopold Stokowski, cond.
Vanguard VRS-1071/VSD 2095. 1961. See: B209
Vanguard VSD-707-08. 1971.
Reviews: ARG 5-62, pp704+;CR 11-61, p34; HF 11-61, p100; HSR 11-
61, p64; MA 11-61, p37; NR 9-61, p1; NYT 9-17-61, pX14. Gr 12-
74, p1157; HF 9-71, p118; SFCh 5-27-73, p27; SR 2-72, p119; St
7-76, pp83-4.

D42.   The Plow That Broke The Plains (Suite: Excerpts: "Cattle" and
       "Blues")

       Amerigo Marino, cond.
       Bowmar Orchestra Library: Music, U.S.A.
       Bowmar Records BOL #65. 1963.

D43.   The Plow That Broke the Plains (Suite for piano)

       Yvar Mikhashoff, pf.
       Spectrum Records, SR-153. With liner notes by the composer.
       1982.
       Reviews: ARG 9-83, p65; NR 7-82, p13.

D44.   Portrait of F.B. ["Frances Blood" by Gertrude Stein]

       Meriel Dickinson, mezzo-soprano; Peter Dickinson, pf.
       Unicorn RHS-353. 1978.
       Unicorn UNI-72017. 1978.
       Unicorn RHS-253. 1978.
       Reviews: Gr 8-78, p367; Na 11-17-79, p508; NR 8-79, p12;
       NYT 7-22-79, pD21; St 9-79, p104.

D45.   Portraits for Solo Keyboard

       Alternations (Maurice Grosser); An Old Song (Carrie Stettheimer);
       Barcarolle (Georges Hugnet);   Bugles and Birds (Pablo Picasso);
       Catalan Waltzes (Ramón Senabre); Chromatic Double Harmonies
       (Sylvia Marlowe); Guggenheim Jeune (Peggy Guggenheim)(Sonata
       No. 4); In a Bird Cage (Lise Deharme); Persistently Pastoral
       (Aaron Copland);   Solitude (Lou Harrison); Tango Lullaby (Flavie
       Alvarez de Toledo); With Fife and Drums (Mina Curtiss).
       Paul Jacobs, pf.
       Nonesuch D-79024. With liner notes by the composer. 1982.
       Reviews:ARG 7 & 8-82, p40; FF 5 & 6-82, p 223. NR 3-82, p6;   NYT
       4-25-82, pD21; St 5-82, p66.

       Alternations (Maurice Grosser); An Old Song (Carrie Stettheimer);
       Bugles   and Birds (Pablo Picasso);   Cantabile (Nicolas de

Chatelain);   Catalan Waltz (Ramón Senabre); In a Bird Cage (Lise
Deharme).
Arthur Tollefson, pf.
Finnadar SR-9027. 1980.
Reviews: ARG 2-81, p34; Contemporary Keyboard 9-80, p71; FF 11 &
   12-80, p188; HF 10-80, pp91-2; NR 12-80, p10; St 1-81, p87.

Album I: Alternations (Maurice Grosser); An Old Song (Carrie
   Stettheimer); Barcarolle (Georges Hugnet); Bugles and Birds
   (Pablo Picasso); Fugue (Alexander Smallens); Solitude (Lou Har-
   rison); Tango Lullaby (Flavie Alvarez de Toledo); With Fife and
   Drum (Mina Curtiss). Album II: The Bard (Sherry Mangan); Canons
   with Cadenza (André Ostier);   Cantabile (Nicolas de Chatelain);
   The Dream World of Peter Rose-Pulham ; Pastoral (Jean Ozenne);
   Prelude and Fugue (Agnes Rindge); Souvenir (Paul Bowles); Tocca-
   ta (Mary Widney).
Nigel Coxe, pf.
Musical Heritage Society, MHS 4804T. With liner notes by the
   composer. 1984.
Reviews:FF 5 & 6-84, p303; Ov 6-84, p58.

Bugles and Birds (Pablo Picasso); Poltergeist (Hans Arp); Solitude
   (Lou Harrison).
Alan Mandel, pf.
Desto DC-6445-47. 3 discs. 1975. See: B209
Reviews: HF 7-76, p102; NYT 4-11-76, pD24.

Cantabile (Nicolas de Chatelain).
Sylvia Marlowe, hpschd.
Decca DL-10021/DL-710021. 1961.
Reviews: HF 6-61, p63; HSR 6-61, p75; MA 9-61, p37; NYT 4-30-61,
   pX21, SR 3-25-61, p50.

Dead Pan (Mrs. Betty Freeman); Drawing (John Wright); Drawing V.T.
   (Franco Assetto); Free-Wheeling (Scott Wheeler); Giving Full
   Attention (Gerald Busby); Intensely Two (Karen Brown Waltuck);
   Loyal, Steady, Persistent (Noah Creshevsky); Round and Round
   (Dominique Nabokov); Showing Delight (Morris Golde); Singing a
   Song (Christopher Cox); Solid, Not Stolid (Richard Flender);
   Something of a Beauty (Anne-Marie Soullière); Untiring (Barbara
   Epstein); Thoughts About Flying(Norma Flender); Wide Awake (Bill
   Katz); With Joy (Sam Byers).
Yvar Mikhashoff, pf.
Spectrum Records, SR-153. With liner notes by the composer. 1982.
Reviews: ARG 9-83, p65; NR 7-82, p13.

Eccentric Dance (Madame Kristians Tonny)
Marga Richter, pf.
MGM E-3147. 1955. See: B208
Reviews: Au 8-55, p44; NR 8-55, p14; NYT 2-13-55, pX10.

Senza Espressione (Bennett Lerner); Thinking Hard (Phillip Ramey).
Bennett Lerner, pf.

Etcetera Records ETC-1019; Digital. 1984.

Reviews: <u>FF</u> 11 & 12-84, p326; <u>Gr</u> 8-84, p 251; <u>HF</u> 9-84, p72; <u>MG</u> 10-84, p8; <u>NYT</u> 11-4-84, pH25; <u>Ov</u> 8-84, p58; <u>St</u> 12-84, p90.

D46. <u>Portraits</u> <u>for</u> <u>Orchestra</u>

Bugles and Birds (Pablo Picasso); Cantabile for Strings (Nicolas de Chatelain); Fugue (Alexander Smallens); Percussion Piece (Jessie K. Lasell); Tango Lullaby (Flavie Alvarez de Toledo).
Philadelphia Orchestra; Virgil Thomson, cond.
Columbia 12154-55D (in set 255); 78 rpm; 2 discs. 1954.
Columbia 12608D; 78 rpm; (Excerpts: Bugles and Birds, Cantabile for Strings). Pre-1956.
Columbia ML-2087; 10". 1950.
CRI-398 (Excerpts: Bugles and Birds, Fugue, and Tango Lullaby). With liner notes by the composer. 1979. Also on CRI ACS 6009. 1985.
Reviews: <u>ARG</u> 10-45, p48; <u>GS</u> 10-45, p8; <u>MM</u> Winter 1946, p66+; <u>NR</u> 10-45, p2. <u>ARG</u> 2-50, p194; <u>JR</u> 3 & 4-50, p30; <u>LJ</u> 4-15-50, p715; <u>Na</u> 2-18-50, p162; <u>NR</u> 3-50, p4; <u>SR</u> 2-25-50, p58 & 3-4-50, p46. <u>ARG</u> 12-79, p58; <u>CR</u> 1-80, p43; <u>HF</u> 12-79, p100.

David Dubal in Flight; Free-Wheeling (Scott Wheeler); In a Hammock (Dennis Russell Davies); Intensely Two (Karen Waltuck Brown); A Love Scene (Mrs. Betty Freeman); Loyal, Steady, Persistent (Noah Creshevsky); Singing a Song (Christopher Cox); Solid, Not Stolid (Richard Flender); Something of a Beauty (Anne-Marie Soullière); Wide Awake (Bill Katz); With Joy (Sam Byers).
Oshkosh Symphony Orchestra; Henri B. Pensis, cond.
Privately recorded. 1983.

D47. <u>Eight</u> <u>Portraits</u> <u>for</u> <u>Violin</u> <u>Alone</u>

Señorita Juanita de Medina Accompanied by Her Mother; Madame Marthe-Marthine; Georges Hugnet, Poet and Man of Letters; Miss Gertrude Stein as a Young Girl; Cliquet-Pleyel in F; Mrs. C.W.L. [Chester Whitin Lasell]; Sauguet, From Life; Ruth Smallens.
Joseph Silverstein, vn.
Nonesuch Records D-79024. With liner notes by the composer. 1982.
Reviews: <u>ARG</u> 7 & 8-82, p40; <u>FF</u> 5 & 6-82, p223; <u>NR</u> 3-82, p6; <u>NYT</u> 4-25-82, pD21; <u>St</u> 5-82, p66.

D48. <u>Praises</u> <u>and</u> <u>Prayers</u>

Betty Allen, mezzo-soprano; Virgil Thomson, pf.
CRI-207. 1966. See: B209
Hi-Fi/Stereo Review Editorial Recording L-165. 1965.
Reviews: <u>AM</u> 10-67, p134; <u>ARG</u> 8-67, p1104; <u>HF</u> 7-67, p79; <u>NYT</u> 4-30-67, pD26.

D49. <u>Praises</u> <u>and</u> <u>Prayers</u>: "Before Sleeping"

Nancy Tatum, soprano; Geoffrey Parsons, pf.

London OS-26053. 1968.

D50. Prelude for Piano

Yvar Mikhashoff, pf.
Spectrum Records, SR-153. With liner notes by the composer. 1982.
Reviews: ARG 9-83, p65; NR 7-82, p13.

D51. Quartet for Strings. No. 1

New Music String Quartet
ASCAP CB-181; Pittsburgh International Contemporary Music Festi-
    val. 1952.
ASCAP CB-169; Pittsburgh International Contemporary Music Festi-
    val. 1954.

D52. Quartet for Strings, No. 2

Juilliard String Quartet

Columbia ML-4987. 1955. See: B208
Columbia CML-4987. 1968. See: B209
Columbia AML-4987. 1974.
Reviews: ARG 8-55, p385; HF 9-55, p57; LJ 9-15-55, p1894; MQ 10-
    55, p551; NR 9-55, p14; NYT 7-10-55, pX12; PP 1-56, p30; SR 8-
    27-55, p38.

Kohon Quartet
Vox SVBX-5305. 3 discs. 1974.
Reviews: HF 12-74, p122; NR 10-74, p7; NYT 9-15-74, pD32; SFCh 11-
    3-74, p22.

D53. The River (Suite)

Los Angeles Chamber Orchestra; Neville Marriner, cond.
Angel SQ-37300. 1976.
Review: HF 9-76, p98; NR 5-76, p4; NYT 5-7-76, pC15; St 7-76,
    pp83-4.

Symphony of the Air; Leopold Stokowski, cond.
Vanguard VRS-1071/VSD-2095. 1961.See: B209
Review: ARG 5-62, pp704+; CR 11-61, p34; HF 11-61, p100; HSR 11-
    61, p64; MA 11-61, p37; NR 9-61, p1; NYT 9-16-61, pX14.

Vienna Symphony Orchestra; Walter Hendl, cond.
American Recording Society ARS-8. 1952.
Desto D-405/DST-6405. 1964.
Reviews: NYT 8-31-52, pX10; SR 9-27-52, p58. ARG 8-65, p1181; HF
    6-65, p84; HSR 9-65, p105; NYT 4-25-65, pX20; SR 6-26-65, p51.

D54. Scenes from the Holy Infancy According to St. Matthew: "Joseph and
    the Angels"

Peloquin Choir; C. Alexander Peloquin, cond.
Gregorian Institute of America EL-19 (in set EL-100).1960.See:

B209

D55. Sea Piece With Birds

Philadelphia Orchestra; Virgil Thomson, cond.
Columbia ML-4919. 1954.
CRI-398. With liner notes by the composer. 1979.
Reviews: ARG 12-54, p153; HF 1-55, p60; MA 2-15-55, p216; Na 1-1-
    55, p19; NR 1-55, p2; SR 1-29-55, p46. ARG 12-79, p58; CR 1-80,
    p43; HF 12-79, p100.

D56. The Seine at Night

Philadelphia Orchestra; Virgil Thomson, cond.
Columbia ML-4919. 1954.
CRI-398. With liner notes by the composer. 1979.
Reviews: ARG 12-54, p153; HF 1-55, p60; MA 2-15-55, p216; Na 1-1-
    55, p19; NR 1-55, p2; SR 1-29-55, p46. ARG 12-79, p58; CR 1-80,
    p43. HF 12-79, p 100.

D57. Serenade for Flute and Violin

David Gilbert, fl.; Kees Kooper, vn.
Turnabout TVS-34508. 1973. See: B209
Reviews: HF 9-73, p96; NR 8-73, p6.

D58. A Solemn Music

Eastman Symphonic Wind Ensemble; Frederick Fennell, cond.
Mercury MG-40011. 1954.
Mercury MG-50084. 1957. See: B208
Reviews: ARG 2-55, p188; HF 10-54, p82; MA 12-1-54, p24; NR 12-54,
    p2.

D59. Sonata for Flute

Angela Lotegelos, fl.
Carlston Records #101. 1984.

Harvey Moskovitz, flute
Musical Heritage Society MHS-3578. 1977.

D60. Piano Sonata No. 1

Nigel Coxe, pf.
Musical Heritage Society MHS 4804T. With liner notes by the com-
    poser. 1984.
Reviews: FF 5 & 6-84, p303; Ov 6-84, p58.

Yvar Mikhashoff, pf.
Spectrum Records, SR-153. With liner notes by the composer. 1982.
Reviews: ARG 9-83, p65; NR 7-82, p13.

D61. Piano Sonata No. 2

Nigel Coxe, pf.
Musical Heritage Society MHS 4804T. With liner notes by the com-
poser. 1984.
Reviews: FF 5 & 6-84, p303; Ov 6-84, p58.

D62. Piano Sonata No. 3

Roger Shields, pf.
Vox SVBX-5303. 3 discs. 1977.
Reviews: ARG 5-77, p9; NYT 7-3-77, pD14.

D63. Piano Sonata No. 4

Paul Jacobs, pf.
Nonesuch D-79024. With liner notes by the composer. 1982.
Reviews: ARG 7 & 8-82, p40; FF 5 & 6-82, p223; NR 3-82, p6; NYT 4-
25-82, pD21; St 5-82, p66.

Sylvia Marlowe, pf.
New Editions 3. 1953. See: B208
Decca DL-10021/DL-710021. 1961.
Reviews: HF 6-61, p63; HSR 6-61, p75; MA 9-61, p37; NYT 4-30-61,
pX21; SR 3-25-61, p50.

D64. Sonata for Violin and Piano

Joseph Fuchs, vn.; Artur Balsam, pf.
CRI-207. 1966. See: B209
Hi-Fi/Stereo Review Editorial Recording L-165. 1965.
CRI ACS 6009. 1985.
Reviews: AM 10-67, p134; ARG 8-67, p1104; HF 7-67, p79; NYT 4-30-
67, pD26.

D65. Sonata da Chiesa

Lillian Fuchs, va.; Peter Simenauer, cl.; Fred   Mills, tpt.; Paul
Ingraham, hn.; Edward Erwin, tbn.; Virgil Thomson, cond.
CRI-207. 1966. See: B209
Hi-Fi/Stereo Review Editorial Recording L-165. 1965.
CRI ACS 6009. 1985.
Reviews: AM 10-67, p134; ARG 8-67, p1104; HF 7-67, p79; NYT 4-30-
67, pD26.

D66. (Five) Songs to Poems of William Blake

Mack Harrell,   baritone; Philadelphia Orchestra; Eugene   Ormandy,
cond.
Columbia ML-4919. 1954.
CRI-398 (Excerpts: "The Divine Image", "Tiger! Tiger!", "The Land
of Dreams", and "And Did Those Feet"). With liner notes by the
composer. 1979.
Reviews: ARG 12-54, p133; HF 1-55, p60; MA 2-15-55, p216; Na 1-1-
55, p19; NR 1-55, p2; SR 1-29-55, p46. ARG 12-79, p58; CR 1-80,
p43; HF 12-79, 100.

D67. Stabat Mater

Jennie Tourel, mezzo-soprano; New Music String Quartet.
Columbia ML-4491. 1952. See: B208
Reviews: ARG 3-53, p211; CR 4-53, p35; GS 2-53, p9; HF 7 & 8-53,
    p46; MA 4-15-53, p17; MQ 7-54, p471; Na 4-11-53, p314; NR 3-53,
    p5; NYT 2-15-53, pX9; SR 2-28-53, pp60 & 75.

D68. Symphony No. 3

New Hampshire Symphony Orchestra; James Bolle, cond.
CRI-411. 1980.
CRI ACS 6009. 1985.
Reviews: ARG 1-81, p43; CR 11-80, p43; FF 9 & 10-80, p223; HF 10-
80, p91-2; NR 8-80, p3.

D69. Symphony on a Hymn Tune

Eastman-Rochester Symphony Orchestra; Howard Hanson, cond.
Mercury MG-50429/SR-90429. 1965.
Mercury SRI-75063. 1976.
Reviews: ARG 3-66, p596; HF 3-66, p92; HSR 5-66, p89; NR 3-66, p2;
NYT 1-30-66, pX22; SR 2-26-66, p51.

D70. Synthetic Waltzes

Arthur Gold, pf.; Robert Fizdale, pf.
Columbia MM-956. 78 rpm. Pre-1952.
Columbia ML-2147; 10" disc. 1952.
Philips S-06614R. Pre-1956.
Reviews: ARG 3-51, p245; GS 12-50, p8; Na 6-16-51, p574; NR 12-
50, p13.

D71. Ten Easy Pieces and a Coda

Yvar Mikhashoff, pf.
Spectrum Records, SR-153. With liner notes by the composer. 1982.
Reviews: ARG 9-83, p65; NR 7-82, p13.

D72. The Tiger

Eleanor Steber, soprano; Edwin Biltcliffe, pf.
St/And SPL-411-12; 2 discs. 1963.
Desto D-411-12/DST-6411-12; 2 discs. 1964. See: B209
Reviews: ARG 5-65, p808; HF 4-65, p103. LJ 6-1-65, p2538; NR 2-65,
    p10; NYT 3-14-65, pX22; PP 1-65, p33; SR 10-30-65, p84.

D73. Tres Estampas de Niñez

Reyna Rivas, mezzo-soprano; Martin Imaz, pf.
Privately recorded. 1983.

D74. Tuesday in November

Motion picture soundtrack using Hollywood musicians;   Virgil

Thomson, cond.
AEI Records, Benchmark Series, ABM 3501. 1982.

D75. Two by Marianne Moore

Meriel Dickinson, mezzo-soprano; Peter Dickinson, pf.
Unicorn RHS-353. 1978.
Unicorn UNI-72017. 1978.
Unicorn RHS-253. 1978.
Reviews: Gr 8-78, p367; Na 11-17-79, p508; NR 8-79, p12; NYT 7-22-
79, pD21; St 9-79, p104.

D76. Two Sentimental Tangos

Bennett Lerner, pf.
Etcetera Records ETC 1019. Digital. 1984.
Reviews: FF 11 & 12-84, p326; Gr 8-84, p251; HF 9-84, p72; MG 10-
84, p8; NYT 11-4-84, pH25; Ov 8-84, p58; St 12-84, p90.

D77. Variations and Fugues on Sunday School Tunes

Marilyn Mason, organ.
Esoteric ES-522. 1954. See: B208 & B209
Counterpoint/Esoteric CPT-522/CPST-5522. 1964/1966.
Reviews: Ha 4-54, p104; HF 5-54, p54; SR 2-27-54, p63.

D78. Wheat Field at Noon

Philadelphia Orchestra; Virgil Thomson, cond.
Columbia ML-4919. 1954.
CRI-398. With liner notes by the composer. 1979.
CRI ACS 6009. 1985.
Reviews: ARG 12-54, p133; HF 1-55, p60; MA 2-15-55, p216; Na 1-1-
55, p19; NR 1-55, p2; SR 1-29-55, p46. ARG 12-79, p58, CR 1-80,
p43; HF 12-79, p100.

Bibliography by Thomson

As one of the major music critics of the twentieth century, Virgil Thomson's writings have been widely circulated and influential. They are here divided into articles (reviews, essays, addresses, and translations) and books. Thomson's New York Herald Tribune articles will be found annotated as a group under the particular anthology in which they have been collected. Reprints are indicated in the annotation of original appearance. "See" references indicate related entries in other sections of this book -- W to "Works and Performances," D to "Discography," B to "Bibliography," and A to archive listings in "Appendix I." Abbreviations are explained in the Preface.

Articles, Essays, Translations, Addresses

T1. "Aaron Copland (American Composers -- VII)," MM 9 (Jan-Feb 1932): 67-73.

>   One of his first major writings and, according to editor Minna Lederman, an article whose "bold, personal approach" influenced subsequent Modern Music contributors (See B159), Thomson here writes a blunt assessment of his friend's music (Copland asked Thomson to write the article). "Aaron Copland's music is American in rhythm, Jewish in melody, eclectic in all the rest." Reprinted in The Life and Death of a Small Magazine ("Modern Music," 1924-1946) by Minna Lederman (See B155).

T2. "About Four Saints," ARG 31 (Feb 1965): 520-21.

>   Thomson briefly reminisces about his collaboration with Gertrude Stein: "happiness was ours working together." See: W1

T3. "The Abstract Composers," Score 12 (June 1955): 62-64.

>   With a focus on the instruments and compositional methods of John Cage, Thomson discusses chance and the abstract in music. "The use of chance in composition gives a result not unlike that of a kaleidoscope...With a large gamut of sounds and a complex

system for assembling them into patterns, all the patterns turn out to be interesting, an arabesque is achieved...I find it only natural that music, usually, in our time, a good quarter century behind the visual arts, should have finally acquired its own 'abstractionist' pressure group.

T4. "Acceptance of The Gold Medal for Music," PAA. Second series, 17 (1967): 47.

Thomson makes a brief, witty acceptance speech.

T5. "Admit," The Gad-fly, Harvard University, April 1925: 1.

This poem about "pathos in life" and the "buttercup virginity" of Harvard professors is the work of student Virgil Thomson.

T6. "America of Age," Boston Symphony Orchestra Concert Bulletin 13 (Jan 21, 1949): 671-75.

Reprinted from the October 31, 1948 New York Herald Tribune, this piece praises American composers, performance practices, and musical pedagogy but advises that "American musicians should make a little effort at this point, lift themselves above their already setting-in complacency and start going places."

T7. "America's Musical Autonomy," The Vanderbilt Alumnus (March 1944): 9.

Reprinted from the March 12, 1949 NYHT, this favorable review of George Pullen Jackson's White and Negro Spirituals (J.J. Augustin, New York, 1944) declares the new book has "clarified the whole question of America's musical resources." Reprinted in VTR.

T8. "America's Musical Maturity," The Yale Review 51 (October 1961): 66-74.

Thomson in this article offers a thumbnail sketch of American musical trends and composers from 1910. "It would be ever so pleasant if music should turn out to be meaningful again and not wholly preoccupied with methodology."

T9. "Amerikanisches Divertimento," Der Monat 1 (March 1949): 98-102.

Thomson discusses the state of American music, reporting on the work of Stravinsky, Arnold Schoenberg, Walter Piston, Darius Milhaud, Otto Leuning, Benjamin Britten, and others. The question of who exactly is an American composer is boiled down in Thomsonian logic to "Any composer who possesses American citizenship." ("Jeder musikalisches Autor, der im Besitz der amerikanischen Staatsbürgerschaft ist.")

T10. "Answers by Virgil Thomson," Possibilities 1 (Winter 1947/48): 21-24.

Thomson fields questions from Lou Harrison, Arthur Berger, Elliott Carter, Paul Bowles, and others about composition. When
asked about "automatic writing" Thomson responds that "most of
our best work...is the product of a concentrated mental state in
which one lets things happen...Concentrated work can always be
polished up later...Half-hearted work is the very devil to
revise."

T11. "Arturo Toscanini's 'Rightness Versus that of Bernard Haggin,"
NYHT Book Review 35 (April 12, 1959): 6.

Thomson reviews B.H. Haggin's Conversations with Toscanini: "Our
author measures every move of his hero with a relentless
assumption of his own 'rightness' about music...He assumes his
judgments of works, tempos, balances, blends and meanings...to
be definitive, and all opposing estimates vain."

T12. "Being a Musician," The Peabody Notes 10 (Spring, 1945): 1+.

In these excerpts from his commencement address to Peabody's
graduating class of 1945, Thomson states: "Musicians own music,
because music owns them. There is no getting around it."

T13. "Berlioz, Boulez, and Piaf, NYRB 14 (Jan 29, 1970): 3-8.

Thomson reviews the following books: The Memoirs of Hector
Berlioz (trans. by David Cairns); Baudelaire-Berlioz; Berlioz
and the Romantic Century (by Jacques Barzun); Berlioz and the
Romantic Imagination (a catalogue of an exhibition at the Victoria and Albert Museum, London, 1969); Pelléas et Mélisande;
and Piaf (by Simone Berteaut). Review reprinted in VTR.

T14. "The Burning Question," ON 30 (March 5, 1966): 9-11.

Thomson opines that opera is in need of reform and that "the
burning question in opera today is making it a part of the
intellectual and artistic world, instead of routine entertain-
ment or a vehicle for vocalism."

T15. "Cage and the Collage of Noises," NYRB 14 (April 23, 1970): 9-14.

Thomson comments on these recent books: Notations by John Cage;
A Year from Monday: New Lectures and Writings by Cage; Silence:
Lectures and Writings by Cage;and Virgil Thomson: His Life and
Music by Kathleen Hoover and John Cage (See B142). Reprinted in
American Music Since 1910 (T188) and VTR.

T16. "Chaplin Scores," MM 18 (Nov-Dec 1940): 15-17.

Thomson reflects on Charlie Chaplin's use of music in his
movies. "His way of integrating music with animated photography
is to admit auditive elements to the rank of co-star with the
poetic and visual effects."

T17. "Composing for the Movies" National Board of Review of Motion Pictures Magazine (Jan 1941): 4-7.

This reprint of a lecture Thomson delivered at the National Board Annual Conference deals mainly with "the real headache in the matter of movie music, and that is: What on earth can they do about music in the naturalistic fiction film?...Music does not go very well with spoken speech. My opinion...is that you have to cut the music out altogether, except at the beginning where it is like an overture, and at the end where it is like a postlude."

T18. "Composition and Review," NYT 83 (March 11, 1934): Sect. 2, p. 6.

In this very brief article Thomson explains that opera is a "tug of war between expression and declamation," and that American composers do not as yet have the complete grasp of prosody needed to produce a good opera. "Very few [composers] know beans about musical declamation."

T19. "El Compositor como Crítico," Buenos Aires Musical (Dec 15, 1954): 5.

In this brief article, written in Caracas for the February 14, 1954 New York Herald-Tribune, Thomson reflects on the special skills and blindspots which a composer brings to music journalism. All things considered, he feels that on the rare occasions when composers themselves bother with criticism, "The result is a maximum of resonance and clarity." ("...La situación adquiere su máximum de resonancia y clarificación.") This article also appeared in German in Melos 21 (Sept 1954): 245-47.

T20. "Conduite d'eau" by Gertrude Stein. Translated from the French by Thomson and Louise Langlois. In Laris. Paris: Lone Gull Press, 1927.

T21. "Conversation Piece: Virgil Thomson," Bravo 1 (1961): 16-19.

Thomson discusses music criticism in general and his career in specific in this interview. "Judgement. happens instantly. What you need the time for actually is careful writing, for explaining what you have on your mind." A continuation of this interview appeared in the February, 1962 (2:41-42) Bravo. In it Thomson comments mainly on radio and tv distribution: "American TV opera...has virtually disappeared."

T22. "Copland on Copland," VF 47 (Sept 1984): 107-8.

Thomson reviews Copland by Aaron Copland and Vivian Perliss (New York: St. Martin's Press, 1984).

T23. "'Craft-Igor' and the Whole Stravinsky," NYRB 7 (Dec 15, 1966): 3-4.

Thomson reviews Stravinsky: The Composer and His Works by Eric

W. White and Themes and Episodes by Stravinsky and Robert Craft.
This article appeared also in Der Monat (April 1967) and was
reprinted in VTR.

T24.   "La Critica Musical," Informaciones (August 1955): 14-15+.

In this article for Buenos Aires readers, Thomson presents ideas
developed in previous essays, especially "The Art of Judging
Music," (See T189) but adds an illustrative metaphor from bull-
fighting. He likens the matador to the musician, observing that
it is necessary for someone (the critic) to say "Olé!" or not.

T25.   "The Criticism of Music," MA 61 (Feb 10, 1943): 5+.

Defining music criticism simply as "the analysis of musical
performance," Thomson suggests in this article that criticism is
not written for composers but for the public.   Having recently
been asked to join the staff of the New York Herald Tribune,
Thomson writes that it "is the most normal thing in the world
that composers should criticize music."

T26.   "A Critique of Criticism," Vg 113 (March 1949): 165.

Originally written for a New York Herald Tribune Fresh Air Fund
Football Program (c.1940-45), this article states: "Art needs no
umpire because art is not a contest...Art can literally...do no
wrong. How can anybody, therefore, be right about it, or wrong
either?...Good reviewing has reality but no authority."

T27.   "The Cult of Jazz," VF 24 (June 1925): 54+.

Reminding his readers that jazz "is dance music and always will
be dance music," Thomson in this article, while allowing that
some diverting and charming pieces have been produced in this
style, states that jazz has almost no "intrinsic musical quality...beyond elementary muscle-jerking," and is not a truly American art. After thumbnail sketches of several contemporary
works, Thomson concludes that jazz is admired simply because it
is "good of its kind, complete, self-assured and unafraid."

T28.   "Current Chronicle: San Francisco," MQ 36 (Jan 1950): 99-105.

Thomson lavishes praise on Milhaud's Sabbath Morning Service in
this analysis of the work. Milhaud's writing has "a freedom
unmatched among the work of living composers," and "every measure is an adventure." Four pages of musical examples are
given.

T29.   Dix Portraits (Ten Portraits) with original English text by Ger-
        trude Stein. Translated into French by Thomson and Georges
        Hugnet. Paris: Editions de la Montagne, 1930.

T30.   "Douglas Moore, 1893-1969," PAA. Second series, No. 20 (1970): 81-
        83.

Thomson sketches the career and gifts of the composer-teacher Douglas Moore.

T31. "A Drenching of Music, but a Drought of Music Critics," NYT 124 (Oct 27, 1974): Sect. 2, p. 1+.

Contending that "the tone of newspaper criticism is blander and less urgent" than earlier in the century, Thomson comments on the work of several non-newspaper music reviewers: Andrew Porter, Robert Craft, and Ned Rorem. Reprinted in VTR.

T32. "Edgard Varèse," PAA. Second series, No. 16 (1966): 91-93.

This short eulogy is a portion of the annual "Commemorative Tributes of the Institute."

T33. "Edwin Denby," Ballet Review, 12 (Spring 1984): 22-23.

Thomson reminisces about his recently departed friend, commenting on their collaboration on Horse Eats Hat , and Denby's dance criticism for Modern Music and his poetry. See: W330

T34. "Elizabeth Lutyens, C.B.E., (1906-1983)," Grand Street 2 (July, 1983): 182-184.

Thomson eulogizes the British composer whose work was "ever distinguished, beautiful, wide in its choices of theme and subject, and technically advanced."

T35. "Ending the Great Tradition," Encounter 12 (Jan 1959): 64-67.

After a brief history of 19th-century compositional evolution, Thomson complains that "both technical advance and expressivity have shown, since World War I...a decline in vigour," and he urges composers to forego modernistic novelties. "The tradition of constant change must be thrown overboard and freshness found through other preoccupations." This article was reprinted in the following: AM (under the title "Music's Tradition of Constant Change") 203 (Feb 1959): 84-90; Cuadernos (under the title "Tradición e Innovaciones") (Jan-Feb 1959); Buenos Aires Musical (title: "La Tradición Musica del Cambio Constante,") (Dec 1959);and Ongakunotomo (Japan: Feb 1960): 94-95.

Two responses to this article were published together in Encounter 5: 563-56 (May 1959): "Two Comments on Virgil Thomson's 'Modest Proposal'" by Frank House and Peter Heyworth.

T36. "Enter: American-Made Music, VF 25 (Oct 1925):71+.

Dismissing the current European musical composers (except for Stravinsky) as "unable to supply enough modernity," Thomson eagerly awaits a new musical season containing many American works. In this article he lists new works to be heard during the upcoming year in New York, including Gershwin's Pianoforte Concerto, Deems Taylor's The Family Ford, and John

Alden Carpenter's ballet <u>Skyscrapers,</u> among others. Thomson prophesies the demise of "high-brow jazz" and the revival of light opera, a "tasty diversion within the limits of that emo- tional detachment which is a psychological necessity in our epoch."

T37. "Equilibrium of the Musical Elements,"<u>Mozart and French Composers,</u> New Friends of Music Program Book 1944-45, 9/1: 19- 23.

Of the music of Mozart and "the Gallic at its best" Thomson writes: "These demand the most glittering execution, the most intelligent phraseology and the most sincere feeling. Any fail- ure to achieve this equilibrium diminishes the music's meaning because...its equilibrium is its meaning."

T38. "Etats-Unis," <u>Inter-Auteurs</u> (1st trimester, 1955): 24-5.

Thomson here writes of the musical difference between the United States and Europe, the most "striking" (<u>différence frappante</u>) of which is that contemporary works are performed publically in the former while broadcast by radio in the latter. This situation influences the type of music written as well as its longevity.

T39. "Eugene Berman, 1899-1972," <u>PAA.</u> Second series, No. 24 (1974): 131-33.

Thomson reminisces on one of his 1920's-30's Paris friends, painter Eugene Berman.

T40. "Fair Game, Fair Play," <u>NYHT</u> Fresh Air Fund Football Program, c. 1940-45, p23.

Thomson explains the workings of the music criticism division of a metropolitan newspaper, how events are chosen for coverage and how writers are selected for the assignments.

T41. "The Feast of Love" from the Latin "Pervigilium Veneris." Published in <u>Art and Literature: An International Review</u>, Summer 1946. New York: G. Schirmer, 1977. See also W148

T42. "Films Seen in New York: A Couple of Nice Movies," <u>MM</u> 14 (May-June 1937): 239-40.

Thomson reviews Silvestre Revueltas's music for "The Wave" ("the core of his inspiration is a trifle soft) and Jean Wiener's for "Knock, où le Triomphe de la Médecine" ("What music is needed is there and what is there is tops.")

T43. "The Flood -- An Opera for Television," <u>Observer Weekend Review</u> (June 17, 1962): 21.

Thomson is completely unimpressed with the visual aspects of this opera and describes Stravinsky's score as "a slender but perfectly real piece...like a master's thumbnail sketch for some grander monument."

T44. "Foreword" for American Music: A Panorama by Daniel Kingman (New York: Schirmer Books, 1979): xx-xxii.

Thomson outlines the high points of this textbook and emphasizes the fact that its author is a composer himself and therefore "knows what music is about."

T45. "Foreword" for The Piano Works of Claude Debussy, by Robert Schmitz (New York: Dvell, Sloan, and Pearce, 1950): xvii-xix.

Thomson highly praises Debussy ("[he] encompassed most fully the French [temperament]...and was the least weighed upon by the dead hand of formula.") and Schmitz ("he early created...a method of playing at once radical and comprehensive...[he displayed] astounding executional and interpretative powers.")

T46. "Foreword" for Rachmaninoff by Victor I. Seroff (New York: Simon and Schuster, 1950): xi-xvi.

Thomson's brief foreward highlights Rachmaninoff's musical gifts and Seroff's ability to "bring Russia's musical ways to life." Thomson admits that before he had read the book he had harbored a "hostile indifference" toward the composer.

T47. "A Forum of Critics" (Virgil Thomson, Eric Newton, and James Johnson Sweeney) Magazine of Art 46 (May 1953): 231-32.

Thomson's response to a request "to define the role of the contemporary critic, his qualifications and his responsibilities." He writes that "a music critic's first obligation is to music...[his] second obligation is to his readers...Nobody has to be right...He merely has to know what he has to talk about, and talk honestly.

T48. "Frederick Kiesler's Opera Sets," Zodiac: A Review of Contemporary Architecture 19 (July 1969).

"Kiesler's sets were all...designed less for the audience to look at than they were for actors to move around in...They were not made for static contemplation...They were made to play a play in."

T49. "French Landscape with Figures," MM 16 (Nov-Dec 1938): 17-22.

Thomson reports on the musical scene of pre-World War II France. He mentions theatre music ("mostly routine stuff"), opera ("The French...would be awfully happy to have another Manon"), and popular music ("the best swing out-fit here is the quintet from the Hot-Club de France").

T50. "The Friends and Enemies of Modern Music" in a catalogue of a memorial exhibition (Feb 23-June 1, 1958), A. Everett Austin, Jr: A Director's Taste and Achievement, (Hartford, CT: John and

Mable Ringling Museum of Art and the Wadsworth Atheneum, 1958).

Thomson delivers a eulogy for A. Everett "Chick" Austin, founder of The Friends and Enemies of Modern Music subscription society, and calls him "a whole cultural movement in one man."

T51. "From 'Regina' to 'Juno'," SR (May 16, 1959): 82-83.

Thomson reviews two recent recordings of the works of Marc Blitzstein: "Juno" (music and songs for Sean O'Casey's Juno and the Paycock) and "Regina" (Blitzstein's full operatic setting of Lillian Hellman's The Little Foxes.)

T52. "The Future of American Music," VF 25 (Sept 1925): 62+.

Thomson expresses hope for a truly American art music in this article, although he feels that at the moment American "musical language is...inadequate for complex personal expression." He denigrates jazz as "a clever and precocious patois...limited in expression by meterical rigidity," but is confident that a more satisfactory national idiom will evolve from the intense contemporary musical activity and enthusiasm.

T53. "The Gallic Approach," Juilliard Review 9 (Winter 1961-62): 9+.

Praising French music as "precise, picturesque, and communicative," Thomson briefly discusses its influence on American music.

T54. "The Genius Type," NYRB 11 (Sept 26, 1968): 56-61.

Thomson comments on Notes of an Apprenticeship by Pierre Boulez; Penser la musique aujourd'hui by Boulez; and Semantique Musicale by Alain Daniélou. Reprinted in VTR.

T55. "George Gershwin," MM 13/1 (Nov-Dec 1935): 13-19.

A hot and cold look at Gershwin with a special emphasis on Porgy and Bess. Thomson points out "the predominance of charm in presentation over expressive substance" in Gershwin's music and yet admits that he is "a gifted composer, a charming composer, an exciting and sympathetic composer...[but] he hasn't learned the business of being a serious composer." Reprinted in VTR.

T56. "Gertrude Stein Portrayed by an Old Friend," NYHT Book Review 24/47 (July 11, 1948): 3.

Thomson has only praise for W.G. Rogers' book, When This You See Remember Me, and for the inimitable Gertrude Stein in this short review.

T57. "A Good Writer," NYRB 26/21-22 (Jan 24, 1980): 6-8.

Thomson reviews Janet Flanner's World: Uncollected Writings

1932-1975, edited by Irving Drutman.

T58. "Greatest Music Teacher -- at 75," Music Educators' Journal 49 (Jan 1949): 42-44.

Nadia Boulanger, of course, is the subject, and Thomson gives a brief account of her teaching methods, her influence on American and other composers, her background, and her talents. "She can understand at sight almost any piece of music, its meaning, its nature, its motivation, its unique existence." Reprinted in: NYT Magazine 111 (Feb 4, 1962): Sect. 6, p. 24+; Piano Quarterly 39 (Jan-March 1962): pp. 16-19; and VTR.

T59. "The Greeks Had No Word For It," The Charioteer 6 (1964): 83-84.

Thomson introduces a modern, musical version of Sophocles' Philoctetes by David Posner. "The musico-poetic theatre is ready...to essay a new words-and-music fusion...And the language most propitious for that today is English."

T60. "A Guide to Contemporary Music," Vg 106 (July 1945): 79+.

Thomson writes: "What everybody looks for in music is comprehensibility...We are seriously bothered only if we cannot find the sense."

T61. "Henri Sauguet," La Revue Musicale Triple Numero 361,362, and 363 (1983): 87-90.

See T94

T62. "High Costs," MJ 6 (Nov-Dec 1948): 19+.

In this article (which originally apeared in the Oct 10, 1948 New York Herald Tribune) Thomson rather idealistically notes that "artistic enterprises which conduct their operations on the model of business must accept the unhappy consequences of a business depression. If our symphony orchestras were more clearly a part of our real cultural life...they would be in a better position...to face money deficits. Their intellectual function would be worth more as capital."

T63. "Home Thoughts," MM 10 (Jan-Feb 1933): 107-109.

Thomson here expresses culture shock on visiting the U.S. after residing for several years in Paris. He laments the triumph of popular music and notes how they order things differently in France.

T64. "How Dead is Arnold Schoenberg?" NYRB 4 (April 22, 1965): 6-8.

Thomson gives a favorable review of Arnold Schoenberg Letters, selected and edited by Irwin Stein. Reprinted in VTR.

T65. "How Modern Can You Be?" Boston Symphony Orchestra Concert

<u>Bulletin</u> 16 (1952-3): 77-81.

Reprinted from the Feb 10,1952 <u>New York Herald-Tribune</u>, this article deals with modernism in musical composition, and Thomson concludes that "musical advance, real technical advance, is taking place today only in the region of rhythmic research."

T66. "How Modern Music Gets That Way," <u>VF</u> 24 (April, 1925): 46+.

After a brief, simplified look at the new uses of musical elements in contemporary music, Thomson reminds befuddled audiences of new music that "there is not a first-rate composer in history who was not an inveterate searcher after novel methods." Thomson advises the concert-goer simply to listen "naively" and to wait patiently for the music to "make sense."

T67. "How 'The Mother of Us All' Was Created," <u>NYT</u> 105 (April 15, 1956): Sect. 2, p. 7.

Thomson recalls the inspiration, collaboration, and composition processes of <u>The Mother of Us All</u> on the eve of its first wholly professional performance in New York at the Phoenix Theatre. Thomson describes the work as a "musico-dramatic spectacle" about "American public and private life in the 19th century." See: W3

T68. "Ideas to Watch in Music," <u>Vg</u> 113 (Jan 1949).

Thomson in this piece looks back over the first half of the century and predicts that American musical style is just about to become "victorious, mature, and serene." He also foresees progress in television opera.

T69. "Igor Markevitch: Little Rollo in Big Time," <u>MM</u> 10 (Nov-Dec 1932): 19-23.

Thomson reviews the debut concert of Markevitch's music, which he finds "a bit self-assertive perhaps and harsh." Thomson finds that Markevitch's "career is more interesting than the music." An excerpt of this review was reprinted in <u>NYT</u> (Dec 25,1932):Sect. 9, p. 10.

T70. "An Inquiry Into Cultural Trends," <u>The American Round Table: People's Capitalism, Part II</u> (published by The Advertising Council, Inc.) (May 22, 1957): 8-48.

This transcript of panel discussions in which Thomson participated at the Yale Club in New York includes the topics "The Quality of American Cultural Achievements," and "Creative Values and Popular Forces in American Life."

T71. "The Interaction of Vernacular and Formal Music," transcript of a panel discussion, UNESCO's <u>Proceedings of the International Music Congress</u>, New York and Washington, D.C., Sept 6-15, 1968.

The comments of Thomson are included in this discussion of the interaction between folk and art music.

T72.   "In the Theatre," MM 14 (March-April, 1937): 170-73.

Thomson reviews the Juilliard production of Garrick by Robert Simon and Albert Stoessel, finding it in a style inappropriate "for depicting our simple U.S.A. motivations or our interpretations of legendary ones, not to speak of...our rapid and racy speech."

T73.   "In the Theatre," MM 15 (Jan-Feb 1938): 112-14.

Thomson opens this review of Blitzstein's The Cradle Will Rock, which he finds "intellectually elegant because clear and...emotionally convincing because felt," with an attack upon Alfred Einstein's myopic view of contemporary music.

T74.   "In the Theatre: Another Negroid Opera," MM 15 (March-April 1938): 183-84.

Thomson calls Denmark Vesey by Paul Bowles and Charles-Henri Ford a "successful and impressive" opera, in which "text and setting are happily united," but feels the use of a Negro cast an artistic mistake.

T75.   "In the Theatre: High-Brows Wow Local Public," MM 14 (May-June 1937): 233-37.

Thomson reviews three premieres -- Gian-Carlo Menotti's Amelia al Ballo, Copland and Edwin Denby's The Second Hurricane, and Stravinsky's The Card Party -- all of which he feels are qualified successes, and, in a coda, predicts a triumph for Marc Blitzstein's The Cradle Will Rock.

T76.   "In the Theatre: Three Shows With Music," MM 14 (Jan-Feb 1937): 101-05.

Thomson reviews incidental music for Erika Mann's Pepper Mill, Kurt Weill's for The Eternal Road, and Paul Bowles's for Dr. Faustus. Although he appreciates Weill's "colossal sens du théatre," he finds Bowles's work here more appropriate, "of a rare musical richness and of a great precision."

T77.   "Introduction" to Commissioning Music, a handbook published by Meet the Composers, Inc. New York: 1984.

Thomson introduces and praises a guide book to promote "goodwill, fair play, and equitable dealings" between patrons and artists.

T78.   "Introduction to La Seine," Parnassus: Poetry in Review 5 (Spring/Summer 1977): 406-16.

Thomson gives a brief sketch of the poet who wrote "La Seine," which he set to music in 1928. His translation of the poem (See T158), plus the original French (by the Duchess of Rohan), as well as a facsimile of the score (in his own hand) are included (See W113). This issue of Parnassus is devoted to pieces by and about Virgil Thomson.

T79. "Introduction" to The Structure of Music: A Listener's Guide by Robert Erickson. (New York, Noonday Press, 1955): vii-xi.

"This uncommonly enlightened book tells the history of music through the history of counterpoint...[it] offers a penetrating experience of music."

T80. "I Say It's Music...Hot," Vg 101 (Feb 15, 1943): 32+.

Thomson comments on the popularity of jazz both in the States and abroad, and discusses jazz style.

T81. "Instruments of Criticism," Prose 4 (Spring 1972): 183-95.

Thomson takes a look at Donald Sutherland's On, Romanticism (New York University Press, 1971) and applies some of its ideas to the art of criticism.

T82. "Is Kindness Killing the Arts?" report on a panel discussion (August 24, 1963), The MacDowell Colony News (Dec 1963).

Thomson, with others, responds to several questions about art and its distribution. He opines: "You have your working life and you have your business life, and the less they see of each other the better."

T83. "Is Opera Dead? One Man Says No..." NYT 117 (June 16, 1968): Sect. 2, p. 13.

Thomson writes that opera "is the grandest theatrical form ever created and the most complete." Much of the article deals with language and opera: "What opera has lacked in our time is...any breakthrough at all into a new language.

T84. "Is Reviewing Fun?" Ha 195 (Nov 1947): 406-09.

Originally written for a NYHT Fresh Air Fund Football Program (c. 1940-45), this amusing article deals mainly with record reviewing. Thomson declares that "judging music from these processed versions is like judging a beauty contest from photographs." This article was reprinted in Neue Auslese (Feb 1948: pp. 38-41) under the title "Ist Musikkritik ein Amusanter Beruf?"

T85. "It Was Like That," foreword to Americans in Paris by George Wickes. New York:Da Capo Press, 1980.

Thomson sketches the major figures of "the great American invasion that took place...from 1903 to 1934." Thomson himself is featured in Chapter 13 of this book. See: B189

T86. "The Ives Case," NYRB 14 (May 21, 1970): 9-11.

After a brief sketch of Ives's life, Thomson offers a hot-and-cold review of Ives's major works. Reprinted in VTR and The Art of Judging Music (T189). In the Sept 3, 1970 issue of NYRB (24:38) Thomson responds to a letter from critic Peter Yates regarding this Ives essay.

T87. "Jazz," The American Mercury 2 (August, 1924): 465-67.

A simple, concise analysis of jazz is the goal of this short article. However, Thomson's view is completely unsympathetic to the contemporary form. He declares that the essence of jazz "remains the foxtrot with a monotonous rhythm underneath," that "the rhythm shakes but it won't flow" and that jazz "never gets anywhere emotionally." Reprinted in: Parnassus:Poetry in Review 5 (Spring/Summer 1977): 439-56; and VTR. Excerpt reprinted in: Tin Pan Alley by Isaac Goldberg. New York: Frederick Ungar Publishing Co., Inc., pp. 271-72.

T88. "John Cage Late and Early," SR (Jan 30, 1960): 38-39.

In this piece Thomson reviews a three-disc set recorded on May 16, 1950 at the 25-Year Retrospective Concert of the Music of John Cage at Town Hall in New York City. The records, with notes by the composer, "give an ample view of a striking personality who is also our most 'far out' composer."

T89. "The Last Time I Saw Kansas City," Junior Bazaar (March, 1948): 68+.

Thomson reminisces about his youth in Kansas City when "one went downtown for everything -- for culture as well as for business." In 1948 he finds it "a vast suburb and not city at all...modernization has decentralized the city's intellectual and social life."

T90. "Leonard Bernstein Conducts a Stimulating Medley of Essays in Music," NYHT Book Review 36 (Nov 29, 1959): 3.

Thomson reviews The Joy of Music by Leonard Bernstein. "Bernstein is readable because he is literate and sincere...[his] is not an original mind, but it is a sound mind and an active one."

T91. "Leonid Berman, 1896-1976" PAA, Second series, No. 28 (1978): 93-4.

Thomson reflects on the life and work of painter and friend Leonid Berman.

T92. "Letter" in Twentieth-Century Composers on Fugue. Leon Stein, editor. Chicago: DePaul University School of Music, 1966, p. 49.

Thomson writes that the fugal form "richly sustains the musical interest without simulating drama" in film scoring and that the fugue "is the bedrock...of instruction in composition" since it "gives the student mastery and sets off his imagination as nothing else will do."

T93. "Letter to the Editor," Helicon Nine: A Journal of Women's Arts and Letters 2 (Spring/Summer 1979): 8-9.

Thomson encourages the publishers of the new feminist journal and writes that "women composers are a rare and special group. There are never enough women artists among all...the disciplines."

T94. "Lettre à Pierre Ancelin." La Revue Musicale, Triple Numero 361, 361, 363 (1983): 87-90.

Asked to discuss the place of Henri Sauguet's music in the United States, Thomson submits an article which appeared in the New York Herald Tribune on May 9, 1953 (and reprinted in Music Reviewed; See T191), and a covering letter lamenting the scarcity of Sauguet performances.

T95. "A Little About Movie Music," MM 10 (May-June 1929): 188-91.

"The trouble with most movie-music is its lack of continuity. The cinema is naturally a discontinuous medium...Musical accompaniment should be an aid to continuity. It should establish and preserve and atmosphere...It should envelope and sustain a narrative..." Thomson goes on to enumerate several problems with film music composition and musical solutions to those difficulties. Reprinted in The Life and Death of a Small Magazine ("Modern Music," 1924-1946) by Minna Lederman (See B155).

T96. "A Little About Movie Music," MM 10 (May-June 1933): 188-91.

Thomson reflects on film music, which he feels should promote continuity, "establish and preserve an atmosphere," and "envelope and sustain a narrative." He points out various problems and cites numerous films as examples.

T97. "Looking for the Lost Generation," NYRB 22 (Feb 19, 1976): 42-44.

Thomson reflects on the life and culture of Paris in the 20's and 30's and comments on Published in Paris: American and British Writers, Painters, and Publishers in Paris, 1920-1939 by Hugh Ford. Thomson responded to remarks about this review in the April 29, 1976 issue of NYRB (23:44).

T98. "Looking Forward," MQ 31 (April 1945): 157-62.

This short but ambitious article contains a simplistic overview of the state of music, both performance and compositions, around the world. Considering both pre-War and current trends, Thomson glances at Russia, France, Germany, England, Central Europe, the

U.S., Brazil, and Mexico. He also predicts the end of the Modernist era in the 1950's and eagerly awaits "the 20th century's right to be itself."

T99.   "Making Black Music," NYRB 21 (Oct 17, 1974): 14-15.

Thomson comments on the following: Bird Lives! The High Life and Hard Times of Charlie (Yardbird) Parker by Ross Russell; Black Music: Four Lives by A.B. Spellman; Black Nationalism and the Revolution in Music by Frank Kofsky; Reflections on Afro-American Music by Dominique-René de Lerma; and Black Talk by Ben Sidran. Thomson responded to comments about this article in the Jan 23, 1975 (21:42) and May 1, 1975 (22:38) issues of NYRB. Reprinted in VTR.

T100. "More and More from Paris," MM 16 (May-June 1939): 229-37.

Thomson reviews a Paris performance of Sauguet's "Chartreuse de Parme" ("probably...the first satisfactory full-eveing radio-opera in any language."), Milhaud's L'homme et son désir ("full of harmonic delicacies"), and other recently produced works.

T101. "More From Paris," MM 16 (Jan-Feb 1939): 104-09.

Thomson discusses the current scene in Paris concentrating on the influx of German exiles and the changes caused by it.

T102. "Most Melodious Tears," MM 11 (Nov-Dec 1933): 13-17.

Thomson discusses the theatre music of Kurt Weill, which he finds well-scored, sensitive to prosody, with "a heaviness that is not far from real power and a melodic line that...doesn't let itself be easily forgotten," but that too often "smells of Hollywood." Reprinted in The Life and Death of a Small Magazine ("Modern Music," 1924-1946) by Minna Lederman (See B155).

T103. "Music," Mademoiselle (Jan 1943): 113+.

After some critical commentary on how the "Star Spangled Banner" (which at the time was standard on concert programs) should be played, Thomson gives a rundown on the musical scene in New York for the 1942-43 season.

T104. "Music," Mademoiselle (May 1944): 185+.

In this column Thomson outlines the musical offerings, both orchestral and operatic, of the 1943-44 season in New York and welcomes Leonard Bernstein to the American musical scene.

T105. "Music and Economics," VF 25 (Dec 1925): 76+.

In this article Thomson first gives a brief history of the economic factors that led to the rise of the large Romantic orchestra and grandiose orchestral work, and then predicts that because of the cuts in European industrial and governmental

patronage "the future music of Europe is undoubtedly some form
of chamber music. The situation in America, however, is different." The American composer will have a choice between the large
symphony and the chamber work, and the future of music is "con-
tingent less upon the talents of our musicians...than upon the
stock market."

T106. "Music Does Not Flow," NYRB 28 (Dec 17,1981): 47-51.

Based on a James lecture delivered at New York University, this
article deals with the history and the future of music composition.   Thomson declares that music is "not a stream in which a
composer drops his line...Nor is it a mysterious wave-force
traveling from past to future...It is merely everything that has
been done or ever will be done with music's materials."

T107. "The Music Flows With the Stream," SR 26 (Jan 30, 1943): 30.

Thomson's merciless review of Songs of the Rivers of America
(edited by Carl Carmer; music arranged by Dr. Albert Sirmany)
points out that the folksongs have been "disgracefully rewritten
in the German Romantic taste."

T108. "Music for Much Ado About Nothing," Much Ado About Nothing,
The Laurel Shakespeare, Francis Fergusson, General Editor. New
York: Dell Publishing Co, 1960.

Following some general remarks about writing music for the
stage, Thomson recounts his experience and methods in composing
for the 1957 American Shakespeare Festival's production of Much
Ado About Nothing. This essay was also printed in Theatre Arts
43 (June 1959): 14-19; and in VTR. See: W344

T109. "Music in Films: A Symposium of Composers," Films: A Quarterly of
Discussion and Analysis 1/4 (Winter 1940): 5-20.

Such composers as Marc Blitzstein, Paul Bowles, Benjamin Britten, Aaron Copland, Dmitri Shostakovich and Virgil Thomson com-
ment on their compositional techniques for film music and the
special needs of the genre. Thomson states: "I don't think it
ever advisable to be obscure when writing for a large number of
people and I did not think it advisable ever to write down to
anybody."

T110. "Music in the 1950s," Ha 221 (Nov 1960): 59-63.

Thomson remarks on a decade of music: "Chromatic complexity and
rhythmic or metrical complexity are surely the mark   of
practically all the ambitious works of the music composed in the
1950s." He laments "an increasingly mass-media and mass-distri-
bution view of music" and blames this for the
"standardized...quality ...that is depressingly characteristic
of so much music written in this time." This article also
appeared with the title "Looking Back on a Decade" in the Nov
1960 issue of Encounter (15: 47-50), and in MJ (19:12-13+) in

Jan 1961.

T111. "Music, Music Everywhere," Cosmopolitan 118 (May 1945): 56-61.

This lyrical piece is a generalized rhapsody on music in America, which "is indeed music's own country."

T112. "Music Now," ON 25 (March 11, 1961): 9-11+.

After a very brief sketch of music history from World War I to 1960, Thomson discusses current trends in composition. "Everybody practices at least a little bit all the techniques, and...everybody's music begins to sound more and more alike...It may well be that our century's styles and devices are coming to be amalgamated into a classical style, or univeral idiom." This article is the Blashfield Address that Thomson gave at the annual meeting of the American Academy of Arts and Letters and the National Institute of Arts and Letters in 1961 and printed in their Proceedings (Second series, No. 11: 17-24). This piece also appeared in The London Magazine (1:72-79) in March, 1962. Similar material is also found in a paper titled "Music's United Front," delivered by Thomson at the Congress for Cultural Freedom's General Conference in Paris, June 16-22, 1960.

T113. "The Music of Scandinavia -- 1954: A Summing Up," The American-Scandinavian Review 42 (Winter 1954): 337-43.

As critic for the New York Herald-Tribune Thomson attended three music festivals in the summer of 1954: Bergen, Norway; Stockholm, Sweden; and Copenhagen, Denmark. Portions of his columns for the paper are reprinted in this article, which highlights the works of: Jørgen Jersild, Niels Viggo Bentzon, Bernhard Lewkowitch, and others.

T114. "The Music Reviewer and His Assignment," PAA. Second series, No. 4 (1954): 36-46.

Thomson declares that "the sole justifiable purpose of reviewing...is to inform the public." He states his case in favor of musically-educated mewspaper critics and goes on to describe how a critic approaches a new or unfamiliar work. This paper had appeared earlier (under the title "The Critic and His Assignment") in the Toronto Royal Conservatory Monthly Bulletin (Jan 1953) and extracts from it also were printed in Magazine of Arts (Pittsburgh; May 1953).

T115. "Music: Vanishing Intellectual," Show 1 (Oct 1961): 120-22.

Opening this piece with the statement "As contemporary music has become more and more intellectual, it has progressively lost its appeal for intellectuals," Thomson traces the social and cultural aspects of modern musical life from World War I to 1960.

T116. "La Musique Americaine Contemporaire," Vingtieme Siecle (Nov

1945).

Thomson considers American composers since 1930 and divides them into three groups: left, right, and center. In the first, he places the atonal, serial, and percussion composers such as Varèse, Cowell, and Cage. In the second, "conservative from a technical and expressive point of view," are Piston, Sessions, Hanson, Barber, Schuman, and Harris. The centrists, "those who express themselves directly, "especially with respect to theater music, are Copland, Gershwin, and himself.

T117. "The New Grove," Notes 38 (Sept 1981): 49-53.

Thomson gives a favorable and realistic review of The New Grove Dictionary of Music and Musicians (edited by Stanley Sadie). See: B229

T118. "The New Musical Mountebankery," NRe 44 (Oct 21, 1925): 226-27.

In this brief article Thomson rails against the demotion of conducting to an American "popular nonsense sport." Stowkowski and others are criticized for their histrionics at the podium, and the American public is condemned for its overattention to the conductor and lack of interest in what is being conducted.

T119. "Neither a Mother Nor a Goose," HST 14 (May 1965): 102.

Thomson scathingly reviews a recording of readings from the works of Gertrude Stein. (Gertrude Stein: Mother Goose of Montparnasse. Addison Metcalf, reader. Folkways FL 9746.)

T120. "A Note About Music in Modern Buildings," The Bulletin (of the Museum of Modern Art, New York City) 1 (Dec 1, 1933): 3.

A glance at the history of acoustics as regards musical composition and at the changes in 20th-century instrumentation due to current architectural trends.

T121. "La Nouvelle Musique en France, aux Etats-Unis et en Russie," Vingtième Siècle (Oct 18, 1945): 1+.

Asked to give his view on contemporary music, Thomson points to France, the United States, and Russia as the countries where one can currently hear outstanding original work. He singles out several composers: Messiaen, Shostakovich, Prokofiev, and especially America's European immigrants.

T122. "Now in Paris," MM 10 (March-April 1933): 141-48.

Thomson surveys the contemporary scene in Paris, focusing in particular on the work of Sauguet, Nabokov, Rieti, Massimo, Cliquet-Pleyel, and he concludes with reflections on the general direction of music in the 20th-century.

T123. "The Official Stravinsky," MM 13 (May-June 1936): 57.

Thomson reviews Stravinsky's Chroniques de ma Vie, (Vol. II. Paris: Denoël et Steel, 1935) and says that the book of "the stiff little man" is interesting "because a good workman writing about his trade is always interesting."

T124. "Of Portraits and Operas," Antaeus, Vols. 21 & 22 (Spring/ Summer 1976): 208-10.

Thomson describes his procedures and goals in composing musical portraits and briefly explains the use of portraiture for opera characterizations.

T125. "Olin Downes: A Free Critical Spirit," NYHT Book Review 33 (Jan 27, 1959): 4.

Thomson reviews Olin Downes on Music (edited by Irene Downes) and calls Downes "the last of the music reviewers to enjoy music" who "wrote passionately, from the heart and with no mean gift of understanding."

T126. "On Being Discovered," NYRB 4 (June 3,1965): 3-4.

This piece is Thomson's hot-and-cold review of Wilfred Mellers' Music in a New Found Land (Knopf, 1965; See B160). Reprinted in VTR.

T127. "On, Donald Sutherland," Denver Quarterly 12 (Fall, 1978): 5-6.

Thomson expounds on the talents and major works of comparative literature specialist and philosopher Donald Sutherland.

T128. "On Good Terms With All the Muses," NYHT Book Review 40 (Sept 8, 1963): 4.

Thomson reviews James Gibbons Huneker by Arnold T. Schwab: "Huneker...for all his love both of music and of 'advance,' never came to grips with the really advanced music of his time."

T129. "On Wooing the Muses," Vg 86 (Sept 15, 1925): 190+.

Thomson reflects on the musical education of children: "We torture our young people with all manner of instruction in music, the usual result being a complete distaste for it and an inability to render in tune or time the simplest popular piece." Thomson gives practical advice ("The only proper music for very young children is...vocal music of a simple, rhythmic charac- ter") and suggests a "family circle of duets, trios, and other forms of concerted music" over the usual student recital.

T130. "On Writing Operas and Staging Them," Parnassus: Poetry in Review 10/2 (Fall/Winter 1982): 4-19.

In this lengthy article Thomson defines and discusses opera, "the most complex operation in music and...in stage-production." He reviews the problems of seeking financial support, finding a

good librettist and libretto, and working out an interpretation
with "a producing director whom you can trust to understand your
dramatic concept." Emphasizing that "singing is what opera is
about," Thomson advises that "singers...must be not allowed to
stagger, lurch, weave about, or make faces. Musical expression
comes from singing the words and the music, not from mugging."

T131. "Opera: It Is Everywhere In America," NYT 112 (Nov 23, 1962):
Sect. 6, Part 2, p. 16+.

Thomson discusses the contemporary state and the future of
American opera in this article. He cites as problems the financial demands of opera production, American composers' lack of
education in opera composition, "ineptitude at handling both the
English language and the human voice," and the dearth of viable,
interesting texts. "The strength of our opera lies in its wide-
spread distribution...but American operas must be created before
they can be distributed."

T132. "Opera: 'The Crucible' and 'The Dove'," Show 2 (Jan 1962): 4-5.

Thomson reviews two operas which were produced in the New York
City Opera's Fall, 1961 season: The Wings of the Dove by Douglas
Moore (libretto by Ethan Ayer) and The Crucible by Robert Ward
(libretto by Bernard Stambler).

T133. "Paris," Town and Country 100 (Feb 1946): 130-31.

Thomson reports on the current cultural life of the French
capital. This article was printed earlier in the October 13,
1945 International Tribune.

T134. "Paris, April 1940," MM 17 (May-June 1940): 203-09.

Thomson reports in letter form on the musical and cultural state
of France. He discusses the radio industry, the popularity of
American music ("their faces light up when it comes on"), opera,
and the "imminence of general European cultural collapse that
has been hanging over us ever since the last war ended."
Reprinted in VTR.

T135. "Paris News," MM 11 (Nov-Dec 1933): 42-46.

Thomson reports on the Spring, 1933 season in Paris, which
included music by Popov, Rieti, Milhaud, Françaix, Nabokov,
Massimo, Satie, Weill, and Markevitch, focusing in particular on
ballets.

T136. "The Philosophy of Style," Showcase 41 (1961-62): 10-11.

Concerning the possible and desirable fusion of Eastern and
Western musical styles, this essay is in essence the lecture
Thomson gave in Tokyo at the 1961 East-West Music Encounter.
This article was also published in Spanish in Buenos Aires
Musicale (Vol. 17, No. 274, p. 1+) in 1962.

T137. "Preface" and notes for Bee-Time Vine and Other Pieces (1913-19) by Gertrude Stein (New Haven, CT: Yale University Press, 1953), pp. v-vii.

According to Thomson "the greatness of the great poets" is judged on "their ability to compose unforgettable lines." In this Miss Stein excelled and Thomson revels in her work.

T138. "Preface" to Folk Songs in Settings by Master Composers, compiled by Herbert Haufrecht (New York: Funk & Wagnalls, 1970), pp. v-vi. Rpt. New York: Da Capo Press, 1977.

Thomson praises the collection not only for its "melodious and poetic gems" but also for its view "of musical masters working simply." See: W141

T139. "Preface" to 40,000 Years of Music by Jacques Chailley (New York: Farrar, Straus, & Giroux, 1964).

Thomson praises the "learning and wisdom...wit and liveliness...and courageousness" of this French musicologist and his book.

T140. "Preface" to Selected Songs by Paul Bowles (Santa Fe, NM: Sounding Press, 1984): 2-3.

In this brief essay, Thomson observes that Paul Bowles's songs "are enchanting for their sweetness of mood, their lightness of texture, for in general their way of being wholly alive and right."

T141. "Preface" to The Three Worlds of Leonid by Leonid Berman. (New York: Basic Book, 1978), pp. ix-xii.

Thomson gives a brief sketch of his long-time friend, painter/writer Leonid Berman.

T142. "Prefacio" (translated into Spanish by Julio Cortázar) to Musica En Buenos Aires by Jorge D'Urbano. (Buenos Aires: Editorial Sudamericana, 1966), pp. 7-8.

Thomson's brief preface to this volume of collected writing by Argentinian music critics underscores the importance of assessing new music rather than contemporary performances of the classics. Thomson cites D'Urbano for his strong, and clearly expressed opinions, and notes that "any opinion about music is legitimate when reached through a musical experience and expressd in clear language." ("Porque toda la opinión sobre la música es legítima cuando se llega a ella a través de una experiencia musical y se es capaz de expresarla con un lenguaje claro.")

T143. "Presentation to Aaron Copland of the Gold Medal for Music," PAA. Second series, No. 7 (1957): 109-10.

Thomson praises Copland's musical language as "straightforward, original, and strong" and his craftmanship for its "power, honesty, and general excellence."

T144. "Presentation to Leopold Stowkowski of the Award for Distinguished Service to the Arts," PAA. Second series, No. 20 (1970): 14.

Thomson presents Stowkowski with the award: "You have trained the public...to hear with refinement and to accept as part of its life contemporary music of all schools and from all nations."

T145. "Presentation to Martha Graham of the Award for Distinguished Service to the Arts," PAA. Second series, No. 21 (1971): 19.

Thomson praises Graham as dancer, choreographer, teacher and producer for work "so fully a reflection of contemporary music and art."

T146. "The Profession of Orchestra Conducting," VF 24 (Aug 1925): 37+.

Thomson laments the Americanization of contemporary European conductors and the American public's content with the standard musical warhorses. Perfection, not variety, dominates program selection. Audiences of "the musically half-educated whose reaction...is wholly emotional and ecstatic" depress Thomson, as does the American habit of "centering the interest in the conductor's personality."

T147. "Putting Space Into Opera Recordings," SR 30 (Aug 30, 1947): 5.

Thomson in this brief article shares his experience in recording his opera Four Saints in Three Acts. He sums up: "The best results...seem to be obtained by producing in the recording hall a performance that resembles as closely as possible, as to sound, a real performance." See: W1 and D23

T148. "Recording Some New Notes on the Scale," NYT Book Review (Dec 10, 1961): 6+.

Thomson reviews two books: The History of Modern Music by Paul Collaer and Introduction to Contemporary Music by Joseph Machlis.

T149. "Remembering Gertrude," Columbia Library Columns 31 (Feb 1982): 2-17.

This transcript of a talk Thomson gave to the Columbia University Friends of the Library in October, 1981 contains an at-home look at Gertrude Stein and personal reminiscences of Thomson on their friendship. Several photos are included. "Gertrude was a great meditator, and by meditating she understood, or thought she understood, what people are like. Her subject was always people...and her main interest in them was to find out exactly how their minds worked and how their destinies and compulsions worked."

T150. "Representational Art Today," (extracts from a panel discussion at the August 27, 1966 meeting at the MacDowell Colony) The MacDowell Colony Newsletter, Dec 1966.

Thomson recalls that in 1961 "It took a good deal of courage in Paris...to sell or announce or even praise representational art because Paris had become with regard to New York a provincial city in art matters, and the New York line was for abstraction."

T151. [Review of] Samuel Barber's Second Essay for Orchestra, Notes 2 (June 1945): 175-6.

In this brief review Thomson gives high marks to Barber for this "sincere, skillful, and mature work." He notes that "the tone is noble, the continuity ingenious, the instrumentation elegant."

T152. [Review of] a recording of Erik Satie's "Socrate," MQ 39 (Jan 1953): 147-49.

Thomson, an ardent admirer of "Socrate" ("a unique work"), has penned a scathing review of Esoteric recording ES-510, denouncing the conductor, singers, and instrumentalists.

T153. "The Rising Pitch," NYHT Fresh Air Fund Football Program (c.1940-45), p. 25.

Thomson discusses the implications of the rising pitch in music (which creates "a desperate difficulty for singers") of middle A from 410 cycles per second in Bach's time to the current 440.

T154. "The Rocky Road of American Opera," HSR 8 (Feb 1962): 49-52.

Thomson discusses the problems of getting 20th-century operas produced and of finding "a poet or playwright whose dramatic ideas are worth putting to music."

T155. "Rzut oka Na Musyke Amerykanska," Ameryka, No. 56, Cena 10ZL, 1963: pp. 7-9.

A very brief survey on "The American World of Music," published for distribution in Poland by Press and Publication Service, U.S. Information Agency, Washington, D.C.

T156. "The Satirical Tendency in Modern Music," VF 24 (May, 1925): 41+.

Pointing out that "irony, burlesque, and mordant parody...are the very essence of modern music," Thomson applaudes the end of the dusky gloom of Romanticism. He is pleased that "laughter has come back to music" because humor has "broken down the fake dignity of style" and "laughter will remove the non-essential...so that only that will remain which, intrinsically, is the stuff of a vital emotional experience."

T157. "Scenes from Show Biz," <u>NYRB</u> 18 (May 4, 1972): 38-40.

Thomson reviews John Houseman's <u>Run-Through: A Memoir</u>. See B145.

T158. "The Seine" (poem) by the Duchess of Rohan. Translated from the French by Thomson. In <u>Parnassus: Poetry in Review</u> 5 (Spring/Summer 1977; See T78). Also music for voice and pf. by Thomson (1928; See W113)

T159. "Socialism at the Metropolitan," <u>MM</u> 12 (March-April 1935): 123-27.

A review of a performance of Shastakovich's opera <u>Lady Macbeth of Mtzensk</u> at the Met in New York. "It is an early work, harsh and green and a little indigestible. But there is a kind of passionate objectivity in it and a kind of idealistic purity that cannot be faked or learned." Reprinted in <u>The Life and Death of a Small Magazine</u> ("Modern Music," 1924-1946) by Minna Lederman (See B155).

T160. "Sound Off At the Center," <u>Observer Weekend Review</u> (London) (Sept 30, 1962).

Thomson reports on the opening festivities of New York's Philharmonic Hall and the unfortunate acoustical difficulties and limitations of the new structure.

T161. "Sports and Diversions" from Erik Satie's <u>Sports and Divertissements</u> (1914). Translated from the French by Thomson. Paris/New York: Editions Salabert, 1975.

T162. "Stravinsky -- Gesualdo," <u>NYT</u> 110 (Oct 2, 1960): Sect. 2, p. 11.

Thomson gives a report on Venice, Italy's 23rd Festival of Contemporary Music.

T163. "Stravinsky's Operas," <u>Musical Newsletter</u> 4 (Fall, 1974): 3-7+.

Thomson surveys Stravinsky's operatic output, work by work, with special emphasis on The <u>Rake's Progress</u> and Oedipus Rex. Reprinted in <u>VTR</u>.

T164. "A Survey of the State of Music in Europe Today," <u>MA</u> 81 (Jan 1961): 11+.

Commenting on West Germany's hegemony in opera, radio, and music publishing, the influence of radio, post-war music business trends, and the advent and development of 12-tone and electronic music, Thomson makes a facile survey of the European music scene in 1961. Thomson responds to Everett Helm's comments on this article in the June, 1961 <u>MA</u> (81:4). On March 7 and 8, 1961, a report on Thomson's original article appeared in <u>Correo de la Tarde</u> under the title "Panorama de la Música Europea, I y II."

T165. "Swing Again," <u>MM</u> 15 (March-April 1938):160-66.

Thomson takes the opportunity of an invitation to review Benny Goodman's Carnegie Hall concert ("a quite uninteresting concert on the whole") to expand on an earlier article on swing (See T166). He differentiates between "beat music," which is accentual, and "quantitative music," which has no accent. Reprinted in <u>Parnassus</u>: <u>Poetry</u> <u>in</u> <u>Review</u> 5 (Spring/Summer 1977): 439-56; and in <u>VTR</u>.

T166. "Swing-Music," <u>MM</u> 13 (May-June 1936): 12-17.

Thomson offers a definition of swing music ("a form of two-step") and reflects on its variations and cultural backgrounds. Reprinted in <u>Parnassus:</u> <u>Poetry</u> <u>in</u> <u>Review</u> 5 (Spring/Summer 197): 439-456; and in <u>VTR</u>.

T167. "The Tenth Muse," <u>NYT</u> <u>Book</u> <u>Review</u> 120 (Oct 4, 1970): Sect. 7, p. 6+.

Thomson reviews <u>A</u> <u>Historical</u> <u>Study</u> <u>of</u> <u>the</u> <u>Opera</u> <u>Libretto</u> by Patrick J. Smith. Reprinted in <u>VTR</u> with the title "Opera Librettos."

T168. "Thanks to the Pop Boys," <u>ASCAP</u> <u>In</u> <u>Action</u> (Fall, 1984): 13+.

In a brief reflective piece on his 45 years as an ASCAP member, Thomson opines that "the popular writers have long been our chief shield and buckler, ever rigorously protective in matters of fair play and copyright."

T169. "Then and Now," (transcript of a round table discussion at a symposium on the expatriate tradition in Paris, held at the American Center for Students and Artists (Paris), Spring, 1964) <u>Paris</u> <u>Revue</u> 9 (Winter 1965): 158-70.

Regarding the "Lost Generation" Thomson comments: "They were never lost...nobody was lost -- in any spiritual or ethical sense, any more than in any other generation."

T170. "Toward Improving the Musical Race," <u>MA</u> 81 (July 1961): 5.

Inspired by the 1961 Tokyo East-West Music Encounter, Thomson writes: "What we are looking for [in music] is a strong cross-breed, a Eurasian, Eurafrican, or Afro-Asian strain that can stand all climates...better built for survival in tomorrow's tough one-world."

T171. "The Tradition of Sensibility," <u>NYRB</u> 5 (Dec 9, 1965): 4-6.

Thomson reviews: <u>Debussy:</u> <u>His</u> <u>Life</u> <u>and</u> <u>Mind</u> by Edward Lockspei-ser; <u>Georges</u> <u>Bizet:</u> <u>His</u> <u>Life</u> <u>and</u> <u>Work</u> by Winton Dean; <u>Alban</u> <u>Berg</u> by Willi Reich; and, <u>The</u> <u>Path</u> <u>to</u> <u>the</u> <u>New</u> <u>Music</u> by Anton Webern (edited by Willi Reich and translated by Leo Black). Reprinted in <u>VTR</u>.

T172. "Transplanted Traditions," <u>MA</u> 75 (Feb 15, 1955): 29+.

Thomson reviews the influence of European music teachers on American composers from the 19th-century to the 1950's and concludes that "the American school is a rising school, and the European is very probably a declining one."

T173. "Twain Meet," NYT 110 (May 21, 1961): Sect. 2, p. 9.

Thomson reports on the Tokyo East-West Music Encounter and Festival of Eastern and Western Music. A similar article appeared in Buenos Aires Musical (Vol. 17, No. 276, p. 5) in 1962.

T174. "Two Festivals," G. Schirmer Newsletter 2 (Winter 1964-65): 3.

Thomson reports on the October 1964 "Festival de Musica de America y España" held in Madrid and on the Coolidge Festival of late October 1964 in Washington, D.C. Thomson's The Feast of Love was performed at the latter, and Autumn Suite for harp at the former. See: W48 & W49

T175. "Untold Tales," NYRB 18 (May 18, 1972): 35-6.

Thomson reviews two books by author-composer-friend Paul Bowles: Without Stopping: An Autobiography and The Thicket of Spring: Poems 1926-69.

T176. "Varèse, Xenakis,Carter," NYRB 19 (Aug 31, 1972): 19-21.

Thomson reviews Edgard Varèse by Fernand Ouellette, Varèse: A Looking Glass Diary, Vol. I by Louise Varèse; Formalized Music: Thought and Mathematics in Composition by Iannis Xenakis; and Flawed Words and Stubborn Sounds: A Conversation with Elliott Carter by Allen Edwards. Reprinted in VTR.

T177. "A Very Difficult Author," NYRB 16 (April 8, 1971): 3-8.

Thomson considers: Gertrude Stein in Pieces by Richard Bridgman; Four Americans in Paris: The Collection of Gertrude Stein and Her Family (a catalogue with seven essays and two word-portraits); Gertrude Stein on Picasso, edited by Edward Burns; Gertrude Stein and the Present by Allegra Stewart; "Gertrude Stein Talking: A Trans-Atlantic Interview" by Robert Haas (Uclan Review, Summer 1962, Spring 1963, and Winter, 1964); The Third Rose: Gertrude Stein and Her World by John M. Brinnin; Gertrude Stein: Her Life and Work by Elizabeth Sprigge; and, Gertrude Stein: A Bibliography of Her Work by Donald Sutherland. Thomson responded to comments on this article in the June 3, 1971 (16:41), July 1, 1971 (16:40),and Oct 7, 1971 (17:41) issues of NYRB.

T178. "Virgil Thomson: American Music and Music Critic: Remarks by Virgil Thomson at the Otterbein Virgil Thomson Festival," edited and prefaced by Barbara A. Zuck, The Otterbein Miscellany 12 (Dec 1976): 1-23.

As a guest at Otterbein College for a festival held in November,

1975 in his honor, Thomson delivered two papers commenting on topics such as the personal element in music criticism, newspaper music criticism from 1910 to the present, reviewing modern music, regionalism in American music, George Gershwin, the absorption of foreign elements in new music, women composers, jazz, 12-tone music, and his own operas.

T179. "Virgil Thomson as Virgil Thomson," A Salute to Virgil Thomson: Symposium of the Society for the Arts, Religion and Contemporary Culture, New York City, May 1977, pp. 4-7.

Thomson expresses his views on the relationship between religion and music: "I suppose that music --when it takes place in churches...is, at best the handmaiden of religion. But when music that has been composed for such usage gets transformed into a concert piece...religion takes on the aspect of being handmaiden to music, largely because there is a different public...I've always thought there was virtually no difference that you can put your finger on between religious and nonreligious musical style...The classical composers who have written both sacred and secular music have written both in manners that can hardly be distinguished."

T180. "Virgil Thomson on the House of Ricordi," MJ 16 (March 1958): 16+.

In the form of a letter to the editor, Thomson comments on the history and success of the famous Italian music publishing company, The House of Ricordi, which in 1958 celebrated its 150th year in business.

T181. "Wanda Landowska," NYRB 3 (Jan 28, 1965): 6-7.

Thomson reviews a "grabbag of casual observations and incomplete analyses" collected and edited by Denise Restout in Landowska On Music. Reprinted in VTR.

T182. "What is Quality in Music?" NYRB 12 (June 19, 1969): 32-34.

Thomson reiterates one of his favorite themes that "in art the doers are the knowers." A discussion of taste and quality follows. This essay appeared also in Quality: Its Image in the Arts, edited by Louis Kronenberger (New York: Atheneum, 1969). Thomson responded to letters concerning this piece in the Sept 11, 1969 NYRB (13:44-45). Excerpts of this article appeared in American Musical Digest (1:30) in Oct, 1969 under the title "Authenticity."

T183. "When the 'Cradle' Was Young," NYHT (April 19, 1964).

In memory of Marc Blitzstein who died in January 1964, a concert version of his The Crade Will Rock was performed at Philharmonic Hall in New York, and the New York Herald Tribune reprinted this November 25th, 1947 review of the opera. The work is called " one of the most charming creations of the American musical theater. It has sweetness, a cutting wit, inexhaustible fancy, faith."

T184. "Where Is Music Going?" Vg 160/6 (1972): 58-60.

> "Apparently nowhere" is Thomson's answer. Electronic music is
> examined and dismissed as "not music at all but just sound
> effects."

T185. "Why Bach Festivals?" NYHT Fresh Air Fund Football Program (13th
Annual), Sept 20, 1951.

> A one-page piece on Bach that makes many points as it enter-
> tains: "Bach...is a model T Ford that anybody can drive...his
> music is as useful as that -- a practical instrument serving any
> and all needs. And here its very obscurity is its
> strength...The mind is occupied, focused, absorbed, but the
> emotions are free."

T186. "Wickedly Wonderful Widow," NYRB 21 (March 7, 1974): 12-15.

> Thomson comments on Staying on Alone: Letters of Alice B. Tok-
> las, edited by Edward Burns.

T187. "William Flanagan," Tribute read by Virgil Thomson at the
Flanagan Memorial Concert, Whitney Museum, New York, April 14,
1970.

> Thomson's eulogy for the   "strong,   self-destructive...and
> self-taught" composer. Reprinted in VTR.

Books

T188. American Music Since 1910. Introduced by Nicolas Nabokov. New
York: Holt, Rinehart, and Winston, 1971. London: Weidenfeld and
Nicolson, 1971. Paperback ed.: New York: Holt, Rinehart, and
Winston, 1972. Contains "The Operas of Virgil Thomson," by
Victor Fell Yellin. See: B61

> Thomson discusses America's musical maturity and musical traits,
> then focuses on individual composers. In supplementary chap-
> ters, Victor Fell Yellin writes on Thomson's operas and Gilbert
> Chase treats 20th-century Latin American music. Finally, there
> are short biographies of 101 American composers.

> Reprints: See T24 & T86 (which also appears in VTR).
> "Ruggles" (Chapter 4), "Aaron Copland" (Chapter 6), and
> "Cage and the Collage of Noises" (Chapter 8) all in VTR.

> Reviews: ARG 38:444 (May 1972); Choice 8:845 (Spring 1971); LJ
> 96:195 (Jan 15, 1971);Clavier 10:8 (No. 4, 1971);Composer (Lon-
> don) 44: 34-5 (Summer 1972); HF 21:MA 31 (July 1971); Music &
> Musicians 20:50-51 (April 1972); Music Educators' Journal 58:
> 61-2 (May 1972); Musical Events 26:12-13 (Aug 1971); Music in
> Education 37:260 (No. 363, 1973); MJ 30:48-9 (Sept 1972); MT

112:861-2 (Sept 1971); Muzyka 19:79-85 (no. 1 1974); Notes 28:224 (Dec 1971); SR 54:82 (Sept 25, 1971); Ruch Muzyczny 18:9 (No. 6 1974); Symphony News 23:20-21 (No. 1, 1972); Times Literary Supplement (Dec 3, 1971): 1532; NYT (March 12, 1971): 35; Yearbook for Inter-American Musical Research 7:186 (1971).

T189. The Art of Judging Music. New York: Alfred A. Knopf, 1948. (Rpt. Westport CT: Greenwood Press, 1969.)

This second collection of essays and reviews which first appeared in the NYHT covers the years 1944 to 1947. The title of the volume comes from a lecture given in 1947 at Harvard where Thomson observed that "the art of formulating musical judgments in chiefly the art of describing music."

Reprints: "Americanisms" in Revue Musicale 242 (1958): 93-95. "Americanisms" (and excerpts from several other articles also) in Composers on Music edited by Sam Morgenstern. New York: Pantheon Books, 1956. "The Art of Judging Music" in AM 180 (Dec 1947): 73-75.; Music and Criticism: A Symposium, edited by Richard F. French. Cambridge: Harvard University Press, 1948, 101-3; The Essay: A Critical Anthology, edited by John L. Stewart. Englewood Cliffs, NJ: Prentice-Hall, 1952, 70-77; Music Educators Journal 51/2 (1964): 37-40; and Amerikaans Cultureel Perspectief, New York: Intercultural Publications, Inc., 1954, pp. 94-103. "Atonality in France" (excerpts) in Score 6 (May 1952): 11-14. "Expressive Content," "Ethical Content," and "Intellectual Content," in Score under the title "Three More Essays" No. 4 (Jan 1951): 19-25. "Modernism Today" (excerpts) in Score 6 (May 1952): 11-14; also in MWW, 504-06. "Schönberg's Music" (excerpts) in Score 6 (May 1952): 11-14; and in Contact (Autumn 1974): 10-12. "Singing Today" (condensed form) in The Musical Digest 1 (Aug 1947): 20-21. "Surrealism and Music" (edited) in Contrepoints 6 (1949): 74-78. "A War's End" in The Life and Death of a Small Magazine ("Modern Music," 1924-1946) by Minna Lederman. (See B155) 28 articles reprinted also in VTR.

Reviews: AM 181:119 (April 1948); Booklist 44:230 (March 1, 1948); Kirkus 16:13 (Jan 1, 1948); LJ 73:476 (March 15, 1948);Notes 5:235 (March 1948); NYHT Weekly Book Review (April 11, 1941): 6; NYT (March 21, 1948): 22; NYer 23:100 (Feb 21, 1948); SFCh (Feb 15, 1948): 12; Springfield Republican (Feb 22, 1948): 15A.

T190. The Musical Scene. New York: Alfred A. Knopf, 1945. Rpt. Westport, CT: Greenwood Press, 1968. See: A13

This is a selection of essays and reviews which, with one exception ("Chaplin Scores" from MM), were first published from 1940 to 1944 in the New York Herald Tribune. The opening essay's theme is "Taste in Music" in which Thomson distinguishes "taste for" and "taste in" music, and he goes on to opine that "if there is any door-opener to taste it is knowledge." Although many of these writings deal with European subjects, some concern creative American musicians, and there is a section on American orchestras. A good picture of New York City musical activity emerges from these pages, and a section headed "Processed Music" contains articles discussing the artistic impact of record and broadcast media.

Reprints: "Band Music" which discusses band music in general and criticizes the Goldman programs, was reprinted as "What Shall Band Music Be?" in The Etude 60: 453+ (July 1942). Dr. R.F. Goldman replied in the Aug 1942 issue.
"The Berlioz Case" (NYHT, Oct 11, 1942) in Fantastic Symphony by Edward T. Cone. Norton Critical Score. New York: W.W. Norton, 1971.
"Britain Wins" and "More Beecham" in Le Grand Baton (journal of the Sir Thomas Beecham Society) 18 (Sept & Dec 1981).
"French Music Here" as "La place de Satie dans la musique du XXe siècle" in La Revue Musicale 214:13-15   (June, 1952). Also in MWW: 475-76.
"Masterpieces" (and excerpts from several other articles also) in Composers on Music edited by Sam Morgenstern. New York: Pantheon Books, 1956.
"Music's Renewal" in La Revue Musicale 212:39-41 (April 1952), with the title "Sur les Perspectives du Ballet et du l'Opéra en Amérique."
"Processed Music" in Music Publishers Journal 3 (Sept-Oct 1945): 33+.
"Surrealism and Music" in The Life and Death of a Small Magazine ("Modern Music," 1924-1946) by Minna Lederman. (See B155)
"Taste in Music" in Town & Country 100 (Feb 1945): 93+ with the title "About Taste in Music There Should Be Dispute." Also in The McGraw-Hill Reader, edited by Gilbert H. Miller. New York: McGraw-Hill Book Co., 1982: 448-452+.
"Taste in Music," "Tempos," and "The French Style" in Score 2 (Jan 1950): 3-9, with the title "Three Essays."
30 articles reprinted also in VTR.

Reviews: Booklist 41:250 (May 1, 1945); Christian Scientist Monitor (May 19, 1945): 15; Commonweal 42:266 (June 29, 1945); Kirkus 13:52 (Feb 1, 1945); LJ 70: 354 (April 15, 1945); Na 160:527 (May 5, 1945); NRe 113:26 (July 2, 1945); NYT (April 15, 1945): 7; SR 28:35 (May 26, 1945); Weekly Book Review (April 15, 1945): 4; MM 22:282-83 (May-June 1945). See: B137

T191. Music Reviewed, 1940-1954. New York: Vintage Books, 1967.

Unlike the three earlier collections of Thomson's New York Herald Tribune writings, which are organized according to subject area (opera, composers, conductors, over-seas, think-pieces, etc.) this volume is chronologically arranged. Most of the reviews and article up to 1950 appear in the three previous books, but those from 1951-54 are reprinted here for the first time.

Reprints: "Modernism Today" (from NYHT, Feb 2, 1947) in MWW, pp. 504-06.
"Scientists Get Curious" in Boston Symphony Concert Bulletin 12 (Jan 8, 1954): 563-67.
"Kurt Weill" in The New Music Lover's Handbook.   Edited by Elie Siegmeister. New York: Harvey House, 1973: 417-18.
24 articles also reprinted in VTR.

Reviews: ARG 34:65-66 (Sept 1967);   HF 19:MA 29-30 (April 1969).

T192. Music, Right and Left.   New York:Holt and Company, 1951. Rpt. Westport, CT: Greenwood Press, 1969.

Another selection of Thomson's writings for the New York Herald Tribune representing the period from 1947 to 1950.

Reprints: "Atonality Today" in Etude 69:18-19+ (Nov 1951).
"On Being American" in MWW: 502-04.
"The Problem of Sincerity," on the subject of emotional honesty in performance in Etude 69:11+ (March 1951).
"Too Many Languages" in Etude 69:17 (June, 1951).
22 articles reprinted also in VTR.

Reviews: Booklist 47:320 (March 1, 1951) and 47:249 (March 15, 1951); Bookmark 10:156 (April 1951); Kirkus 18:748 (Dec 15, 1950); LJ 76:518 (March 15, 1951); MA 71:31 (June 1951); MC 143:29 (April 1, 1951); Music News 43:21 (June 1951); Notes 83:346 (March 1951); Na 173:242-43 (Sept 22, 1951); NYHT Book Review (March 11, 1951): 6; NYT (March 25, 1951): 6; NYer 27:131 (March 17, 1951); Op 16:24 (March 1951); SFCh (June 14, 1951): 19; SR 34:20 (May 26, 1951); Springfield Republican (April 1, 1951): 16A; U.S. Quarterly Book Review 7:138 (June 1951).

T193. The State of Music. New York: Morrow, 1939. Second edition. New York: Vintage Books, 1962. Rpt. Westport, CT: Greenwood Press, 1974.

Thomson here discusses the status of the musician, the economics of music, and musical politics, advocating professional solidarity.   The revised edition adds bracket sentences passim to indicate what has changed or remained.

Reprints: "A 1961 Preface" and Chapters 1-4,6,7,10, and "A 1961 Postlude" in VTR.
Chapter 4, "Life Among the Natives, or Musical Habits and Customs" in Contemporary Composers on Contemporary Music. Edited by Elliott Schwartz and Barney Childs.   New York: Holt, Rinehard and Winston, 1967. Rpt. New York: Da Capo Press, 1978, pp. 170-181.
Chapter 6, "How Composers Eat" in The American Composer Speaks: A Historical Anthology, 1770-1965. Baton Rouge, LA: State University Press, 1966, pp. 178-183.
Chapter 7, "Why Composers Write How, or The Economic Determinism of Musical Style" in slightly different form as "Les Comptes

d'Orphée" in Contrepoints 5:17-45 (1946); this same version
reappeared in La Revue Musicale 305-6:87-106 (1977).

Reviews: Books (Oct 19, 1939): 3; MM 17:63-65 (Oct-Nov 1939)
[reprinted in Copland on Music by Aaron Copland. New York: W.W.
Norton, 1963. Pp. 237-41.]; NYT (Dec 10, 1939): 2; NYer 15:55
(Dec 30, 1939); NRe 102:416 (March 25, 1940); SR 21:19 (March
16, 1940); Theatre Arts 24:219 (March 1940).

T194. Virgil Thomson. New York: Alfred A. Knopf, 1966; London:Weidenfeld
& Nicolson, 1967; Paperback eds. New York:Da Capo Press, 1977;
and New York: Dutton/Obelisk, 1985.

In his autobiography Thomson records the details of his busy
life, offers numerous character sketches of his friends, and
discusses his works and their performances. Two portraits of
Thomson by Maurice Grosser appear on the cover of the 1985
paperback edition.

Reprints: Chapter 1, "Missouri Landscape with Figures," Chapter 8,
"Antheil, Joyce, and Pound," and Chapter 9, "Langlois, Butts,
and Stein" all in VTR.
Chapter 3, "A Musician's Adolescence," in Perspectives: An An-
thology edited by Marianne H. Russo and Edward G. Groff.
Dubuque, IA: Kendall Hunt Publishing Co., 1976. Pp. 52-56.
Chapter 15, "A Portrait of Gertrude Stein," appeared previous to
book publication in NYRB 6: 13+ (July 7, 1966). Also in VTR and
in: Linda Simon. Gertrude Stein: A Composite Portrait. New York:
Avon, 1974. Pp. 123-37.
Chapter 27, "The Paper," [Thomson's account of his career as
music critic for the NYHT] appeared in HSR 17:53-58 (Nov 1966).
Also in VTR.
Chapter 35, "A Distaste for Music," in Vg 148:292-95+
(Sept 1, 1966).

Reviews: ARG 33: 460-03 (Feb 1967); Best Sell 26:297 (Nov 15,
1966); Book Week (Oct 9, 1966): 3; Christian Science Monitor
(Oct 27, 1966): 11; Commentary 43:96+ (May, 1967); Ha 233:120
(Dec 1966); HF 16:MA21+ (Nov 1966); LJ 91:4650 (Oct 9, 1966);
Music & Letters 48: 268-70 (No. 3, 1967);Music & Musicians 15:17
(Aug 1967);MJ 25:89 (Jan 1967); Musical Opinion 91:214 (Jan
1968);MR 29:53-56 (No. 1, 1968);MT 108:710-11 (Aug 1967); Music
Teacher & Piano Student 46:25 (May 1967); Na 203:421-22 (Oct 10,
1966); NRe 155:40-42 (Nov 24, 1966); Newsweek 68:98 (Nov 7,
1966); NYT (Oct 18, 1966): 43; NYT Book Review (Oct 9, 1966): 5;
NYer 42:248 (Nov 19, 1966);ON 31:32 (Dec 10 1966);PP 60:49+ (No.
2,1968);Tempo 80:36-7 (Spring 1967); Commentary 43:96 (May
1967); The Times Literary Supplement (March 23, 1967): 232;
Virginia Quarterly Review: 43:lxxxix (Spring 1967); Yale Review
56:580 (June 1967).

T195. A Virgil Thomson Reader. Introduction by John Rockwell.
Boston: Houghton Mifflin Co., 1981. Paperback: New York:
Dutton/Obelisk, 1984.

This anthology of Thomson's writings includes excerpts from his autobiography, selected articles from Modern Music, a substantial portion of The State of Music, numerous articles from the New York Herald Tribune, various writings since 1954, and two conversations -- one with John Rockwell and the other with Diana Trilling. The Reader received the National Book Critics Circle Award for criticism.

Reprints: See T86.
"A Conversation with Virgil Thomson" appeared previous to book publication in Partisan Review 4: 544-557 (1980).

Reviews: Cal 7:99 (Jan 1982); Central Opera Service Bulletin 24:32 (No. 1; 1982); Choice 19:933 (March 1982); HF 32:MA14-15 (March 1982); LJ 106:2395 (Dec 15, 1981): National Review 34:966 (Aug 6, 1982); NRe 186:31+ (Jan 20, 1982); NYRB 29:8-9 (Feb 4, 1982); NYT Book Review 86:9 (Dec 6, 1981) and 89:1 (April 29, 1984); NYer 57:131 (Feb 8, 1982);Nineteenth-Century Music 8:64+ (Summer 1984); Village Voice 28:35+ (Jan 4, 1983).

Bibliography about Thomson

In order to organize the vast amount of material about Virgil Thomson and his work, this section has been arranged as follows: articles from journals and magazines, then books and dissertations, followed by entries in dictionaries, encyclopedias, and various indices. Two sections at the end cite sources in other books and articles which may be of interest but which did not warrant full annotation. "See" references indicate related entries in other sections of this book -- W to "Works and Performances," D to "Discography," B to "Bibliography," and A to the archive listings in "Appendix I." Abbreviations are explained in the Preface.

Periodical and Newspaper Articles

B1.   Alcaraz, José Antonio. "Virgil Thomson: 'Leyenda Viviente,'"
       Heterofonia 9/49 (1976): 24-29.

       Interweaving reflective and explanatory interludes, Sr. Alcaraz
       here interviews Thomson on such subjects as his collaboration
       with Stein, idiomatic text-music relationships, and his asso-
       ciations with Satie, Boulez, and especially John Cage. At the
       end of the piece, Cage gives his side of the story.

B2.   Anonymous. "Homage: Virgil Thomson," NYer 47 (Dec 25, 1971): 39.

       A charmingly light portrait of Thomson amidst the numerous
       celebrations of his 75th birthday.   "He talks at a rate faster
       than most people can think...[and] it seems he has known every-
       one in the world for fifty years and has forgotten no one."

B3.   -------. "An Interview with Virgil Thomson, Seventy-five Years
       Sassy," Symphony News, 22 (Dec 1971): 4-5.

       In this interview Thomson airs opinions about the financial
       aspects of managing orchestras, the effects of current financial
       arrangements on composers, and modern musical training and con-
       ducting trends.   "The American symphony orchestra is a three-
       headed body...You have a musical director. You have an office
       director. And then you have the sacred trustees or board, which

raises the money and has the final veto. Any one of those three entities can have the dominating role in an orchestra, depending on whether it is raising the largest amount of money."

B4.   Ardoin, John. "Recitals: Alice Esty," MA 80 (May, 1960): 41.

A review of an April 3, 1960 recital by soprano Alice Esty in Carnegie Recital Hall during which Thomson's Songs for Alice Esty (later called Mostly About Love) were premiered: "melodically naive...full of charm and wit." See: W142

B5.   Balada, Leonard. "Entrevista con Virgil Thomson," Ritmo (Nov-Dec 1945): 35.

Introducing Thomson to Spanish readers as "one of the three greatest contemporary North American composers, together with Barber and Copland ("uno de los tres más grandes compositores norteamericanos actuales, junto con Barber y Copland"), Balada elicits generally known information and opinions from his inter- viewee.

B6.   Barlow, Samuel L.M.   "American Composers, XVII: Virgil Thomson," MM 18 (May-June 1941): 242-49.

A generalized article about Thomson's Paris experience and ca- reer to date. Barlow concludes that "Thomson is one of the best grounded musicians in our country. Therefore, what he launched, what he brought home, what he advocates, and what he writes must be taken seriously." Included is a sketch of Thomson by B.F. Dolbin.

B7.   Beeson, Jack. "Virgil Thomson's Aeneid," Parnassus: Poetry in Review 5 (Spring/Summer 1977): 457-478.

An historical and analytical article on Thomson's three operas and his powers of declamation. (Several musical examples are included.) "Thomson's operas share many of the generalities of French opera and the particularities of opéra comique. They abjure both the greater chromaticism and the decidedly greater contrapuntal and denser orchestral texture of German opera and the soaring and emotionally stressful vocal lines of Italian opera." See: W1, W3, & W6

B8.   Bennett, Elsie M.   "Virgil Thomson," The School Musician 32 (Nov 1960): 36+.

This article announces the publication of Thomson's "Lamenta- tions -- Theme and Variations" for accordion and quotes the composer's opinion of the instrument: "The accordion has huge accents...It has volume; also a soft sustained effect...it will mix easily with other instruments...it can be used...to hold a passage together rhythmically." A slightly condensed version of this article also appeared in MJ 18 (Feb 1960): 36-7. See: W193

B9.   Blau, Eleanor.   "Three Composers Liken Secular to Sacred Works,"

NYT (April 14, 1973): 18.

Virgil Thomson, Richard Felciano, and Ned Rorem discuss their sacred compositions and compositional techniques. Thomson opines that composers who write religious music today do so as "a rather pleasurable outlet for religious memories...They can remember their parents...a whole background filled with religious feeling."

B10. Briggs, John. "The Role of the Critic," Showcase 41/3 (1962): 6-7+.

Principles and practices of newspaper music criticism and the writing of Olin Downes, Virgil Thomson, and Noel Straus are discussed in this article. It is concluded that Thomson's "witty, sparkling articles were widely quoted and discussed, and that is good for business. His sprightly tour of duty with the New York Herald Tribune was stimulating."

B11. Burgin, Richard and Dominique Nabokov. "A Conversation With Virgil Thomson, Parts I and II," New York Arts Journal 21 (1981): 16-19; and 22 (1981): 25-28.

A frank, verbatim interview from May, 1980. Among other things Thomson's career and his opinions on electronic music, funding for the arts, and film music are discussed.

B12. Cazden, Norman. "Virgil Thomson: Serenade for Flute and Violin," Notes 10 (Dec 1952): 144.

A review of the score: "brief, unpretentious, and dedicated to the premise that any two tones may be sounded together if they form some diatonic relation...as music the Serenade is inoffensive and yet subtle." See: W175

B13. Cook, Eugene. "Virgil Thomson: The Composer in Person," HFS 14 (May 1965): 58-61.

In this interview contemporary musical affairs in France, Germany, and the U.S.A. are discussed.

B14. Copland, Aaron. "The American Composer Gets A Break," The American Mercury 34 (April 1935): 488-92.

In this article about four American composers (Roger Sessions, Walter Piston, Roy Harris, and Virgil Thomson), Copland praises Thomson's "gift for allowing English to be natural when sung" and prophesies that Thomson's "future lies on the stage, or at any rate in vocal writing."

B15. -------. "America's Young Men of Promise," MM 3 (March-April 1926): 13-20.

In this survey article, Thomson is mentioned briefly and his work is characterized as displaying "a melodic invention of no mean order and a most subtle rhythmic sense growing out of a fine feeling for prosody." (See B17 for a sequel to this article.)

B16.   -------. "From a Composer's Notebook," MM 6 (May-June 1929): 15-19.

A section in this potpourri article states "Virgil Thomson can teach us all how to set English to music...he allows words to have the naturalness of speech."

B17.   -------. "Our Younger Generation: Ten Years Later," MM 13 (May-June 1936): 3-11.

A sequel to Copland's article of March, 1926 (See B15). By now Thomson is quite well-known, especially for his Four Saints in Three Acts which Copland calls "a thoroughly characteristic Thomson piece...In it he proves himself to be essentially a vocal composer." See: W1

B18.   Cowell, Henry. "Current Chronicle," MQ 34 (July 1948): 410-15.

An analysis of Thomson's The Seine at Night: "Thomson has...produced a work apparently far more conventional in richness of perfumed sound than usual. In reality the change from his plainest writing is very slight indeed...He is fond of unadorned major and minor triads, and equally unadorned major scale passages...He has also been attracted by the most extreme dissonance. The use of these elements with unyielding consistency...has produced a really glaring simplicity." See: W29

B19.   -------. "Current Chronicle: New York," MQ 35 (Oct 1949): 619-22.

Cowell offers a brief analysis of A Solemn Music: "A serious and well-wrought piece, dramatic in its clash of musical forces, serene and lovely in its grave chord progressions." See: W34

B20.   -------. "Current Chronicle: New York," MQ 42 (July 1956): 389-90.

Cowell reviews Thomson's Concerto for Flute: "a work of charm." Thomson's "impression of Impressionisn" and his "indifference to keys" are praised. See: W39

B21.   Cunkle, Frank. "Afternoon at Lincoln Center," The Diapason 54 (Feb 1963): 23.

A review of a recital to inaugurate the new organ in Philharmonic Hall held on December 15, 1962, which included Thomson's Pange Lingua: "A work of prodigious difficulty which [E. Power] Biggs made exciting and intelligible." See: W195

B22.   Dale, S.S. "Contemporary Cello Concerti: Virgil Thomson," The Strad 84 (Aug 1973): 225-29.

An amusing article on the British premiere of Thomson's Cello Concerto in Edinburgh in 1951 with Sir Thomas Beecham conducting the French National Orchestra and Anthony Pini as soloist. An analysis of the work is also included. "Altogether a most successful fusion of form and content, with much picturesque orchestration." See: W36

B23. Davis, Peter G. "Composers' Showcase," HF 17 (Feb 1967): MA11.

A report on a Composers' Showcase concert at New York University in November, 1966, featuring Thomson's Nine Etudes for Piano. The "sprightly" pieces "combine a fine sense of proportion, and occasional references to a popular song...with the freshness and innocence that are hallmarks of this composer." See: W188

B24. Dilworth, Thomas. "Virgil Thomson and James Joyce," James Joyce Quarterly 20 (Fall 1982): 136-8.

A brief article about Thomson's unwillingness to collaborate with James Joyce on a contata or other musical work because, per Thomson, such a joint effort would have been "a wounding blow to Gertrude [Stein]."

B25. -------. "Virgil Thomson on George Antheil and Ezra Pound: A Conversation," Paideuma 12 (Fall/Winter 1983): 349-56.

Thomson on Antheil: "George was really launched...by literary people because with his violence and infantile boyish charm, he was a literary man's idea of a musical genius." On Pound: "Ezra was a man of great mental powers and great creative powers. But he was always jumping ahead of himself. He said foolish things, and then he began to believe them because he'd said them."

B26. Dlugoszewski, Lucia. "The Aristocracy of Play," Parnassus: Poetry in Review, 5 (Spring/Summer 1977): 486-97.

An analysis of Thomson's personality and works with an emphasis on the aesthetics of play. "Thomson's music requires the lightest touch in performance as he has given the lightest touch in its creation...Its airiness lifts the whole thing off the ground." Works mentioned include the Second Symphony, Wheatfield at Noon, and Four Saints in Three Acts. See: W1, W12, & W32

B27. Dubal, David. "Virgil Thomson Talks With David Dubal," Keynote 5 (Nov 1981): 6-11.

On the occasion of his 85th birthday, Thomson discusses his childhood, his musical training and style, and his operas. Numerous photos of Thomson from 1918 to the scene of the current interview are included.

B28. Dudar, Helen. "It's Home Sweet Home for Geniuses, Real or Would-be," Smithsonian 14 (Dec 1983): 94-105.

An entertaining article on the colorful, 100-year-old Chelsea Hotel where Thomson has lived for 40 years. A photo of Thomson and an anecdote about former neighbor Edgar Lee Masters are included.

D29. Dulman, Martin. "Independent Spirit," ON 41 (July 1976): 15-18.

In an interview, "the Mark Twain of American opera" reflects on American opera, its composition and production. "Other countries are perfectly at home with their own language on the stage, but Americans are not quite so comfortable...There are no real proper quality opera directors with original ideas and understanding anywhere. Choreography is the fashion of the times."

B30. Ellsworth, Ray. "Americans on Microgroove," HF 6 (Aug 1956): 60-66.

In this survey article on American music available on records, Thomson is called "an eclectic of a peculiar sort" whose "impish radicalism is not in his technique...but rather in his irreverent attitude toward the stuffy."

B31. Ericson, Raymond. "'Four Saints' For Bridgeport," NYT (Oct 24, 1971): Sect. 2, p. 13.

A report on the upcoming Thomson celebration during the second week of January, 1972 in Bridgeport, Connecticut in honor of Thomson's 75th birthday. Featured were: three performances of Four Saints in Three Acts, and a "reading" of The Mother of Us All. Also mentioned are other celebratory concerts in New York. See: W1 & W3

B32. Eyer, Ronald F. "Meet the Composer: Virgil Thomson," MA 64 (April 25, 1944): 7+.

This article, liberally sprinkled with quotes, written from an interview, deals with Thomson's background, career, and writings. "There are no preconceived ideas of goal or destination for his musical production as a whole; there are only the exigencies and the obvious desiderata of the work in hand at the moment."

B33. -------. "Thomson Opera Revived at Phoenix," MA 76 (May 1956): 23.

This review of the April 16th, 1956 first fully professional performance of The Mother of Us All at the Phoenix Theater in New York, declares Thomson's score to be "secure, lucid, and purposeful...a marvel of clarity and simplicity." See: W3

B34. Fain, Kenneth. "Oakland: Mills College," HF 32 (Sept 1982): MA22-23.

A report of Mills College's birthday concert for Lou Harrison on May 10, 1982. Thomson was unable to attend but sent a piece Gending Chelsea to premiere there. Originally a gamelan piece, the work was arranged for two vocalists and small chorus by Jody Diamond. The performance raised "a bit of Virgiliana to new heights of cross-cultural campiness." See: W201

B35. Field, Michael G. "Virgil Thomson and the Maturity of American Music," The Chesterian 28 (April 1954): 111-14.

This condescending British overview of the state of music in the U.S. applauds Thomson for his courage in working toward and for "truly American" music, and for his "sophistication of mind which only Europe could provide."

B36. Fleming, Shirley. "Orchestra of Our Time: Thomson's 'Four Saints,' Satie's 'Socrate,'" HF 28 (March 1978): MA23-24.

A brief review of a performance of a concert form of Four Saints in Three Acts in New York on November 10, 1977: "Four Saints remains irresistible. Thomson's Southern Baptist ear for the American musical idiom caught a spirit that is as pertinent today as it was fifty years ago." See: W1

B37. Frankenstein, Alfred. "'The Mother of Us All' -- A Brilliant Exhibition," HF 26 (Dec 1976): MA21-23.

A lengthy review of the 1976 Santa Fe, New Mexico performance of The Mother of Us All. Thomson is proclaimed "the master of a marvelously flexible idiom, based on that of American hymnody but imitating or quoting nothing; this idiom is capable of the finest nuances of expression and reaches true grandiloquence in the towering, passionate outbursts wherein Susan B. protests the frustration of her cause." See: W3

B38. -------. "Virgil is as Virgil Does," Parnassus: Poetry in Review 5 (Spring/Summer 1977): 498-500.

A brief piece on Thomson's simplicity of style, in both music and prose, and his honesty. "Virgil Thomson won his reputation as a wit simply by telling the truth--and telling it simply."

B39. -------. "Virgil Thomson: Concerto for Violoncello and Orchestra," Notes 10 (June 1953): 482-83.

This review of the score declares "that it is the best cello concerto since Haydn...the texture of the work is distinguished for its lightness, its luminosity, and its superbly well aerated balance of forces." See: W36

B40. Freedman, Guy. "Everbest, Virgil Thomson," MJ 35 (March 1977): 8-10+.

In this interview Thomson comments on his collaboration with Gertrude Stein, musical trends in the 20th century, and music

criticism.   "Aesthetic trends are just like a new strain of
grippe or disease of some kind that goes all over the world.
Sometimes it hits Europe first and sometimes it hits America
first. And many of them hit at the same time."

B41. Fremantle, Anne. "Virgil Thomson," A Salute to Virgil Thomson.
      Symposium of the Society for the Arts, Religion and Contemporary
      Culture, New York City, May, 1977, p. 3.

      Brief introductory remarks made to the Society before Thomson's
      address (See T179).   "I know of no one else but the late George
      Bernard Shaw who could convey an understanding of what music is
      about in cold, cold print."

B42. Fuller, Donald. "More on the New York Season," MM 20 (March-April
      1943): 182-3.

      Fuller feels that Thomson displays "aptness for evolving atmos-
      phere and underlining dramatic significance" in his two orches-
      tral suites from the documentary film scores, The Plow that
      Broke the Plains and The River. "When he is able to achieve
      this quite personal music of solid human foundations, with its
      moving sadness and good humor, Thomson offers something very
      real, which is not at all in his salon or conceited efforts, or
      in his skillful essays based on prosodic knowledge, frequently
      said to represent the composer at his best." See: W13 & W14

B43. Giffin, Glenn. "Santa Fe," ON 41 (Nov 1976): 88.

      A brief review of the August 1976 Santa Fe production of The
      Mother of Us All "which opened with a burst of fireworks, an
      onstage band, large floats rising up on the stage's back eleva-
      tor and a jumble of individual personalities." See: W3

B44. Glanville-Hicks, Peggy.   "Virgil Thomson," MQ 35 (April 1949):
      209-225.

      This assessment of Thomson and his music includes brief analyses
      of the Sonata da Chiesa, Symphony No. 2, The River, and Louisia-
      na Story, among other works, with musical examples. "Thomson
      has a style, and a very definite one, but it is almost
      impossible to put one's finger on any detail...It is un-idiosyn-
      cratic." Includes worklist. See: W12, W162, W317, & W320

B45. -------. "Virgil Thomson: Four Saints in Three Acts," Notes 6
      (March 1949): 328-30.

      A highly favorable review of the complete vocal score of the
      opera.   "Two unique attributes equipped Thomson as an artist to
      make this work a classic...These were a hymn-tune element that
      is deeply a part of his musical esthetic, and his fastidiousness
      and expertness in the setting of words." See: W1

B46. Gold, Arthur and Robert Fizdale."Food Surprises from Virgil Thom-
      son," Vg 162 (Aug 1973): 110-11+.

A thumbnail sketch of Thomson's colorful life and career, with an accent on his culinary talents. Recipes include those for Crab Meat Thomson and Shrimp Maurice Grosser.

B47. Goldbeck, Eva. "A Thomson Soirée," MM 13 (Nov-Dec 1935): 50-51.

In reviewing a recital of Thomson's music (Sonata for Violin and Piano, Stabat Mater, five of the portraits) at the New School in New York City on November 8, 1935, Goldbeck reflects that much of the composer's music is written for an intimate theatre -- the salon. "Often it seems pretentious and frivolous, although it is intrinsically honest and serious." She also expresses respect for Thomson's "severe and fluent technique." See: W121, W171, & W's 209-229

B48. Goldman, Richard Franko. "Music Criticism in the United States," Score (London) 12 (June 1955): 86-7.

In this general survey Goldman praises Thomson as a critic who is "both lively and informed...who could write English with grace and sense, and whose prejudices were at least literate and musical."

B49. Grosser, Maurice. "Virgil Thomson among the Painters," Parnassus: Poetry in Review 5 (Spring/Summer 1977): 506-18.

This article is a slice of a memoir of Paris in the 1920's and 30's. The friendship between the author and Thomson is the subject, along with anecdotes involving other painters. Mentioned are: Eugene and Leonid Berman, Christian Bérard, Pierre Roy, Max Jacob, Ramón Senabre, Marcel Duchamp, Florine Stettheimer, and Pablo Picasso.

B50. Gruen, John. "Thomson Conducts World Premiere of His Requiem Mass," MA 80 (June 1960): 17.

A review of the premiere of Missa Pro Defunctis on May 14, 1960 in Potsdam, New York with the Crane Chorus and Symphony: "One of this century's great ecclesiastical works...simplicity and economy of statement are everywhere in evidence." See: W87

B51. Haggin, Bernard H. "The Imagined World of Virgil Thomson," The Hudson Review 20 (Winter 1967-68): 625-35.

A lengthy article on Thomson's career as a critic. Haggin maintains repeatedly that Thomson "lives in, and writes about a world imagined as he would like it to be." This acerbic essay denigrates Thomson's professional standards and critical criteria and has the flavor of personal vengeance being vented.

B52. -------. "Music," Na 154 (Jan 3, 1942): 20.
Thomson's performance during his first year as music critic for the New York Herald-Tribune is assessed. "Discussing large questions like a five-year plan for the New York Philharmonic, or mere pet ideas like the wow technique of Toscanini, Mr.

Thomson has occasionally been terrible; but about pieces of
music and performances he has often been wonderful."

B53.   -------. "Music," <u>Na</u> 154 (Jan 17, 1942): 74.

In response to his column on January 3rd in <u>The Nation</u>, the
author defends his estimate of Thomson as a critic who "often
writes with exciting penetration," and discusses the purpose of
music criticism.

B54.   -------. "Music: Mr. Thomson's Imagination," <u>Na</u> 158 (Jan 22,
1944): 110.

Another appraisal of Thomson's performance as critic for the <u>New
York Herald Tribune</u>: "Into a discussion of things of this world
as they exist and happen Mr. Thomson disconcertingly introduces,
as though they were equally real, things from some private world
as he would like them to exist and happen...The mixture of real
and unreal is disconcerting."

B55.   -------. "Music: Virgil Thomson as a Critic," <u>Na</u> 179 (Dec 4,
1954): 499-500.

A review of a Concert Society of New York performance conducted
by Thomson and featuring his <u>Stabat Mater</u> and <u>Four Songs to
Poems of Thomas Campion</u>. Haggin goes on to lament Thomson's
departure from the <u>New York Herald Tribune</u>: "He had the equip-
ment of critical perception that is the one essential in
criticism,...and it produced the only newspaper criticism of
music worth reading." See: W121 & W129

B56.   Hall, David. "A Thomson Discography," <u>HSR</u> 14 (May 1965): 57.

A brief, annotated discography of currently-available recordings
and some suggestions or requests for future releases.

B57.   Harrison, Lou. "Happy Birthday, Virgil," <u>Parnassus: Poetry in
Review</u> 5 (Spring/Summer 1977): 436-38.

A short collection of Thomson anecdotes in the form of a birthday salute: "[Thomson] has complained that he is 'troubled by
Jingle Bells' (it kept cropping up in the spontaneous tunes);
and in an age of unplayful, fierce plotting of composition, he
was perfectly sound in inventing and naming an 'Idiot
Style'...'The main difference between you and me (as composers)
and other people is that we are never bored,' he has said...I
think that perhaps it is the wild man in him that is the source
of the endurance of his works and he who guards the tenderness
and clarity of them."

B58.   Heinsheimer, Hans. "New York 'Phantasien in einem Rathskeller',"
<u>Neue Zeitschrift für Musik</u> 132 (Dec 1971): 661-63.

A survey article on Thomson's cosmopolitan musical background
and career in a report on a celebration of his 75th birthday at

the Plaza Hotel in New York.   In particular Thomson's relationship with Gertrude Stein is discussed.

B59.   -------.   "A Well-Tempered Composer: Birthday Greetings to Virgil
Thomson," ASCAP Today 5 (Jan 1972): 14-17.

This article by Schirmer's director of publications reviews
Thomson's career and gives special attention to his "precise and
well organized business mind" and his negotiations with Gertrude
Stein about royalties.   Also discussed is the foundation of the
American Composers Alliance in 1938 and the classical composer's
relation to ASCAP through the years.

B60.   Helm, Everett.   "Virgil Thomson's Four Saints in Three Acts," MR
15 (May 1954): 127-32.

This review praises "the seemingly naive score" as "extremely
skillful and sophisticated," and Thomson for his "uncanny
feeling for prosody and for finding the just declamation of
English...The entire piece might well be considered a parody of
19th-century opera...But the parody is so skilfully and
discreetly carried out that it can pass unnoticed." See: W1

B61.   Henahan, Donal.   "And Now, Virgil's Odyssey," NYT (March 21,
1971): Sect. 2, p. 15+.

A major interview-article with Thomson as he approaches his 75th
birthday.   Topics of discussion include Aaron Copland, Charles
Ives, Thomson's book American Music Since 1910, his opera Lord
Byron, and contemporary trends in music and culture.   "I'm an
old Confederate, always agin' the government, but I believe in
the country, in its energy, in its power of organization. In my
century, we've seen extraordinary things." See: T188 and W6

B62.   -------.   "The Brow That Broke the Mold," Parnassus: Poetry in
Review 5 (Spring/Summer 1977): 481-85.

A charmingly written look at Thomson's powers of criticism and
prose, with quotes throughout.   Thomson's style is said to mix
"elegant and blunt talk, gravity and levity, objectivity and
passion, all in exquisitely right proportions...Only a critic
who has been brought up in Kansas City and polished in Paris can
hope to acquire such distinctive, easy-riding style."

B63.   -------. "Choral Performances," American Choral Review 9/4 (1967):
53-4.

A review of the Rockefeller Chapel Choir's premiere of Thomson's
The Nativity (May 7, 1967) under the direction of Richard Vikstrom at the University of Chicago: "Though the dissonance level
is fairly high throughout, there always is a solid key feeling
and a gently mellifluous effect. Much of the time the chorus is
knitting dulcet chains of thirds, while the orchestra compli-
cates the texture with discreet seconds." See: W94

B64. Hiemenz, Jack. "New York," HF 32 (May 1982): MA32-3.

A review of the American Composers Orchestra concert on November 30, 1981 at Tully Hall, which featured Thomson's Cello Concerto, with Janos Starker as soloist. "The sophisticated virtuosity of the cello part, the playfulness of the harmonies, and Thomson's expert orchestration keep it from slipping into simplicity." Also played were Sea Piece and The Seine at Night. See: W29, W36, & W38

B65. Hitchcock, H. Wiley. "Homage to Virgil Thomson at Eighty-Five," Institute for Studies in American Music Newsletter 11 (Nov 1981): 1-2.

This is the text of the keynote address delivered at the ceremony in which Thomson, on his 85th birthday, was awarded the honorary degree of Doctor of Humane Letters by Brooklyn College of the City University of New York. Thomson's achievements are summarized, and Prof. Hitchcock concludes that "for all his cultivation, sophistication, and savoir faire, Virgil Thomson's thought and expression are those of the bright, unspoiled, uninhibited, and boundlessly inquisitive child." A photograph of sculptor Marisol's "Portrait of Virgil Thomson" accompanies the article.

B66. Huntley, J. "Music in Films," MT 98 (Dec 1957): 662-63.

In this survey article Thomson is praised as "a supreme technician, with an uncanny grasp of the effects to be obtained by the accurate use of a stop-watch."

B67. Igo, John. "Bringing Back the Expatriots," San Antonio Monthly (May 1983): 39-60.

A rambling and genial interview which, as usual, covers Thomson's friendships with the famous of Paris in the 20's, his operas, and his work with Gertrude Stein. See: W1, W3, & W6

B68. Keller, Hans. "Louisiana Story -- I and II," Music Survey 2 (Autumn 1949): 101-02; and 2 (Winter 1950): 188-89.

Analysis of the film score for which Thomson won a Pulitzer Prize in 1949 and of Frederick Sternfeld's analysis of the music (See B95 & B96). "A remarkable attempt to use the still more remarkable musical opportunities of a highly dramatic, but at the same time unhurried and largely speechless picture." See: W320

B69. Larson, Jack. "The Word on Byron," Parnassus: Poetry in Review," 5 (Spring/Summer 1977): 519-26.

The librettist for Thomson's Lord Byron recalls their long collaboration on the opera. See: W6

B70. Levy, Alan Howard. "Paris in the Twenties: Nadia Boulanger,

Virgil Thomson and America's Musical Maturation," <u>Contemporary</u>
<u>French</u> <u>Civilization</u> 4 (Fall 1979): 23-43.

This article discusses the subtleties and sources of Thomson's
music and other American expatriate composers in Paris in the
20's and credits the broadening influence of Boulanger.

B71. Luten, C.J. "Thomson at Seventy-Five," <u>ON</u> 36 (April 15,
      1972): 12-13.

      A thumbnail sketch of Thomson and his work, with emphasis on his
      achievement in opera: "Thomson's music is not insistent; it is
      easy to live with. It is classic in that content is always more
      important than style; in an age of mannerism, gadgetry and
      chance, his work seems the more treasurable."

B72. Mandel, Alan and Nancy. "Composers to Re-emphasize: Virgil Thom-
      son," <u>Clavier</u> 14 (April 1975): 16-17.

      A brief sketch of Thomson's music and career, with emphasis on
      the portraits and other piano works. "Thomson reveals in his
      music an ironic brevity, a quixotic, impish humor, a clarity of
      realization, a gravitation toward simplicity."

B73. Margrave, Wendell. "Current Chronicle: Washington, D.C.," <u>MQ</u> 51
      (April 1965): 409-13.

      In this review of the October 1964 Coolidge Festival, Thomson's
      <u>Feast</u> <u>of</u> <u>Love</u> for baritone and chamber orchestra is called "a
      sort of cantata." "The writing is professional, not very
      advanced in harmonic basis, but fluent and ingenious in its use
      of instruments." See: W48

B74. Merkling, Frank. "New York," <u>ON</u> 36 (June 1972): 23-4.

      A review of the Juilliard American Opera Center's premiere of
      <u>Lord</u> <u>Byron</u> on April 20, 1972: "There is beautiful writing for
      voice and instruments; there are few concessions to
      theatricality...The prevailing freshness of melody and
      rhythm...lends <u>Lord</u> <u>Byron</u> a real 'English' flavor." See: W6

B75. Movshon, G. "Virgil Thomson -- an informal album," <u>HF</u> 19 (Jan
      1969): MA17+.

      A report on a concert at the Hotel Pierre in New York put on by
      the sponsors of the Sunday Afternoon Cafe Concerts. Thomson was
      there to explain his concept of musical portraiture before five
      of his portraits were played. There followed the <u>Cantabile</u> <u>for</u>
      <u>Strings</u>, and several excerpts from all three of Thomson's ope-
      ras. In general: "Thomson's music is bright, economical, busy,
      and pointed. If the musical idiom does not seem unduly topical
      ...neither does it appear in any way out of date." See: W1, W3,
      W6, & W21

B76. Oja, Carol J. "The Copland-Sessions Concerts and their Reception in the Contemporary Press," MQ 65 (April 1979): 212-29.

Thomson's name comes up several times in this article as one of the composers for a series of concerts held in New York and Paris, 1928-31. Mentioned briefly are Thomson's Five Phrases from "The Song of Solomon", and Capital, Capitals. See: W107 & W109.

B77. Paris, Matthew. "Interview with Virgil Thomson," Brooklyn College Alumni Literary Review 5 (1984): 315-351.

One of the very few intelligent interviews with Thomson. Among the many topics discussed are: American music, performance practices, various 20th-century composers and their work, Lord Byron, The Mother of Us All, Gertrude Stein and feminism, songsetting, and Thomson's mid-Western roots and their influence. The piece goes into greater depth than most of the interviews and includes more than witty generalizations and personal anecdotes of famous folk. See: W3 & W6

B78. Porter, Andrew. "The Memory of Byron," NYer 52 (Jan 17, 1977): 106-08.

A review and analysis of Lord Byron written after the WNYC radio broadcast of the Julliard School recording aired in December of 1976: "Thomson's score limns sentiments with sure, easy strokes and does not aim to stir emotion in the listeners. The music is distinguished by the peculiar justness of word setting...Like Purcell and Britten, Thomson has the gift to declaim English lines in melodies that not merely are fitting in rhythm and pitch inflections but make a music in which words and musical contour seem indissolubly joined...Lord Byron is a new combination of Thomson's previous operatic elements found in his choral and orchestral music." Reprinted in Music of Three Seasons: 1974-1977. New York: Farrar Straus Giroux, 1978, pp. 482-6. See: W6

B79. Ramey, Phillip. "Virgil Thomson at 85: A Candid Conversation," Ov 2 (Nov 1981): 12-15+.

Many photos accompany this engaging interview. Thomson describes himself ("I'm kind of salty and spicy, you know. Anyway, I'm not a smoothie.") and his life at 85, and talks about his career and works. About style he says, "it is not something you do, style is something you have. And if you have it, you don't have to think about it."

B80. Rich, Alan. "America's Living Musical Treasure," H&G 154 (July 1982): 14+.

A retrospective article on the 85-year-old composer-critic's career: "If Thomson had a hand in inventing American music, he played an even greater role in inventing American music criticism...He worked at a time when American culture in all areas was actively...building an identity. Not content to kibitz from the sidelines, he demanded and obtained the right to participate in that process."

B81.   -------.   "Eternal Virgil," New York Magazine 13 (Nov 24, 1980): 69-70.

A sketch of Thomson's career and literary style: "Thomson invented contemporary journalistic music criticism; he gave it its language and its integrity and defined its horizons."

B82.   Rockwell, John.   "A Conversation with Virgil Thomson," Parnassus: Poetry in Review 5 (Spring/Summer 1977): 417-35.

A nearly verbatim interview transcript with Thomson who discusses 20th-century trends in art and music and his own long career in music and criticism. This interview was reprinted in VTR.

B83.   Rorem, Ned.   "Lord Byron in Kansas City," NRe 166 (May 6, 1972): 23-4.

A lengthy review of the premiere of Lord Byron: "The music is pure Thomson...Carefully planned, with appropriate airs and witty ensembles, the vocal conceptions are at all times what singers call gracious...The sound is lean, harmonic opulence and rhythmic complication being...foreign to Thomson." Reprinted in Pure Contraption: A Composer's Essay. New York: Holt, Rinehart and Winston, 1974: pp. 69-74. See: W6

B84.   Rosenfeld, Paul.   "Prepare for Saints," NRe 78 (Feb 21, 1934): 48.

A hot-and-cold review of the premiere of the "queer little piece" Four Saints in Three Acts. "As the opera progresses, the expressions wax more earnest and pathetic. The prose grows sonorous...Thomson's score...is too frequently the work of a musical juggler, and too infrequently that of a composer who feels a little something, and he has a knack with the American idiom..." Reprinted in Rosenfeld's Discoveries of a Music Critic (New York: Harcourt, Brace, 1936),p. 297. For a response to this article see B110. See: W1

B85.   Rosenwald, Hans.   "Speaking of Music: Contemporary Music," Music News 43 (Feb 1951): 10-11.

From this survey article on contemporary composers and their work: "There is a sense of simplicity in most of his music which makes many of his contributions tuneful and amicable. There is, on the other hand, a poignant sarcasm about much that Thomson writes. Finally, there is music in which one is doubtful as to what is meant seriously and what is plain satire."

B86.   Rossi, Nick.   "Virgil Thomson at 75," MJ 29 (Nov 1971): 11-12+.

Thomson's colorful career is recalled in this light article, and the upcoming Thomson Festival held by the Music Department of the University of Connecticut at Bridgeport is announced.

B87. Schonberg, Harold C. "Virgil Thomson: Parisian from Missouri,"
      HFS 14 (May 1965): 43-56.

      Schonberg presents a well-written biographical sketch of Thom-
      son: "The perfect cosmopolite -- sophisticated, bilingual, ur-
      bane, cultivated, witty...He has a keen sense of paradox and
      often comes out with outrageous ideas simply because they sound
      amusing or contradictory. He is fiercely antipathctic to aca-
      demic intellectualism, is not afraid of anything, delights to
      puncture concepts that everyone takes for granted, and has an
      immense curiosity coupled to a retentive memory."

B88. Seldes, Gilbert. "Delight in the Theatre," MM 11 (March-April
      1934): 138-41.

      Although he expresses some reservations about Stein's surrealis-
      tic libretto for Four Saints in Three Acts, Seldes finds Thom-
      son's setting of it impressive. He concludes that "this opera
      pleased me more than all but half a dozen in the traditional
      repertory.   It has fantasy and vigor. It can be taken as a
      gigantic piece of mystification and a huge joke; it certainly
      should not be taken without laughter. It has taste and kind-
      ness, humor and feeling." See: W1

B89. Simon, Robert. "Opera Uptown," NYer 23 (May 17, 1947): 103-4.

      Review of the Columbia Theatre Associates' production of
      The Mother of Us All: "The production was ingeniously worked
      out.   The   singing   was   generally   good,   and   the
      orchestra...handled   the   clear,   meaningful   orchestration
      neatly...Mr. Thomson's musical setting for the libretto is right
      on every count. Its imagination, directness, and simplicity
      perfectly set off the intricate words and the action." See: W3

B90. Smith, Patrick J. "Musician of the Month," HF 21 (Nov 1971): MA8-
      9.

      An amusing report on an interview with Thomson during which
      music publishing, criticism, and compositions were discussed:
      "'I   see   very   little of interest   in   most   electronic
      pieces...First of all, it's canned...Then, the composers do not
      understand what they are doing...it is fun and games.'"

B91. -------. "New York," Op 23 (May 1972): 518-20.

      A review of the premiere of Lord Byron: "Thomson's music is as
      resolutely melodic and conservative as the libretto...The ob-
      viousness of a good deal of the opera, combined with some heavy-
      handedness contributed to the coolness of the reception...Thom-
      son has rejected most the current models of opera-writing...to
      resurrect that out-of-fashion genre, the French 19th-century
      opera...It is certainly Thomson's most personal opera...The
      Juilliard cast...performed the work well, but this opera re-

quires a fully-professional group, since much of the tessitura is demanding." See: W6

B92. -------. "Thomson's 'Lord Byron'," HF 22 (July 1972): MA11+.

A major review of the premiere of Lord Byron: "What Lord Byron makes evident is that Gertrude Stein's avoidance of being pinned down was equally part of Thomson's artistic make-up...In this Thomson is akin to Vladimir Nabokov in the technique of never revealing himself and of hiding behind puns and games, and it is apt because it is consistent with Byron's endless poses...[The opera] handles the problem of work and music...and is...a genuine musical entity of great beauty." See: W6

B93. Smith, Rollin. "American Organ Composers: Virgil Thomson," Music (The AGO and RCCO Magazine) 10 (July 1976): 42-3.

A review of Thomson's career and major works, especially those for organ. Also quoted is Thomson's August 5, 1945 New York Herald Tribune column, "The Organ."

B94. Soria, Dorle. "Virgil Thomson," HF 32 (Feb 1982): MA8-9+.

An amusing and informative light sketch of Thomson's personality and philosophy of life, and a review of all the various festivi- ties centered around his 85th birthday. "'I worked hard all my life. But even when I was young and didn't have any money, I decided I could do practically everything in music. I decided I would not do anything that I didn't want to.'"

B95. Sternfeld, Frederick W. "Current Chronicle: New York." MQ 35 (Jan 1949): 115-21.

An analysis of Louisiana Story: "Thomson's unmuddled discords have a distinctly contemporary flavor...the prospect for the course of contemporary music in the films looks bright." See: B68 & B96 and W320

B96. -------. "'Louisiana Story': Teamwork Between Producer and Composer," Music Teachers' National Association Studies in Musi- cal Education, History, and Aesthetics 43 (1949): 40-45.

An analysis of the score for Louisiana Story similar to the author's Musical Quarterly (Jan 1949) article. (See above.) Thomson is applauded not only for his sensitive score but also for knowing "where and where not to place the music." See: B68 & B95 and W320

B97. Stevenson, Florence. "A Continuous Present," ON 35 (April 10, 1971): 8-13.

An extensive and interesting article on Gertrude Stein with passing references and anecdotes regarding her librettos for Four Saints in Three Acts and The Mother of Us All. See: W1 & W3

B98. Sutherland, Donald. "A Short but Far-Flung Collaboration with V.T.," Parnassus: Poetry in Review 5 (Spring/Summer 1977): 501-04.

The author reminisces about his brief collaboration with Thomson on the translation of some French poetry for songs.

B99. Swan, Annalyn. "Yankee Doodle Dandy," Newsweek 98 (Dec 7, 1981): 84+.

A brief sketch of Thomson's colorful life and career upon his 85th birthday. His music is dubbed "a sort of cosmopolitan corn pone," and he is praised for his refusal "to become a period piece."

B100. Tcherepnin, Ivan. "The Imperial Court of the Chelsea Hotel," Parnassus: Poetry in Review 5 (Spring/Summer 1977): 479-80.

The author reminisces about a 1961 visit to Thomson: "His piercing yet light manner...has a disarming effect of putting one at ease while remaining on one's toes."

B101. Tommasini, Anthony. "The Musical Portraits by Virgil Thomson," MQ 70 (Spring 1984): 234-47.

Adapted from his book on Thomson's musical portraits (See B182), Tommasini's article focuses on the procedure that Thomson has developed for musical portait composition. The discussion is preceded by a description of Gertrude Stein's abstract word portraits which gave Thomson the impetus for experimentation. See: W209 through W315

B102. Trilling, Diana. "A Conversation with Virgil Thomson," Partisan Review 4 (1980): 544-57.

Part of an oral history series now on deposit in the Oral History Department of the Columbia University Library, this interview focuses on the relation of music to "the advanced literary-intellectual culture of New York City," discusses Stein, Pound, Stravinsky, Blitzstein, Weill, Joyce, and the political climate between 1925 and 1975. Reprinted in VTR.

B103. Van Vechten, Carl. "On Words and Music," NYT (Feb 18, 1934): Sect. 9, p. 2.

A review of the premiere of Four Saints in Three Acts. Van Vechten applauds the performance and "this rather miraculous music drama." Reprinted in ARG 31 (Feb 1965): 521-22. See: W1

B104. Walsh, Michael and Nancy Newman. "Red, White and Blue Boulevardier," Time 118 (Nov 30, 1981): 91.

Anecdotal sketch of Thomson's works and career upon his 85th birthday. "'I am essentially a predecessor...Some artists close things. I am the kind who opens things.'"

B105. Weinstock, Herbert.   "V.T. of the H.T.," <u>SR</u> 37 (Aug 28, 1954): 48+.

This article reviews the colorful career of the critic who "assaulted, delighted, affronted, titillated, outraged, and very well pleased for nearly a decade and a half." Thomson is described as "the most thoroughly American of Americans, just as he is one of the most constantly musical of musicians."

B106. Wickes, George. "A Natalie Barney Garland." <u>Paris Review</u> 16 (Spring 1975): 113-18.

Thomson responds to questions about Natalie Barney (American expatriot in Paris in the 1920's), Gertrude Stein, and others.

B107. Williams, Jonathan. "Super-Duper Zuppa Inglese," <u>Parnassus: Poetry in Review</u> 5 (Spring/Summer 1977): 527-31.

Eleven surrealistic poems inspired by two statements culled from Thomson's autobiography.

B108. Wintour, Anna. "Neighborhood Style," <u>New York Magazine</u> 16 (Sept 26, 1983): 33-62.

In this entertaining survey of Manhattan's neighborhoods, Thomson's Chelsea Hotel apartment serves as the quintessential Chelsea experience. A description and photos of his suite are accompanied by his comments on his 40 years there.

B109. Wolf, Robert Erich. "Current Chronicle: France," <u>MQ</u> 47 (July 1961): 400-07.

An analysis of <u>Missa pro defunctis</u>: "Thomson has recently demonstrated with characteristic skill and unpretentiousness still viable diatonic-chromatic possibilities outside the serial system...A work...fresh and inventive and...full of deep and touching sentiment." See: W87

B110. Young, Stark. "One Moment Alit," <u>NRe</u> 78 (March 7, 1934): 105.

In response to Paul Rosenfeld's earlier review of <u>Four Saints in Three Acts</u> (See B84), Young defends the opera as "the most important event of the theatre season...the first free, pure theatre...seen so far." He goes on: "It lives in itself, and is in essence a constant surprise." See: W1

References in Books

B111. Anagnost, Dean Z.   <u>The Choral Music of Virgil Thomson</u>.   Ed.D. dissertation. Columbia University Teachers College, 1977. [Order No.: AAD79-00649]

Anagnost's dissertation provides an overview of Thomson's choral music composed between 1920 and 1973, published and in available

manuscript. He analyzes the composer's style, provides a catalogue of choral works, and discusses pertinent writings both by
and about Thomson.

B112. Arlton, Dean. American Piano Sonatas of the Twentieth Century:
Selective Analysis and Annotated Index.   Ed.D. dissertation.
Columbia University, 1968. [Order No.: 69-9903]

Arlton here examines Thomson's piano sonatas in detail, with
special reference to structure and interpretation. See: W169,
W170, W173, & W244

B113. Austin, William W. Music in the 20th Century From Debussy Through
Stravinsky. New York: W.W. Norton, 1966. Pp. 385f, et passim.

Surveys Thomson's place and influence, building on the composer's own image of his work as "a large railway station, not
particularly attractive, though details of it [are] interesting,
but massive and full of variety, with many people going in and
out of it."

B114. Barzun, Jacques.   Music in American Life.   Garden City, NY:
Doubleday, 1956. Pp. 55-58.

In his chapter on music in academic life, Barzun contrasts
statements by Paul Henry Lang and Thomson, the former maintain-
ing that music should be studied as a social phenomenon and the
latter that, because of the low level of musical literacy, the
subject is best approached as an auditory experience.

B115. Beebe, Lucius.   Snoot If You Must.   New York: Appleton-Century,
1943. Pp. 166-172.

A witty and facetious account of the premiere of Four Saints in
Three Acts.   "...The field was strewn with murdered unities,
decapitated conventions, smashed tophats, and...Chandon magnums." See: W1

B116. Bowers, Jane Palatini.   The Writer in the Theater: The
Plays of Gertrude Stein.   Ph.D. dissertation.   University of
California at Berkeley, 1981. [Order No.: AAD82-11866]

Bowers includes a discussion of Four Saints in Three Acts and
The Mother of Us All, as well as the Thomson-Stein relationship,
in her analysis of Stein's dramatic style. See: W1 & W3

B117. Carman, Judith Elaine. Twentieth-Century American Song Cycles: a
Study in Circle Imagery. D.M.A. dissertation.   University of
Iowa, 1973. [Order No.: 74-7452]

Carman discusses the circular imagery and form in music, focusing on English song cycles from the 16th to the 20th centuries,
and analyzing 15 selected works by 20th century American composers. Music examples included.

B118. Chase, Gilbert. <u>America's</u> <u>Music</u>, 2nd edition. New York: McGraw-Hill, 1966. Pp. 530-34, <u>et</u> <u>passim</u>.

Surveys "a small measure of the abundant, extraordinarily varied, and unique musical production of Virgil Thomson," placing it in perspective <u>vis</u> <u>à</u> <u>vis</u> American music.

B119. Clarke, Garry E. <u>Essays</u> <u>on</u> <u>American</u> <u>Music</u>. Westport, CT: Greenwood Press, 1977. Pp. 161-78.

Clarke discusses Thomson's influence and style quoting musical examples. "The significance of Thomson's work as a composer, as a critic, and as a champion of American music cannot be questioned."

B120. Copland, Aaron. <u>The</u> <u>New</u> <u>Music,</u> <u>1900-1960</u>. Revised and enlarged edition. New York: W.W. Norton, 1968. Pp. 135-39, <u>et</u> <u>passim</u>. (Previously published in 1941 with the title <u>Our</u> <u>New</u> <u>Music</u>.)

Copland observes that Thomson "is about as original a personality as America can boast, in or out of the musical field," and discusses his contribution to American music, especially opera.

B121. Copland, Aaron and Vivian Perlis. <u>Copland:</u> <u>1900</u> <u>Through</u> <u>1942</u>. New York: St. Martin's/Markek, 1984. Pp. 197-201, <u>et</u> <u>passim</u>.

Thomson is quoted or referred to frequently throughout this first volume on Copland's life and works. A portion of Thomson's interview, on deposit in Yale University's <u>Oral</u> <u>History,</u> <u>American</u> <u>Music</u>, is reprinted and reads, in part, that Copland "had the great gift of being a good colleague, and we became good, loyal colleagues...He has said and written that I'm one of the few composers who influenced him."

B122. Craft, Robert. <u>Present</u> <u>Perspectives:</u> <u>Critical</u> <u>Writings</u>. New York: Knopf, 1984. Pp. 68-75.

Thomson's career in music criticism (mainly his years for the New York <u>Herald</u> <u>Tribune</u>) are examined. His reviews are described as "consistently...the best written in any of the arts during the decade [40's]" and his language is praised for being "well seasoned with vernacular." His critical powers are described as "unrivaled."

B123. Davies, Lawrence. <u>Paths</u> <u>to</u> <u>Modern</u> <u>Music</u>. New York: Charles Scribner's Sons, 1971. Pp. 274-86.

Chapter 22 of this book deals with Thomson, "a figure as American as Edison or Henry Ford, yet who has had the sophistication to spend much of his long life window-shopping in Europe and who possesses a degree of articulacy so uncommon among musicians as to have made him a veritably unique sopkesman for his country." Thomson's working relationship with Gertrude Stein is also discussed.

B124. Davis, Ronald L.   A History of Music in American Life.   3 vols.
Malabar, FL: Robert Krieger Publishing Co., 1980-82. Vol. II,
p. 128; Vol III, pp. 153-64, et passim.

Summarizes Thomson's life and mentions significant works.

B125. Downes, Irene, ed. Olin Downes On Music.   New York: Simon &
Schuster, 1957. Pp. 187-90 and 211.

New York Times critic Olin Downes reviews the 1934 New York
performance of Four Saints in Three Acts in his February 21st
column: "[Thomson] has produced music which is in the happiest
contrast to the labored or lumpish scores by Americans that have
been heard of late." In a later article (Oct 20, 1935) Four
Saints is called a nearly "complete and unified opera." See: W1

B126. Duke, Vernon.   Listen Here! A Critical Essay on Music Deprecia-
tion.   New York: Ivan Obolensky, Inc., 1963. Pp. 230-37, et
passim.

This eccentric and generally negative book finds fault with
Thomson's critical writings with respect to accuracy as well as
judgment.   Duke focuses on the shortcomings of Thomson's Modern
Music article on Gershwin. (See T55) in particular. "Thomson's
comments...are shot through with capricious ambiguity of the
cattiest sort."

B127. Edwards, Arthur C. and W. Thomas Marrocco.   Music in the
United States.   Dubuque, IA: Wm. C. Brown, 1968. Pp. 101 and
155.

Thomson's style is described as "more Classic than Romantic,"
and his compositional style is considered "direct, devoid of
extraneous frills and affectations."

B128. Ewen, David.   The World of Twentieth-Century Music.   Englewood
Cliffs, NJ: Prentice-Hall, 1969. Pp. 831-39, et passim. (A
revised and expanded version of the earlier The Complete Book of
Twentieth-Century Music. Englewood Cliffs, NJ: Prentice-Hall,
1959.)

Thomson's life and musical style are discussed ("He has wit and
feeling...charm and sophistication") and the major works are
given superficial analysis. Works:Symphony on a Hymn Tune, Four
Saints in Three Acts, The Suite from "The Plow that Broke the
Plains", Filling Station, The Mother of Us All, Louisiana Story,
Concerto for Cello and Orchestra, Concerto for Flute, Strings,
Harp, and Percussion, Missa Pro Defunctis, A Solemn Music and A
Joyful Fugue. See: W1, W2, W3, W10, W13, W36, W39, W45, W87, &
W320

B129. Geppert, Eunice Claire Peevy. A Comparative Study of the Reviews
of Olin Downes and Virgil Thomson.   M.M. thesis. University of
Texas at Austin, 1950.

Geppert compares and contrasts the music criticisms of Downes and Thomson during two periods of six months each (October 1940-April 1941 and October 1946-April 1947) and finds that although they disagree on a few points, they agree that "the fundamental purpose of the artist is to make beautiful music as simply, artistically, and convincingly as possible" and that a performance should "reveal to...listeners what the composer had in mind." Geppert also surveys briefly the history of music criticism and discusses the main ideas of representative critics from each period.

B130. Gillespie, John. Five Centuries of Keyboard Music. New York: Dover, 1972. Pp. 413-14 and 425.

Gillespie discusses Thomson's style and surveys the solo keyboard works, singling out the Ten Etudes ("they combine technical problems...with highly diverting keyboard writing."), and the last two sonatas as especially worthwhile. See: W181

B131. Goldman, Richard Franko. "Virgil Thomson and Others," in The New Oxford History of Music, Vol. X, The Modern Age, 1890-1960. Edited by Martin Cooper. London: Oxford Univeristy Press, 1974. Pp. 602-05, et passim.

Goldman discusses Thomson's style and contributions to American music. "The deceptive simplicity of his usually diatonic and triadic idiom was as representative of a new spirit in music as the complex constructions of many of his contemporaries." There is a brief analysis of Four Saints in Three Acts, with music examples, an assessment of his role as a music critic, and a conclusion which states that "Thomson is one of the few contemporary artists in any field with a true sense of high comedy." See: W1

B132. Goss, Madeleine. Modern Music-Makers: Contemporary American Composers. New York: E.P. Dutton, 1952; Westport, CT: Greenwood Press, 1970. Pp. 238-47.

A general survey of Thomson's career with an emphasis on Four Saints in Three Acts and its mixed critical reception. His other major works are mentioned in passing, and a Samuel Barber quote closes the section: "[Thomson] possesses the snappiest brain in the [music] confraternity." See: W1

B133. Greer, Thomas H. Music and Its Relationship to Futurism, Cubism, Dadism, and Surrealism, 1905-1950.. Ph.D. dissertation. North Texas State University, 1969. [Order No.: 69-13218]

In his investigation of music as it related to four twentieth-century art and literary movements, Greer explores the dada spirit in the collaboration of Thomson and Gertrude Stein.

B134. Grosser, Maurice. Painter's Progress. New York: Clarkson N. Potter, Inc., 1971. Pp. 24, 31, 68, 85, and 95.

Dedicated to Virgil Thomson, Grosser's book -- part memoir, part theoretical treatise, and part aesthetic speculation -- recalls Harvard and Paris days with his friend and some of the circumstances connected with the first production of Four Saints in Three Acts, for which Grosser realized the scenario. See: W1

B135. Gruen, John. Close-Up. New York: Viking, 1968. Pp. 198-206.

Gruen interviews Thomson on such subjects as taste, his experience on the New York Herald Tribune, Stravinsky, style, imagination, and religion. When asked to describe his character Thomson responds: "I think I had better leave that to other people...I don't want to describe or analyze my character or anything like that."

B136. Haggin, Bernard H. A Decade of Music. New York: Horizon, 1973. Pp. 30-31, 41-53, 70-73, 241-2, et passim.

Haggin here reprints articles from The Hudson Review, The Sewanee Review, and Commonweal in which Thomson's critical writings are frequently quoted and discussed, sometimes in passing, and sometimes, as in "The Imagined World of Virgil Thomson" at length. See: B51

B137. -------. Music in the Nation. New York: William Sloane Associates, Inc., 1949. Pp. 52-54, 71-72, 79-81, and 229235.

Haggin offers reprints of reviews of Thomson's Four Saints in Three Acts, of his music criticism in the New York Herald Tribune, and of his collection The Musical Scene. See: T190 and W1

B138. -------. The New Listener's Companion and Record Guide. Third edition. New York: Horizon Press, 1971. Pp. 177-78, 197-200, et passim.

Haggin discusses Thomson's criticism ("the only newpaper music criticism worth reading") and, briefly, his first two operas. See: W1 & W3

B139. Hansen, Peter S. An Introduction to Twentieth Century Music. Fourth edition. Boston: Allyn and Bacon, 1978. Pp. 288 and 312-13.

Hansen contrasts Thomson's "witty, sophisticated, and highly objective" music with the more serious and personal style of Howard Hanson. Thomson's life is sketched briefly, his important works are mentioned, and his criticism is compared to his music. "Urbanity and sophistication, lack of reverence, and a refusal to be proper and dull" characterize both modes of expression. Pp. 312-13 are reprinted in The New Music Lover's Handbook. Edited by Elie Siegmeister. New York: Harvey House, 1973. Pp. 525-27. See: W165

B140. Hipsher, Edward Ellsworth. American Opera and Its Composers, 1871-1948. New York: Presser, 1934; Da Capo Press, 1978.

Pp.407-11.

A report on the premiere production of Four Saints in Three Acts. Emphasis is placed on the unusual libretto and unconventional sets, costumes, and cast, but a few words are left for Thomson's score: "He [Thomson] excruciatingly parodies everything, from recitative and aria to ensemble, from the Handel chorus to Gilbert and Sullivan...There are take-offs of a Spanish serenade...the coloratura feats of two sopranos while the chorus gathers agape at their prowess, and other similar musical witticisms." See: W1

B141. Hitchcock, H. Wiley. Music in the United States: A Historical Introduction. Englewood Cliffs, NJ: Prentice-Hall, 1969; rev. ed. 1984. Pp. 201-5, et passim.

Hitchcock places Thomson in historical perspective and summarizes his contributions, offering keen critical comments on Four Saints in Three Acts. Music examples are given. See: W1, W10, W162, W165, W316, W317, & W319

B142. Hoover, Kathleen and John Cage. Virgil Thomson: His Life and Music. New York: Thomas Yoseloff, 1959. Rpt. Freeport, NY: Books for Libraries Press, 1970.

The only life-and-works study to date, this volume consists of a biographical section by Hoover and an analytical section by Cage. A chronological list of works is appended. Also published in French (Virgil Thomson: sa vie, sa musique. Paris: Buchet-Chastel).

Reviews: ARG 7-59, pp769-71; Booklist 5-1-59, p475; HF 10-59, p41; LJ 5-1-59, p1516;London Times Literary Supplement 9-25-59, p546; Musical Opinion 12-59, p171; MT 1-60, pp25+; NYHT Book Review 4-26-59, p6; Notes 12-5-59, p47+; ON 12-5-59, p24; SR 5-30-59, p54. NYRB 4-23-70, p9+ (See T15)

B143. Houseman, John. Final Dress. New York: Simon & Schuster, 1983. Pp. 463-71, et passim.

As a close friend of Houseman's, Thomson crops up throughout this memoir. Houseman discusses his direction of the premiere production of Lord Byron, and Thomson's and his earlier collaboration on music for King John, Othello, Hamlet, and Measure for Measure. See: W6, W331, W340, W341, & W342

B144. -------. Front and Center. New York: Simon & Schuster, 1979. Pp. 108-10, et passim.

Of special interest are Houseman's comments on his work with Thomson on the film "Tuesday in November" and his account of a two-week drive across the country with Thomson in the summer of 1943. See: W319

B145. -------. Run-through: a Memoir. New York: Simon & Schuster,

1972. Pp. 99-127, et passim.

Houseman gives a detailed, behind the scenes account of the historic premiere production of Four Saints in Three Acts. "I soon discovered that what Virgil needed was not just someone to stage his opera, but some sort of director-producer-impressario who would combine, coordinate, and regulate the various artistic elements he had already selected. I accepted the assignment without diffidence and without question." Many other works are also mentioned. See: T157 and W1

B146. Howard, John Tasker.   Our American Music: 300 Years of It. New York: Crowell, 1965.   Fourth edition. Pp. 432-34, et passim. Similar material in A Short History of Music in America by J.T. Howard and George Kent Bellows. New York: Crowell, 1967. Pp. 295-98, et passim.

Howard describes Thomson's French influences, association with Gertrude Stein, and early success of Four Saints in Three Acts. He briefly discusses the Symphony on a Hymn Tune, the Cello Concerto, Five Songs After William Blake, and The Mother of Us All, and Thomson's music criticism ("widely read" because "informed and direct.") See: W1, W3, W10, W36, & W130

B147. Howard, John Tasker and Arthur Mendel.   Our Contemporary Compos-ers: American Music in the Twentieth Century. New York: Crowell, 1941. Rpt. Freeport, CT: Books for Libraries Press, 1975. Pp. 237-66, et passim.

In a chapter on "Experimenters," Thomson is said to be "as unexpected as anyone else." Much of the focus is on Four Saints in Three Acts. See: W1

B148. Howard, John Tasker and James Lyons. Modern Music. New York: Thomas Y. Crowell, 1957. Revised edition. Pp. 128-30, et passim.

A survey of Thomson's career and musical style. "While he shuns the towering and lofty flights of the German romanticists, he never hesitates to become sentimental, even though he may at times have his tongue in his cheek." Copland's appraisal of Four Saints in Three Acts is quoted. See: W1

B149. Jackson, Richard. The Operas of Gertrude Stein and Virgil Thom-son: A Binomial Study. M.A. thesis. Tulane University, 1962.

After a sketch of the historical setting in which Stein and Thomson worked and met, Jackson discusses Stein's aesthetic principles and artistic intentions with respect to the theater. "It is the sychronization of emotional tempo between stage and audience that Gertrude Stein attempted to establish in her plays and operas." Jackson goes on to analyze Thomson's early musical style and describe his preparation for the collaboration with Stein. Subsequent chapters discuss the operas themselves in an admirably thorough way. See: W1 & W3

B150. Jeffers, Grant Lyle. Non-Narrative Music Drama: Settings by Virgil Thomson, Ned Rorem, and Earl Kim of Plays by Gertrude Stein
and Samuel Beckett; and "What Happened," an Original Chamber
Opera Based on a Play by Gertrude Stein. 2 vols. Ph.D.
dissertation. University of California at Los Angeles, 1983.
[Order No.: AAD83-21922]

Approximately one-third of the first volume analyzes Four Saints
in Three Acts focusing on the relationship between Stein's
dramatic language and Thomson's musical structure. See: W1.

B151. Kendall, Alan. The Tender Tyrant, Nadia Boulanger. London: Mac-
Donald and Jane, 1976. Passim.
As a student of Boulanger, Thomson's name appears frequently
throughout this volume on the life and work of the great teacher
whom Thomson called "a one-woman musical U.N."

B152. Kingman, Daniel. American Music: A Panorama. Foreword by Virgil
Thomson. New York: Schirmer Books, 1979. Pp. 389-94, 411-12,
433, et passim.

Kingman summarizes Thomson's life and works, briefly analyzing
The Plow That Broke the Plains, The Mother of Us All, and the
String Quartet No. 2. Music examples are included. See: W3,
W176, & W316

B153. Kolodin, Irving. The Metropolitan Opera, 1883-1966. Fourth edition. New York: Alfred A. Knopf, 1966. Passim.

In this "Candid History" of the Met, Thomson's views as published in the New York Herald Tribune on such subjects as the Met
management and various new performances are briefly quoted.
("An opera house cannot wait til it gets rich to give modern
works.")

B154. Krenek, Ernst. Musik in goldenen Westen. Vienna: Hollinek, 1949.
P. 16.

Basically unsympathetic to Thomson's musical style and aesthetic
goals, Krenek looks closely at Four Saints in Three Acts, which
he finds resembles "primitive church music" and "hackneyed
Italian opera." Krenek grudgingly admits that the work has "an
undeniable if not easily explainable charm." See: W1

B155. Lederman, Minna. The Life and Death of a Small Magazine ("Modern
Music," 1924-1946). New York: Institute for Studies in American
Music, 1983. Passim.

Thomson figures prominently in this memoir by the editor of
Modern Music. Portions of several articles are reprinted (See
T1, T95, T102, & T159), several letters are quoted, and his
mentor-like role is described. Lederman writes that "there was
a marked sensitivity to the quality of writing which I attrib-
uted to his [Thomson's] example."

B156. Longstreet, Stephen. We All Went to Paris. New York: Macmillan, 1972. Pp. 377-84.

In a chapter on the musical American expatriate community in Paris in the 1920's, Thomson's relationship with Gertrude Stein and his collaboration with her on Four Saints in Three Acts are discussed. "In terms of just plain good feeling France was in those days, even for the poor, the richest life an artist ever knew." See: W1

B157. Machlis, Joseph. American Composers of Our Time. New York: Thomas Y. Crowell, 1963. Pp. 76-86.

A chapter on Thomson offers a good general summary of the life, training, and career of this "American romantic." Three reasons are given for Thomson's success as a music critic: "He complimented his readers by never writing down to them...He approached his task with enormous gusto...He brought into his writing the spirit of a brilliant performance." Many of his major compositions are mentioned but only Four Saints in Three Acts, The Mother of Us All, and his film score for "Louisiana Story" receive more than a passing remark. See: W1, W3, & W320

B158. -------. Introduction to Contemporary Music. Second edition. New York: W.W. Norton, 1979. Pp. 411-14, et passim.

Machlis surveys Thomson's life, influences, and major works, especially the film scores which "set a new standard for film music." Thomson is either mentioned or quoted frequently throughout the book. See: W1, W3, & W320

B159. Meckna, Michael. The Rise of the American Composer-Critic: Aaron Copland, Roger Sessions, Virgil Thomson, and Elliott Carter in the Periodical "Modern Music," 1924-1946. Ph.D. dissertation. University of California at Santa Barbara, 1984. [Order No.: DA8428624]

This study examines music criticism by the four composer-critics in the periodical Modern Music. It assesses their approach, methods, and degree of success. Observing that they differed widely in background, training, and artistic aims, the author notes that the four complemented and balanced each other, and discusses how they attracted almost eighty American composers to the pages of the journal, thus establishing the composer-critic as a vital part of American musical life. See: T1

B160. Mellers, Wilfrid. Music in a New Found Land. Second edition. New York: Hillstone, 1975. Pp. 206-220, and 448.

Thomson's musical style and background are discussed ("There is an American insouciance and cheek in Thomson's bizaare juxtapositions") and several works are briefly analyzed. "Thomson's vision...is too direct, and therefore disturbing, to make him a widely popular composer." See: T126 and W1, W3, W10, W87,

W109, W130, W162, W165, W316, W317, & W320

B161. Nathan, Hans. "The United States of America" in A History of Song. Edited by Denis Stevens. Revised edition. New York: W.W. Norton, 1970. Pp. 441-43.

Nathan cites Thomson's settings of "Preciosilla" (Stein), "The Little Black Boy" (Blake), and "Follow Your Saint" (Campion) to illustrate Thomson's vocal style. "He aims at an appearance of disarming simplicity, freely resorting to the well known, the well worn and the outright trivial." See: W110, W129, & W130

B162. Norman, Gertrude and Miriam Lubell Schrifte, editors. Letters of Composers: 1603-1941. New York: Knopf, 1941. Pp. 379-81.

This collection contains Thomson's letter from Paris on March 20, 1939 to Aaron Copland. He mentions The Second Hurricane, "a very rich work," and What to Listen for in Music, "a bore." He also asks about the Arrow Music Press ("What the hell has happened to our music-printing business?"), the American Composers' Alliance, and refers to his own book, The State of Music (See T193) in progress.

B163. O'Connell, Charles. The Other Side of the Record. New York: Knopf, 1948. Pp. 77-78.

In this memoir a former musical director of RCA Victor recalls how the acerbic New York critics (even "the feline Virgil Thomson") were eventually won over by Eugene Ormandy. Although Ormandy invited Thomson to conduct the Philadelphia Orchestra, the former knew the latter was "not a man to be suborned with bribery."

B164. Porter, Andrew. A Musical Season. New York: The Viking Press, 1974. Pp. 91-92, 176-79, 279.

Porter offers succinct reviews, which originally appeared in the New Yorker, of productions of Four Saints in Three Acts (at the Forum, winter, 1973; settings "so sensitively precise that once heard, they sing again in the mind at a mere reading of the text."), The Mother of Us All (in the auditorium of the Guggenheim Museum, December, 1973; "Mother is a kind of masterpiece."), and Thomson's "brilliant, acute and salutary" address on music criticism (Manhattan School of Music; May, 1973; "well worth hearing; he remains the master of us all.") See: W1 & W3

B165. Prindl, Frank Joseph. A Study of Ten Original Compositions for Band Published in America since 1946. Ed.D. dissertation. Florida State University, 1956. [Order No.: 00-17029]

Prindl's dissertation discusses Thomson's A Solemn Music as well as works by eight other composers, to show how, for a variety of reasons, contemporary composers have turned to the concert band as an appropriate medium of expression. See: W34

B166. Reis, Claire R. Composers, Conductors, and Critics. New York:
Oxford University Press, 1955. Passim.

Thomson's name appears in chapters dealing with music criticism,
the League of Composers, and the League's work with the American
Lyric Theatre in 1939 to produce Thomson's ballet Filling
Station. See: W2

B167. Rickert, Lawrence G. Selected American Song Cycles for Baritone
Composed Since 1945. D.M.A. dissertation. University of
Illinois, 1965. [Order No.: 66-4275]

Rickert presents a detailed examination of Thomson's Five Songs
of William Blake, in which the composer is "eclectic in his
choice of a variety of suitable musical styles," and unity "is
achieved by the use of similar accompaniments in different
songs." See: W130

B168. Rogers, Harold Emery. An Analysis of Six American Operas. M.A.
thesis. University of Denver, 1962.

Rogers discussses The Mother of Us All, in addition to
Menotti's The Medium, Weill's Down in the Valley, Copland's The
Tender Land, Floyd's Susanna, and Barber's Vanessa. See: W3

B169. Rorem, Ned. Critical Affairs: A Composer's Journal. New York:
George Braziller, 1970. Passim. Also: Music and People. New
York: George Braziller, 1968.

Rorem left the Curtis Institute in 1944 to "seek Manhattan
fortune as Virgil Thomson's copyist," and his subsequent
writings, especially the two cited here make frequent though
brief reference to his first employer.

B170. Rosenfeld, Paul. An Hour With American Music. Philadelphia: J.B.
Lippincott, 1929. Rpt. Westport, CT: Hyperion Press, 1979. Pp.
96-99.

This early assessment of Thomson's music points out an affinity
with Satie yet also "an individual cast." Rosenfeld discusses
several early works and finds them "musically effective" with a
winning "simplicity of line and purity of expression."

B171. -------. Discoveries of a Music Critic. New York: Harcourt,
Brace, 1936. Pp. 297-302.

A reprint of Rosenfeld's 1934 review of Four Saints in Three
Acts. Also reviewed is a 1932 Yaddo Festival performance by Ada
MacLeish of Thomson's Stabat Mater, "neoclassic in politics,
Catholic in ideology, royalist in style, and most effective
theater." See: W1 & W121

B172. Sahr, Hadassah Gallup. Performance and Analytic Study of
Selected Piano Music by American Composers. Ed.D. dissertation.
Columbia University, 1969. [Order No.: 70-4586]

Sahr analyzes structural and interpretive elements in the piano etudes and observes that they "represent the simplicity of style which is recognized as one of Thomson's most significant contributions to American music." See: W181 & W188

B173. Salzman, Eric. <u>Twentieth-Century Music: An Introduction</u>. Second edition. New York: Prentice-Hall, 1947. Pp. 66, 87, and 101-02.

Salzman mentions Thomson briefly, focusing on the text-music relationship with Stein collaborations, which he feels resulted in "a kind of popular surrealism" as well as "an anticipation of minimalism."

B174. Saminsky, Lazare. <u>Living Music of the Americas</u>. New York: Howell, Soskin and Crown, 1949. Pp. 61-65.

In Saminsky's colorful writing style Thomson is dubbed "a storm center. His is a mind off the worn highways with, perhaps, too much mental champagne in it...Of a more manifold and more gifted musical mind, Thomson could not long remain in the Satie parish. He veered from his first viewpoint and from his own creative line as well...He is no Narcissus forever enchanted by his own talk; he falls in with the Emersonian mark of a civilized man -- the ability to change his mind." Thomson's influence is called "a good one. Depontification, dismantling of everything stilted...this is valuable work."

B175. Service, Alfred R., Jr. <u>A Study of the Cadence as a Factor in Musical Intelligibility in Selected Piano Sonatas by American Composers</u>. Ph.D. dissertation. State University of Iowa, 1958. [Order No.: 58-5859]

Service discusses Thomson's piano sonatas, along with those of sixteen other native Americans in order to discover solutions to the general problem of musical intelligibility. See: W169, W170, W173, & W244

B176. Slonimsky, Nicolas. "Chamber Music in America" in <u>Cobbett's Cyclopedic Survey of Chamber Music</u>. Second edition. Edited by Walter W. Cobbett. London: Oxford University Press, 1963. Vol. III, pp. 165-66.

Surveys Thomson's chamber music, in which "modernism finds its expression in a unique genre of sophisticated simplicity and stylistic paradox," focusing on the two string quartets, the <u>Stabat Mater</u>, and especially the <u>Sonata da Chiesa</u>. See: W121, W162, W174, & W176

B177. -------. <u>Music Since 1900</u>. Fourth edition. New York: Charles Scribner's Sons, 1971. <u>Passim</u>.

Slonimsky quotes Thomson on Roy Harris's <u>Third Symphony</u> ("It is earnest, clumsy, pretentious, imaginative, and terribly sincere"), discusses his tepid attraction to Schoenberg's dodecaphonic method, and notes premier dates, frequently with capsulized but pungent critical comments, of the Cello Concerto, Fanfare for France, The Feast of Love, Filling Station, Four Saints in Three Acts, The Suite from "Lousiana Story", The Mayor LaGuardia Waltzes, Missa pro defunctis, The Mother of Us All, Sea Piece with Birds, The Seine at Night, Concerto for Flute, Strings, Harp and Percussion, Symphony on a Hymn Tune, Second Symphony, and Wheatfield at Noon. See: W1, W2, W3, W10, W12, W17, W22, W29, W30, W32, W36, W38, W39, W87, & W148.

B178. Smith, Cecil Michener. Worlds of Music. New York: Lippincott, 1942. Pp. 79-83, et passim.

Thomson's views on the Community and Civic Concert Series, which were originally aired in his Sunday Herald Tribune column in 1951, are analyzed. The major issue was program selection and whether or not Thomson is correct in his assertions that the "recitalists whose careers are taken over by management chains find their programs censored...and local organizers of concerts...find that they have virtually no choice about programs."

B179. Stein, Gertrude. The Autobiography of Alice B. Toklas. New York: Harcourt Brace, 1933. Pp. 257, 277-81, and 283.

Stein's personal narrative mentions Thomson as one of the many prominent creative people attracted to her Parisian salon. Although Miss Toklas was slow to like Thomson, he and Miss Stein became friends and eventually collaborators, she admiring his sense of prosody as well as his taste in art.

B180. Sternfeld, Frederick. Music in the Modern Age. London: Weidenfeld and Nicolson, 1973. Pp. 378-9.

"Thomson's remarkable ear for the inflections of words makes him an excellent composer of songs, sometimes simple to the point of audacity." Sternfeld discusses Five Songs from William Blake and other works. Musical examples are included. See: W130

B181. Tawa, Nicholas E. Serenading the Reluctant Eagle: American Musical Life, 1925-1945. New York: Schirmer Books, 1984. Pp. 197-201, et passim.

Tawa discusses Thomson's life and works. "He is preeminent in his ability to capture a solitary atmosphere or emotional feeling through the simplest of means." There are brief analytical discussions of the Symphony on a Hymn Tune, Four Saints in Three Acts, Filling Station, and The Plow that Broke the Plains. See: W1, W2, W10, & W316

B182. Teasley, Elizabeth Kincaid. An Analysis and Comparison of the Critical Works of Virgil Thomson and Olin Downes. M.A. thesis. North Texas State University, 1947.

This brief (43 pages) but worthy thesis opens with a chapter on the purposes of criticism in general, then focuses on the work of Thomson and Olin Downes during the years 1940-45. Using criteria set up by W.H. Hadow, M.D. Calvocoressi, and T.M. Greene, the author favors Thomson's writing "because he brings more issues to light" but feels that both writers "have made fundamental and distinctive contributions to the maintenance of high standards of music."

B183. Tommasini, Anthony Carl. The Portraits for Piano by Virgil Thomson. D.M.A. dissertation. Boston University, 1982. [Order No.: AAD82-20903]

Tommasini describes Thomson's intent and method, presents an overview of all the portraits (115 at the time of writing), focuses on those for piano (the majority), analyzes four, and appends a thematic catalogue. Thomson's taped remarks are quoted extensively throughout. (Note: Dr. Tommasini has revised, updated, and expanded his dissertation for publication by Pendragon Press. See B182. An essay adapted from his book appears in the Spring, 1984 issue of The Musical Quarterly. See B101.) See: W209 through W315

B184. -------. Virgil Thomson's Musical Portraits. New York: Pendragon Press, 1985.

A revision and expansion of the author's DMA dissertation (See W183), Tommasini's book discusses musical portraiture in general, describes Gertrude Stein's abstract word portraits and their influence on Thomson, details Thomson's compositional procedure, surveys the entire body of portraits (140 at his writing), focuses closely on four portraits, and offers a comprehensive thematic catalogue. Tommasini presents biographical information about, comments from, and photographs of the subjects themselves. (Note: some of the material was adapted for an article in MQ, Spring, 1984; See B101) See: W209 through W315

B185. Upton, William Treat. Art Song in America. New York: Oliver Ditson, 1930. With a supplement, 1930-1938. Pp. 27-28 and 39.

In the supplement to a history of art song, Thomson's Stabat Mater is discussed ("the part writing is excellent throughout...the viola perhaps...most eloquent of them all"), and Thomson's views on prosody and song composing are quoted ("The English and Americans have never attacked the problem seriously.") See: W121

B186. Van Alen, Janice Kay. Stylistic and Interpretative Analysis and Performance of Selected Choral Compositions for Women's Voices by three American Composers: Vincent Persichetti, Virgil Thomson, and Daniel Pinkham. Ed.D. dissertation. Columbia University Teachers College, 1973. [Order No.: 74-9653]

Van Alen surveys Thomson's choral music for women, looking closely at his Mass and Seven Choruses from the "Medea" of Euripides, which illustrate the composer's "unique and uncomplicated use of percussion to aid the singers...and also to highlight the dramatic qualities of the texts." See W73 & W74

B187. Vinton, John. <u>Essays After a Dictionary: Music and Culture at the Close of Western Civilization</u>. Lewisburg, PA: Bucknell University Press, 1977. Pp. 29-77.

In order to show how Thomson honed his music criticism skill for daily use in the <u>New York Herald Tribune</u>, Vinton reprints fourteen of Thomson's early reviews paired with responses by Thomson's mentor, Geoffrey Parsons, who wrote "Sometimes I almost despair of your ever becoming a newspaper writer" on May 2, 1941.

B188. Ward, Kelly Mac. <u>An Analysis of the Relationship Between Text and Musical Shape, an Investigation of the Relationship Between Text and Surface Rhythmic Details in "Four Saints in Three Acts" by Virgil Thomson</u>. Ph.D. dissertation. The University of Texas at Austin, 1978. [Order No.: AAD79-00649]

Ward's dissertation shows that a "musical opulence" lies under the "placid surface" of <u>Four Saints in Three Acts</u>, and he discusses text-music relationship in it. See: W1.

B189. Wickes, George. <u>Americans in Paris</u>. New York: Doubleday and Co., Inc., 1969. Rpt. New York: Da Capo Press, 1980. Pp. 213-33.

"I regard Paris as my home town," wrote Thomson once. This chapter outlines his work there, especially his relationship with Gertrude Stein, and their collaboration on <u>Four Saints in Three Acts</u>. See: T85 and W1

B190. Yates, Peter. <u>Twentieth Century Music</u>. New York: Pantheon Books, 1967. Pp. 104-08, <u>et passim</u>.

In a chapter entitled "Stein-Thomson," the collaboration of the two artists and the atmosphere around the American expatriots of the 1920's are examined. <u>The Mother of Us All</u> is praised as "the most satisfactory -- and the most beautiful American opera." <u>Four Saints in Three Acts</u> is also reviewed. The influence of Satie on Thomson is also discussed. See: W1, W3, & W87

B191. Zinsser, William. <u>On Writing Well</u>. New York: Harper and Row, 1985. Third edition. Pp. 176-79, <u>et passim</u>.

Several of Thomson's critical writings are quoted as examples of how "a good critic can make sense of what happened by writing good English and by using references that mere mortals can understand."

B192. Zuck, Barbara A. <u>A History of Musical Americanism</u>. Ann Arbor, MI: UMI Research Press, 1980. Pp. 147-49, 262-64, <u>et passim</u>.

Zuck refers to the work and influence of Thomson, focusing in

particular on the expression of musical Americanism in <u>Filling</u>
<u>Station</u>, <u>Four Saints in Three Acts</u> ("melodies rooted in Anglo-
American hymnody"), <u>The Plow That Broke the Plains</u> ("the first
large work by a major American composer to incorporate cowboy
songs"), <u>The River</u>, and <u>Symphony on a Hymn Tune</u> ("the earliest
major work [to treat] hymn and folk materials"). See: W1, W2,
W10, W316, & W317

Dictionary, Encyclopedia, and Index Citations

B193. <u>The ASCAP Biographical Dictionary</u>. Fourth edition. Compiled for
the American Society of Composers, Authors and Publishers by
Jacques Cattell Press. New York: R.R. Bowker Co., 1980. P. 505.

B194. <u>American Society of Composers, Authors and Publishers Symphonic</u>
<u>Catalogue</u>. Third edition. New York: R.R. Bowker Co., 1977. P.
461.

B195. Ammer, Christine. <u>Harper's Dictionary of Music</u>. New York: Harper
& Row, 1972. P. 372.

B196. Anderson, E. Ruth. <u>Contemporary American Composers: A Biographical</u>
<u>Dictionary</u>. Second edition. Boston: G.K. Hall, 1982. P. 518.

B197. <u>BMI Orchestral Program Survey, 1967-68 Season</u>. New York: Broadcast
Music, Inc., 1968.

B198. <u>Baker's Biographical Dictionary of Musicians</u>. Seventh edition.
Completely revised by Nicolas Slonimsky. New York: Schirmer
Books, 1984. Pp. 2306-07.

B199. Basart, Ann Phillips. <u>Serial Music: A Classified Bibliography of</u>
<u>Writings on Twelve-Tone and Electronic Music</u>. Berkeley: Univer-
sity of California Press, 1961. Pp. 3 and 11.

B200. <u>Bio-Bibliographical Index of Musicians In the United States of</u>
<u>American From Colonial Times</u>. Second edition. Washington, DC:
Music Section, Pan-American Union, 1956. P. 375.

Lists ten writings by or about Thomson. N.B.: Sources listed in
this publication will also be found in the present volume.

B201. Blom, Eric. <u>Everyman's Dictionary of Music</u>. Revised by Sir Jack
Westrup. New York: St. Martin's Press, 1971. P. 698.

B202. Bloom, Julius, editor. <u>The Year in American Music: September</u>
<u>1946-May 1947</u>. New York: Allen, Towne, and Heath, 1947. <u>Passim</u>.

B203. Broder, Nathan. "Virgil Thomson" in <u>Die Musik in Geschichte und</u>
<u>Gegenwart</u>. 16 vols. Edited by Friedrich Blume. Kassel und
Basel: Bärenreiter-Verlag, 1949-79. Vol. XIII (1960), cols.
371-72.

B204. Bull, Storm. <u>Index to Biographies of Contemporary Composers</u>. New

York: Scarecrow Press, 1964. Vol. I, p. 367. Vol. II (1974),
p. 504.

B205. Butterworth, Neil. A Dictionary of American Composers. New York:
Garland Publishing Co., 1983. Pp. 468-72.

B206. "Chronological Catalogue of the Works of the American Composer
Virgil Thomson" in Music y Artes 74-76 (April-June 1956): 38-57.

B207. Claghorn, Charles Eugene. Biographical Dictionary of American
Music. West Nyack, NY: Parker Publishing Co., 1973. P. 437.

B208. Cohn, Arthur. The Collector's Twentieth-Century Music in the
Western Hemisphere. New York: J.B. Lippincott, 1961. Rpt. New
York: Da Capo Press, 1972. Pp. 204-212.

Introduces, lists, and briefly criticizes 15 recordings. See:
D1, D2, D6, D9, D18, D21, D35, D36, D39, D45, D52, D58, D63,
D67, & D77

B209. -------. Recorded Classical Music. New York: Schirmer Books,
1981. Pp. 1913-17.

Lists and briefly criticizes 16 of Thomson's recordings, only
two of which are mentioned in Cohn's previous volume. (See
B206) See: D3, D8, D13, D29, D34, D41, D45, D48, D52, D53, D54,
D57, D64, D65, D72, & D77

B210. Composers of the Americas (Compositores de América), 18 Vols.
Washington, DC: Pan American Union, 1955-. Vol. III (1957), pp.
96-119.

B211. Cooper, Martin, editor. The Concise Encyclopedia of Music and
Musicians. London: Hutchinson, 1971. P. 441.

B212. Current Biography. New York: H.W. Wilson, 1940. Pp. 802-03; and
1966, pp. 405-08.

B213. Dictionnarie de la Musique. 2 vols. Edited by Marc Honegger.
Paris: Bordes, 1970.

B214. Eagon, Angelo, editor. Catalog of Published Concert Music by
American Composers. Second edition. Metuchen, NJ: Scarecrow
Press, 1969. See also supplements in 1971 and 1974.

B215. Edmunds, John and Gordon Boelzner, editors. Some Twentieth Century American Composers: A Selective Bibliography. 2 vols. Introduction by Peter Yates.   New York: The New York Public Library, 1959. Vol. I, pp. 52-53, et passim; Vol. II, p. 24.

B216. Enciclopedia della Musica. 4 vols. Edited by Claudio Sartori.
Milan: G. Ricordi, 1963-64.

B217. Entziklopedichesky Muzĺkalnĺi Slovar [Encyclopedic Dictionary of
Musicians]. Edited by B.S. Sheinpress and I.M. Yampolsky. Mos-

cow: Izdatelstvo "Sovetskaya Entziklopediya," 1966.   See entry
under Tómcoh.

B218. Ewen, David. <u>American</u> <u>Composers</u>: <u>A</u> <u>Biographical</u> <u>Dictionary</u>. New
York: G.P. Putnam's Sons, 1982. Pp. 663-68.

B219. --------. <u>Composers</u> <u>Since</u> <u>1900</u>: <u>A</u> <u>Biographical</u> <u>and</u> <u>Critical</u> <u>Guide</u>.
New York: H.W. Wilson, 1969. Pp. 585-89. Also First Supple-
ment, 1981. Pp. 300-02.

B220. --------. <u>Encyclopedia</u> <u>of</u> <u>Concert</u> <u>Music</u>. New York: Hill and Wang,
1959. Pp. 514-15, <u>et</u> <u>passim</u>.

B221. --------. <u>The</u> <u>New</u> <u>Encyclopedia</u> <u>of</u> <u>the</u> <u>Opera</u>. New York: Hill and
Wang, 1971. Pp. 247-48, 459-60, and 689-90.

B222. --------.   <u>The</u> <u>Year</u> <u>in</u> <u>American</u> <u>Music</u> <u>(June</u> <u>1947-May</u> <u>1948</u> <u>inclu-</u>
<u>sive)</u>. New York: Allen, Towne, & Heath, 1948. <u>Passim</u>.

B223. Flanagan, William and John Gruen, "Virgil Thomson," in <u>The</u> <u>Inter-</u>
<u>national</u> <u>Cyclopedia</u> <u>of</u> <u>Music</u> <u>and</u> <u>Musicians</u>. Edited by Oscar
Thompson. Tenth edition edited by Bruce Bohle. New York: Dodd,
Mead, 1975. Pp. 2272-76.

B224. Gleason, Harold and Warren Becker. <u>Twentieth</u> <u>Century</u> <u>American</u>
<u>Composers</u>. Second edition. Bloomington, IN: Frangipani Press,
1980. Pp. 203-21.

B225. Griffiths, Paul. "Virgil Thomson," in <u>The</u> <u>New</u> <u>Oxford</u> <u>Companion</u> <u>to</u>
<u>Music</u>. Edited by Denis Arnold. 2 vols. Oxford: Oxford Univer-
sity Press, 1983. Vol. 2, p. 1819.

B226. <u>International</u> <u>Who's</u> <u>Who</u> <u>in</u> <u>Music</u> <u>and</u> <u>Musicians</u> <u>Directory.</u>   Tenth
edition. Cambridge: Melrose Press, 1984. P. 898.

B227. Jablonski, Edward. <u>The</u> <u>Encyclopedia</u> <u>of</u> <u>American</u> <u>Music</u>.   Garden
City, NY: Doubleday & Co., 1981. Pp. 300-01, <u>et</u> <u>passim</u>.

B228. Jacobs, Arthur. <u>A</u> <u>New</u> <u>Dictionary</u> <u>of</u> <u>Music</u>.   Third edition.
Harmondsworth, England: Penguin Books, 1973. P. 384.

B229. Jackson, Richard.   "Virgil Thomson," <u>The</u> <u>New</u> <u>Grove</u> <u>Dictionary</u> <u>of</u>
<u>Music</u> <u>and</u> <u>Musicians</u>.   20 vols.   Edited by Stanley Sadie. Lon-
don: Macmillan, 1980. Vol. XVIII, pp. 786-89.

Jackson succinctly surveys his subject's life and discusses his
basic style in this most complete and analytical of the many
dictionary-encyclopedia articles on Thomson. Attention is drawn
to the great variety of Thomson's work, his early use of
Gregorian chant and modal polyphony, his preoccupation with
Baptist hymns and 19th-century popular, his wit and playfulness,
and his meticulous prosody.   (Jackson has revised and expanded
his article for <u>The</u> <u>New</u> <u>Grove</u> <u>Dictionary</u> <u>of</u> <u>Music</u> <u>in</u> <u>America</u>,
forthcoming late in 1986.) See: T117 and W6, W10, W29, W32, W34,
W36, W38, W87, W121, W181, W320 & W321

B230. -------. United States Music: Sources of Bibliography. New
York: Institute for Studies in American Music, 1973. Revised
1976. Pp. 3 and 61-65.

B231. Johnson, H. Earle. Operas On America Subjects. New York: Coleman-
Ross, 1964. P. 95.

B232. Karp, Theodore. Dictionary of Music. New York: Galahad Books,
1973. P. 394.

B233. Katalog der Abteilung Noten. Darmstadt: Das Institut, 1966.
(Supplement 1967).

B234. Keats, Sheila. "American Music on LP Records: an Index," Juilliard Review 2 (Spring 1955): 42-43.

B235. -------. "Reference Articles on American Composers,"
Juilliard Review 1 (Fall, 1954): 34.

B236. Kennedy, Michael. The Concise Oxford Dictionary of Music. Based
on the original publication by Percy Scholes. London: Oxford
University Press, 1980. P. 656.

B237. Kinscella, Hazel G. "Americana Index to The Musical Quarterly,
1915-1957" Journal of Research in Music Education 6 (Fall,
1958): 132-33.

B238. Krummel, D.W., Jean Geil, Doris J. Dyer, and Deane L. Root.
Resources of American Music History. Urbana, IL: University of
Illinois Press, 1981. Passim.

This volume lists the archival sources for Thomson's
manuscripts, publications, correspondence, and personal papers.
For complete information, see the "Archives" appendix to this
book, which lists separate entries numbered A1 through A23.

B239. Loewenberg, Alfred. Annals of Opera, 1597-1940. Third edition.
Totowa, NJ: Rowman. Col. 1426.

B240. Malá Encykolopédia Hudby. Compiled by Marián Jurick. Edited by
Ladislav Mokry. Bratislava, Czech.: Obzor, 1969.

B241. Michel, François, editor. Encyclopédie de la Musique. 3 vols.
Paris: Fasquelle éditeurs, 1958-61.

B242. La Musica. 2 vols. Edited by Guido M. Gatti. Turin: Unione
Tipografico-Editrice Torinese, 1968-71.

B243. Musikkens Hvem Hvad Hvor. 3 vols. Edited by Nelly Backhausen and
Axel Kjerulf. Copenhagen: Politikens Forlag, 1950. Revised
edition 1961.

B244. Oja, Carol J. American Music Recordings: A Discography of 20th-
Century U.S. Composers. New York: Institute for Studies in
American Music, 1982. Pp. 295-98.

The entries in this volume are included and expanded in the "Discography" chapter of the present book.

B245. Osborne, Charles E., editor. Dictionary of Composers. New York: Taplinger, 1978. Pp. 348-49.

B246. Pavlakis, Christopher. The American Music Handbook. New York: The Free Press, 1974. Passim.

B247. Randel, Don Michael. Harvard Concise Dictionary of Music. Cambridge, MA: Harvard University Press, 1978. P. 507.

B248. Reis, Claire R. Composers in America. New York: Macmillan, 1947. Rpt. NY: Da Capo Press, 1977. Pp. 358-60.

B249. Rosenthal, Harold, and John Warrack. The Concise Oxford Dictionary of Opera. Second edition. London: Oxford University Press, 1979. Pp. 176, 337, and 498-99.

B250. Rowland-Entwistle, Theodore and Jean Cooke. Famous Composers. London: David & Charles, n.d. Pp. 115-16.

B251. Sandved, Kjell, editor. The World of Music: An Illustrated Encyclopedia. 4 vols. New York: Abradale Press, 1963. Vol. 3, pp. 1378-79.

B252. Shirley, Wayne D. Modern Music, Published by the League of Composers, 1924-1946: An Analytic Index. Edited by William and Carolyn Lichtenwanger. New York: AMS Press, 1976. Pp. 222-24. See B157.

Anything in the journal Modern Music pertaining to Thomson is also cited where appropriate in the present volume.

B253. Skowronski, JoAnn. Aaron Copland: A Bio-Bibliography. Westport, CT: Greenwood Press, 1985. P. 222, et passim.

B254. Twentieth Century Authors. New York: Wilson, 1942. First supplement, 1955.

B255. Vinton, John, editor. Dictionary of Contemporary Music. New York: E.P. Dutton, 1974. Pp. 761-2.

B256. Watson, Jack M. and Corinne. A Concise Dictionary of Music. New York: Dodd, Mead & Co., 1965. Pp. 297-98.

B257. Westrup, Jack and Frank Lloyd Harrison, editors. The New College Encyclopedia of Music. Revised by Conrad Wilson. New York: W.W. Norton, 1976. P. 547.

B258. Who's Who in America. 43rd edition. 1984-85. 2 vols. Chicago: Marquis Who's Who, Inc., 1984. Vol. II, pp. 3258-59.

B259. Weir, Albert, editor. Macmillan Encyclopedia of Music and Musicians. New York: Macmillan, 1938. P. 1859.

B?60. Young, Percy M. __A Critical Dictionary of Composers and Their Music__. London: Dennis Dobson, 1954. P. 337. See: W1, W2, & W10

Unannotated Brief References: Books

B261. Alcaraz, José A. __Hablar de Música__. Mexico City: Universidad Autónoma Metropolitana, 1981.

B262. Bauer, Marion. __Twentieth Century Music__. Revised edition. New York: G.P. Putnam, 1947. Pp. 333-34, __et passim__.

B263. Broder, Nathan. "The Evolution of the American Composer," in __One Hundred Years of Music in America__. Edited by Paul Henry Lang. New York: G. Schirmer, 1961. Pp. 31 and 35.

B264. Collaer, Paul. __A History of Modern Music__. Translated from French by Sally Abeles. Cleveland: World Publishing Co., 1961 and 1963. P. 44.

B265. Cowell, Henry, editor. __American Composers on American Music__. Stanford, CA: 1933. P. 6.

B266. Demuth, Norman. __Musical Trends in the Twentieth Century__. London: Rockliff, 1952. P. 250.

B267. Deri, Otto. __Exploring Twentieth-Century Music__. New York: Holt, Rinehart and Winston, 1968. P. 493.

B268. Ewen, David. __David Ewen Introduces Modern Music__. Philadelphia: Chilton, 1962. Revised 1969. Pp. 45, 47, 48, 117, 189, and 216.

B269. -------. __Music Comes to America__. New York: Thomas Y. Crowell, 1942 and 1947. Pp. 226, 278, 289, and 296.

B270. Flanner, Janet. __Paris Was Yesterday, 1925-1939__. New York: The Viking Press, 1972. Pp. xix and 46.

B271. Goldin, Milton. __The Music Merchants__. London: The Macmillan Co., 1969. P. 194.

B272. Greenfield, Howard. __They Came to Paris__. New York: Crown Publishers, 1975. Pp. 4, 6, 16, and 103-04.

B273. Grout, Donald Jay. __A History of Western Music__. Third edition with Claude V. Palisca. New York: W.W. Norton, 1980. P. 699.

B274. Layton, Robert. "Music in the United States," in __Twentieth Century Music: A Symposium__. London: Calder and Boyars, 1968. Pp. 125, 129-31, 135-9, and 236.

B275. Leichtentritt, Hugo. __Serge Koussevitsky, The Boston Symphony Orchestra and the New American Music__. Cambridge: Harvard University Press, 1947. Pp. 125 and 128.

B276. Mueller, John Henry. <u>The American Symphony Orchestra: A Social History of Musical Taste</u>. Bloomington: Indiana University Press, 1951. Pp. 181, 277, and 278.

B277. Peyser, Joan. <u>The New Music: The Sense Behind the Sound</u>. New York: Delacorte Press, 1971. Pp. 124, 128, 163, and 180.

B278. Pleasants, Henry. <u>Serious Music--And All That Jazz!</u>. New York: Simon & Schuster, 1969. Pp. 104 and 205.

B279. Rosenstiel, Léonie. "The New World" in <u>Schirmer History of Music</u>. Edited by Léonie Rosenstiel. New York: Schirmer Books, 1982. Pp. 940 and 943.

B280. Sablosky, Irving. <u>American Music</u>. Chicago: The University of Chicago Press, 1969. Pp. 158 and 181.

B281. Salazar, Adolfo. <u>Music in Our Time</u>. New York: W.W. Norton, 1946. Pp. 315-16.

B282. Schickel, Richard. <u>The World of Carnegie Hall</u>. New York: Julian Messner, 1960. Rpt. Westport, CT: Greenwood Press, 1973. Pp. 321-23, <u>et passim</u>.

B283. Silverman, Faye-Ellen. "The Twentieth Century" in <u>Schirmer History of Music</u>. Edited by Léonie Rosenstiel. New York: Schirmer Books, 1982. Pp. 776-77.

B284. Slonimsky, Nicolas. "The United States" in <u>Music of the Western Nations</u>. Edited by Hugo Leichtentritt. Cambridge: Harvard University Press, 1956. Pp. 291-92.

B285. Spalding, Walter Raymond. <u>Music at Harvard</u>. New York: Coward-McCann, 1935. Rpt. New York: Da Capo Press, 1977. P. 215.

B286. Sternfeld, Frederick W. "Music and the Cinema" in <u>Twentieth Century Music</u>. Edited by Rollo Myers. New York: Orion Press, 1968. P. 236, <u>et passim</u>.

B287. Stevenson, Robert Murrell. <u>Protestant Church Music in America</u>. New York: W.W. Norton, 1970. Pp. 122n., 126 and 126n.

B288. Woodworth, George Wallace. <u>The World of Music</u>. Cambridge: Harvard University Press, 1964. P. 155.

Unannotated Brief References: Periodicals

<u>MM</u> 3:18 (Nov-Dec 1925); <u>MM</u> 4:9 (Jan-Feb 1927); <u>MM</u> 6:18 (Nov-Dec 1928); <u>MM</u> 6:5-6 (May-June 1929);<u>MQ</u> 18:14 (1932); <u>MM</u> 9:122 (March-April 1932); <u>MM</u> 10:90 (Jan-Feb 1933); <u>MM</u> 11:145 (March-April 1933); <u>MM</u> 11:193 (May-June 1934); <u>Newsweek</u> 6:40-41 (Nov 2, 1935); <u>NYT</u> (Nov 9, 1935): 18; <u>NYT</u> (Feb 17, 1936): 20; <u>MM</u> 13:58 (March-April 1936); <u>MM</u> 14:43 (Nov-Dec 1936); <u>MM</u> 14:168 (March-April 1937); <u>MM</u> 15:50 (Nov-Dec 1937); <u>MQ</u> 24:24-25 (1938); <u>MM</u> 15:95 & 112

(Jan-Feb 1938); MM 15:249 (May-June 1938); MM 16:264 (May-June 1939); MM 17:64 (Nov-Dec 1939); MQ 26:106 (1940); MM 17:239 (May-June 1940); MM 18:63 & 66(Nov-Dec 1940); Newsweek 16:60 (Dec 16, 1940); MQ 27: 54 & 163 (1941); MM 18:135 (Jan-Feb 1941); MM 18:154 & 178-179 (March-April 1941); MM 19:137 (Nov-Dec 1941); MQ 28:140 (1942); MM 19:110 & 129 (Jan-Feb 1942); Time 39:53 (May 11, 1942); MM 20:57 (Nov-Dec 1942); MM 20:101, 117 & 126 (Jan-Feb 1943); MM 20:166 & 175-6 (March-April 1943); MM 20:256 (May-June 1943); MM 21:9 (Nov-Dec 1943); Musician 48:147-8 (Dec 1943); MM 21:164 & 182 (March-April 1944); MM 21:241 (May-June 1944); MM 22:53 (Nov-Dec 1944); MM 22:13 & 106 (Jan-Feb 1945);MM 22:261 (May-June 1945); Christian Science Monitor Weekly Magazine (May 19, 1945): 15; MQ 32:357 (1946); MM 23:114 (Spring 1946); MM 23:166, 208 & 230 (Summer 1946); MM 23:246, 274, & 323 (Fall 1946); MM 23:114, 190 & 298 (Winter 1946); MQ 33:324 (1947); MQ 32:6 (1948); SR 31:41 (Dec 25, 1948): MQ 35:115 & 121 (1949); MQ 36:55, 259, & 584 (1950); MA 70:12 (Sept 1950); MQ 37:484 (1951); NYT (April 2, 1951): 27; Time 57:76-78 (April 2, 1951); SR 34:20 (May 26, 1951); Variety (Dec 10, 1952): 62; PP 45:69 (Jan 1953); NYT (Nov 21, 1953): 27; Na 178:157-8 (Feb 20, 1954); MA 74:14-15 (March 1954); NYT (April 11, 1954): 84; Variety (May 12, 1954): 43; NYT (July 28, 1954): 28; MA 74:4 (Aug 1954); Time 64:43-44 (Aug 2, 1954); MC 150:14 (Sept 1954); NYT (Nov 25, 1954): 30; PP 47:69 (Jan 1955) Variety (Jan 19, 1955): 71; Revista Musical Chilena 10:29-30 (July 1955); Variety (Sept 21, 1955): 73; Music Teacher 35: 159 (March 1956); Music of the West 11:18 (May 1956); NYT (June 7, 1956): 24; MC 154:9 (Oct 1956); Compositores de America 3:96+ (1957); MC 155:5 (May 1957); NYT (Feb 16, 1958): 71; Le Guide du Concert et du Disque 38:59+ (Oct 3, 1958); NYT (Feb 3, 1959):33; NYT (Dec 5, 1959): 8; NYT (May 26, 1960): 38; NYT (Dec 3, 1960): 25; Variety (June 14, 1961): 48; Neue Zeitschrift Für Musik 122:477 (Nov 1961); Time 78:41 (Dec 15, 1961); Music Magazine/Musical Courier 164:22 (Feb 1962); Show (June 1962): 42; NYT (June 4, 1962): 34; Perspectives of New Music 1:190n. (1963); MR 24:269+ (Nov 1963); Perspectives of New Music 2:14,16, & 18 (1964); Perspectives of New Music 4:121, 152, & 160 (1965); ON 30:5 (Dec 25, 1965); Music and Musicians 13:15 (Aug 1965); NYT (Feb 15, 1966): 34; HF 16:158 (April 1966); NYT (April 5, 1966): 4; Music Educators' Journal 51: 44 (Sept 1966); Facts on File 26:360 (Sept 15, 1966); HSR 18:67 (Jan 1967); NYT (March 7, 1968): 53; NYT (April 30, 1969): 40; HF 20:MA22-23 (May 1970); NYT (April 7, 1971): 49; NYT (Nov 14, 1971): 79; NYT (Nov 19, 1971): 51; Time 98:84 (Dec 6, 1971); Music Clubs Magazine 51:17 (1972); NYT (Jan 9, 1972): Sect. 2, p. 15; Richmond [VA] Times-Dispatch (Feb 25, 1972); Norwalk [CT] Fair-press (Jan 13, 1973); The Choral Journal 13:1 (March 1973); The Baltimore Sun (Nov 11, 1973); HF 24:MA7 (Aug 1974); NYT (Nov 17, 1974): Sect. 2,p. 19; Clavier 14:34 (April, 1975); HF 25:MA24-26+ (April 1975); Le Courrier Musical de France 55:91+ (1976); NYT (Nov 25, 1976): 38; Soundings 5:88+ (1977); The Music Trades 125:44 (Jan 1977); Variety (June 7, 1968): 68; St 41:147 (Nov 1978); Central Opera Service Bulletin 21:14-15 (No. 3: 1979); New York Magazine 12:73-4 (Jan 22, 1979); Notes 36:78 (Sept 1979); Virtuoso 1:34 (1980); Variety (Nov 5, 1980): 85; Virtuoso 2:14-15 (1981); NYer 57:196+ (Oct 19, 1981); New York Magazine 14:89-90 (Oct 19, 1981); San Antonio Light (Nov 1, 1981):4+; The Boston

Globe (Nov 29, 1981): 62; HF 31:MA13-14 (Dec 1981); Central Opera Service Bulletin 23:36 (1982); Nutida Musik 26:40-42 (1982-3); Ov 3:17+ (Feb 1982); Publishers' Weekly 211:44+ (Feb 12, 1982); Notes 39:77 (Sept 1982); Central Opera Service Bulletin 25: 41+ (No. 1: 1983); VF 46:41 (June 1983); HF 33:MA25+ (Nov 1983); Variety (Dec 7, 1983): 2+; Music Clubs Magazine 64:30 (No. 1, 1984); U.S. News & World Report 96:66 (Jan 9, 1984); American Organist 18:133 (April 1984).

Appendix I
Archival Materials

This section is arranged alphabetically by state in which various libraries or archives hold Thomson manuscripts, correspondence, and other memorabilia. "See" references, e.g. See W123, refer to the "Works and Performances" section of this volume.

A1. Holograph score of Ten Etudes for pf. in the Music Library, Mills College, Oakland, CA 94613. See: W181

A2. Holograph manuscript and inscribed first edition of The Seine at Night in the Music Library, Stanford University, Stanford, CA 94305. See: W29

A3. Personal papers, a definitive collection including holograph music manuscripts and sketches, published literary and musical writings, correspondence, and memorabilia at the John Herrick Jackson Music Library, Yale University, 98 Wall St., New Haven, CT 06520. An excellent finding aid, compiled by Victor Cardell, is available.

A4. Several interviews with Virgil Thomson on both audio and video tape are available in the Oral History collection, American Music, Yale School of Music, 96 Wall Street, New Haven, CT 06520.

A5. Original program of Four Saints in Three Acts, Hartford, 1934, in the Mildred P. Allen Memorial Library, Hartt College of Music, 200 Bloomfield Ave., West Hartford, CT 06117. See: W1

A6. Videotaped interview with Virgil Thomson conducted by Robert Jacobson on February 23, 1984, for the Kennedy Center Honors Oral History Program. Printed transcript available. Kennedy Center Honor Oral History Program, Washington, DC 20566

A7. Letters of Virgil Thomson are in the correspondence collections of Erno Balogh, Ross Lee Finney, Serge Koussevitzky, Listen magazine, Modern Music journal, Hans Nathan, Willard Rhodes, Arnold Schoenberg, Irving Schwerké, Charles Seeger, Nicolas Slonimsky, Burnett Tuthill, and William Treat Upton in the Music Division, Library of Congress, Washington, DC 20540.

A8.   Musical score for Countee Cullen's Medea in the collection of
      Countee Cullen's papers, Trevor Arnett Library, Atlanta Univer-
      sity, 273 Chestnut St. S.W., Atlanta, GA 30314.

A9.   Letters of Virgil Thomson in the Joseph Regenstein Library,
      University of Chicago, 1100 E. 57th Street, Chicago, IL 60637.

A10. Holograph manuscript of Two Sentimental Tangos in the Music Col-
      lection, St. Mary College, Leavenworth, KS 66048. See: W9

A11. Photographs of 1934 production of Four Saints in Three Acts in the
      Eva Jessye Collection in the Potter Library, Pittsburg State
      University, Pittsburg, KS 66762. See: W1

A12. Papers of Geneve Lichtenwalter (1869-1951), local pianist and
      teacher of Virgil Thomson, in the Music Library, Conservatory of
      Music, University of Missouri, 4420 Warwick Blvd., Kansas City,
      MO 64111.

A13. Scrapbook of Thomson's Herald Tribune writings, some of which are
      included in The Musical Scene (1945), compiled by the Music
      Department of the Boston Public Library, 666 Boylston St., Box
      286, 02117-0286. See: T190

A14. Holograph manuscript of Cantabile: A Portrait of Nicolas de
      Chatelain and assorted letters to Hans Moldenhauer in the
      Moldenhauer Archives, Houghton Library, Harvard University,
      Cambridge, MA 02138. See: W253

A15. A file of correspondence containing approximately 300 items relat-
      ing to Thomson's membership in the American Academy and
      Institute of Arts and Letters, 633 W. 155th St., New York, NY
      10032.

A16. Oral history interview featuring discussion of childhood in Kansas
      City, studies with Nadia Boulanger, and collaboration with film-
      maker Robert Flaherty in Oral History Collection, Butler
      Library, Columbia University, New York, NY 10027.

A17. Notes and manuscripts for Thomson's early articles, published and
      unpublished, in the Columbia University Library, Columbia
      University, New York, NY 10027.

A18. A one hour film entitled "Virgil Thomson, Composer," produced and
      directed by John Huszar, co-produced by FilmAmerica, Inc. and
      WNET/Thirteen, which aired on PBS on December 27, 1980 in honor
      of Thomson's 80th birthday. Distributed by Arthur Cantor, Inc.
      33 West 60th St., New York, NY 10023.

A19. Holograph manuscripts of portraits of Agnes Rindge and Minna
      Curtiss (1936-41) in the Pierpont Morgan Library, 29 E. 36th
      Street, New York, NY 10016.

A20. Holograph manuscripts of Ah, Love, Could You and I With Fate
      Conspire, Agnus Dei, Dirge, I Attempt from Love's Sickness to

Fly, and _Susie Asado_; xeroxes of holograph manuscripts of _A Hymn for the Pratt Institute_ and _Ten Easy Pieces and a Coda_; and a scrapbook of _Herald Tribune_ writings in the Music Division, New York Public Library, 111 Amsterdam Ave., New York, NY 10023. See: W66, W96, W106, W127, & W164

A21.   Holograph manuscripts of _Two Sentimental Tangos_ and _Synthetic Waltzes_ in the Sibley Music Library, Eastman School of Music, University of Rochester, 26 Gibbs St., Rochester, NY 14604. See: W9 & W161

A22.   Oral history interview concerning WPA Theater Project (1935-39) in the Fenwick Library, Special Collections, George Mason University, 4400 University Drive, Fairfax, VA 22030.

A23.   Letters from Virgil Thomson to Percy Grainger in the Grainger Museum at the University of Melbourne, Parkville, Victoria, Australia 3052.

Appendix II
Chronological List of Compositions

The "W" number following each title, e.g. W123, refers to the "Works and Performances" section of this volume.

1920 De Profundis, W61
      The Sunflower, W104
      Vernal Equinox, W103

1921 O My Deir Hert, W62
      Prelude, W154
      Sanctus, W63

1922 Fanfare, W156
      Passacaglia, W158
      Pastorale on a Christmas Plainsong, W155
      Prelude, W157
      Three Antiphonal Psalms, W65
      Tribulationes Civitatum, W64

1923 Two Sentimental Tangos, W9 & W159

1924 Agnus Dei, W66
      Fête Polonaise, W68
      Five Chorale-Preludes, W160
      Missa Brevis, W67
      Three Sentences from "The Song of Solomon," W105

1925 Agnus Dei, W69
      Synthetic Waltzes, W161

1926 Benedictus, W70
      Five Phrases from the "The Song of Solomon," W107
      Five Two-Part Inventions, W163
      Sanctus, W71
      Sonata da Chiesa, W162
      Susie Asado, W106
      Ten Easy Pieces and a Coda, W164
      The Tiger, W108

Variations on Sunday School Tunes, W165

1927 Capital Capitals, W109
      Preciosilla, W110
      La Valse Grégorienne, W111

1928 Le Berceau de Gertrude Stein, W112
      Commentaire sur Saint Jérome, W114
      Four Saints in Three Acts, W1
      Portraits for Violin Alone, W166
      Saints' Procession, W72
      Les Soirées Bagnolaises, W115
      Symphony on a Hymn Tune, W10
      Trois Poèmes de la Duchesse de Rohan, W113

1929 Alternations: A Portrait of Maurice Grosser, W210
      Le Bains-bar, W168
      Catalan Waltz: A Portrait of Ramón Senabre, W211
      Five Portraits for Four Clarinets, W167
      Piano Sonata No. 1, W169
      Piano Sonata No. 2, W170
      Portrait of F.B., W116
      Travelling in Spain: Alice Woodfin Branlière, W209

1930 Air de Phèdre, W119
      Clair Leonard's Profile, W212
      Le Droit de Varech, W326
      Film: Deux Soeurs qui ne sont pas soeurs, W120
      Madame Dubost chez elle, W213
      Oraison Funèbre de Henriette-Marie de France, Reine de la Grande-
        Bretagne, W118
      Pastoral: A Portrait of Jean Ozenne, W214
      Piano Sonata No. 3, W173
      Portraits for Violin and Piano, W172
      Russell Hitchcock, Reading, W215
      Sea Coast: A Portrait of Constance Askew, W216
      Le Singe et le léopard, W117
      Sonata for Violin and Piano, W171

1931 La Belle en dormant, W123
      Chamber Music, W122
      Serenade for Flute and Violin, W175
      Stabat Mater, W11 & W121
      String Quartet No. 1, W174
      Symphony No. 2 in C Major, W12

1932 String Quartet No. 2, W176
      Symphony No. 2 in C Major (arr. for pf., 4 hands), W177

1934 A Bride for the Unicorn, W327
      Mass for Two-Part Chorus and Percussion, W74
      Pigeons on the Grass Alas, W124
      Seven Choruses from the "Medea" of Euripides, W73

1935 Connecticut Waltz: A Portrait of Harold Lewis Cook, W228

A Day Dream: Portrait of Herbert Whiting, W229
Ettie Stettheimer, W219
Go to Sleep, Alexander Smallens, Jr., W125
Helen Austin at Home and Abroad, W226
The Hunt: A Portrait of A. Everett Austin, Jr., W222
Hymn: A Portrait of Josiah Marvel, W223
Meditation: A Portrait of Jere Abbott, W227
An Old Song: A Portrait of Carrie Stettheimer, W220
A Portrait of R. Kirk Askew, W217
Prelude and Fugue: A Portrait of Miss Agnes Rindge, W225
Souvenir: A Portrait of Paul Bowles, W218
Tennis: A Portrait of Henry McBride, W221

1936   Hamlet, W331
       Horse Eats Hat, W330
       Injunction Granted, W329
       Macbeth, W328
       The Plow That Broke the Plains, W316
       Suite from "The Plow That Broke the Plains," W13 & W178

1937   Antony and Cleopatra, W332
       Filling Station, W2 & W179
       Go to Sleep, Pare McTaggett Lorentz, W126
       The John Mosher Waltzes, (arr. for orch.), W16
       My Shepherd Will Supply My Need, W75
       The River, W317
       Scenes from the Holy Infancy According to St. Matthew, W76
       The Spanish Earth, W318
       Suite from "Filling Station," W15
       Suite from "The River," W14

1938   Androcles and the Lion, W333
       A French Boy of Ten: Louis Lange, W231
       Maurice Bavoux: Young and Alone, W232
       Portrait of Claude Biais, W230

1939   Dirge, W127

1940   Aria: A Portrait of Germaine Hugnet, W250
       Awake or Asleep: A Portrait of Pierre Mabille, W252
       Barcarolle: A Portrait of Georges Hugnet, W238
       The Bard: A Portrait of Sherry Mangan, W233
       Bugles and Birds: A Portrait of Pablo Picasso, W243
       Canons With Cadenza: A Portrait of André Ostier, W256
       Cantabile: A Portrait of Nicolas de Chatelain, W253
       Church Organ Wedding Music, W180
       Dora Maar or the Presence of Pablo Picasso, W248
       The Dream World of Peter Rose-Pulham, W247
       Duet: A Portrait of Clarita, Comtesse de Forceville, W254
       Eccentric Dances: Portrait of Madame Kristians Tonny, W240
       Fanfare for France: A Portrait of Max Kahn, W237
       Five-Finger Exercise: A Portrait of Léon Kochnitzky, W246
       Fugue: A Portrait of Alexander Smallens, W257
       In a Bird Cage: A Portrait of Lise Deharme, W234
       Invention: Theodate Johnson Busy and Resting, W242

Lullaby Which is Also a Spinning Song: A Portrait of Howard
    Putzel, W245
Pastoral: A Portrait of Tristan Tzara, W249
Piano Sonata No. 4: Guggenheim jeune, W244
Poltergeist: A Portrait of Hans Arp, W236
Stretching: A Portrait of Jamie Campbell, W255
Swiss Waltz: A Portrait of Sophie Tauber-Arp, W239
Tango Lullaby: A Portrait of Mlle. Alvarez de Toledo, W241
Toccata: A Portrait of Mary Widney, W251
The Trojan Women, W334
With Trumpet and Horn: A Portrait of Louise Ardant, W235

1941   Insistences: A Portrait of Louise Crane, W259
       The Bugle Song, W77 & W128
       The Life of a Careful Man, W335
       Oedipus Tyrannos, W336
       Parades: A Portrait of Florine Stettheimer, W261
       Percussion Piece: A Portrait of Jessie Lasell, W260
       Surrey Apple-Howler's Song, W78
       Welcome to the New Year, W79
       With Fife and Drums: A Portrait of Mina Curtiss, W258

1942   Aaron Copland, Persistently Pastoral, W266
       Canons for Dorothy Thompson, W18
       James Patrick Cannon, Professional Revolutionary, W262
       The Mayor LaGuardia Waltzes, W17
       Prisoner of the Mind, Schuyler Watts, W264
       Scottish Memories: Peter Monro Jack, W263
       Wedding Music: A Portrait of Jean Watts, W265

1943   Five-Finger Exercise: Portrait of Briggs Buchanan, W267
       Sonata for Flute Alone, W182
       Ten Etudes for Piano, W181

1944   Barcarolle for Woodwinds, W19 & W183
       Bugles and Birds, W20
       Cantabile for Strings, W21
       Fanfare for France, W22
       Fugue, W23
       Meditation, W24
       Pastorale, W25
       Percussion Piece, W26
       Tango Lullaby, W27
       Sonorous and Exquisite Corpses, W184

1945   Fugue and Chorale on "Yankee Doodle," W28
       Solitude: A Portrait of Lou Harrison, W268
       Tuesday in November, W319

1947   The Mother of Us All, W3
       The Seine at Night, W29

1948   Acadian Songs and Dances from "Louisiana Story," W31
       Louisiana Story, W320
       Suite from "Louisiana Story," W30

Wheatfield at Noon, W32

1949 At the Beach, W33 & W185
      Hymns from the Old South, W80
      A Solemn Music, W34
      Suite from "The Mother of Us All," W35

1950 Concerto for Violoncello and Orchestra, W36 & W186

1951 Chromatic Double Harmonies: Portrait of Sylvia Marlowe, W269
      Five Songs from William Blake, W37 & W130
      For a Happy Occasion, W190
      Four Songs to Poems of Thomas Campion, W129 & W187
      Nine Etudes for Piano, W188
      Walking Song, W189

1952 Bayou, W4
      The Grass Harp, W338
      The Harvest According, W5
      King Lear, W337
      Sea Piece with Birds, W38

1953 Kyrie Eleison, W81

1954 Concerto for Flute, Strings, Harp, and Percussion, W39 & W191
      Ondine, W339

1955 At the Spring, W134
      The Bell Doth Toll, W135
      Consider, Lord, W131
      Four Songs to Poems of Thomas Campion (arr. for mixed chorus), W84
      The Holly and the Ivy, W132
      If Thou a Reason Dost Desire to Know, W137
      John Peel, W138
      Look, How the Floor of Heaven, W136
      Never Another, W82
      Remember Adam's Fall, W133
      Song for the Stable, W83
      Tiger! Tiger!, W85

1956 Eleven Chorale Preludes for Organ, W40
      Homage to Marya Freund and to the Harp, W270
      King John, W340
      Measure for Measure, W341
      Shakespeare Songs, W139

1957 The Goddess, W321
      The Lively Arts Fugue, W41
      The Merchant of Venice, W343
      Much Ado About Nothing, W344
      Othello, W342
      Tres Estampas de Niñez, W140

1958 Crossing Brooklyn Ferry, W86
      Power Among Men, W322

A Study in Stacked-Up Thirds, W192

1959   Collected Poems, W43 & W143
       Bertha, W345
       Fugues and Cantilenas, W42
       Lamentions: Etude for Accordion, W193
       Mostly About Love, W142
       My Shepherd Will Supply My Need (arr. for voice and pf.), W141

1960   Mass for Solo Voice, W88 & W144
       Missa pro defunctis, W87
       Stabat Mater (arr. for voice and pf.), W145

1961   Crossing Brooklyn Ferry (arr. for chorus and orchestra), W44
       Variations for Koto, W194
       A Solemn Music and a Joyful Fugue, W45

1962   Dance in Praise, W89
       Five Auvergnat Folk Songs, W92
       Mass for Solo Voice (arr. for voice and orch.), W46
       Pange Lingua, W195

1963   The Holly and the Ivy (arr. for mixed chorus), W90
       My Master Hath a Garden, W91
       Praises and Prayers, W146
       Two by Marianne Moore, W147

1964   Autumn: Concertino for Harp, Strings, and Percussion, W49
       The Feast of Love, W48 & W148
       Journey to America, W323
       Pilgrims and Pioneers, W47
       When I Survey the Bright Celestial Sphere, W93

1965   Ode to the Wonders of Nature, W50

1966   Ballet Music from III:2 of "Lord Byron," W197
       Edges: A Portrait of Robert Indiana, W271
       Etude for Cello and Piano, W196
       Fantasy in Homage to an Earlier England, W51
       Lord Byron, W6
       The Nativity as Sung by the Shepherds, W94

1967   From Byron's "Don Juan," W52
       How Will Ye Have Your Partridge Today?, W95

1968   A Hymn for the Pratt Institute, W96

1969   Edges: A Portrait of Robert Indiana (arr. for orch.), W54
       For Eugene Ormandy's Birthday, 18 November 1969: A Study in
          Stacked-Up Thirds, W272
       Metropolitan Museum Fanfare: Portrait of an American Artist, W53
       Study Piece: Portrait of a Lady, W55

1970   The Baby Maker, W324

1972   From "Sneden's Landing Variations," W149
       Man of Iron: A Portrait of Willy Eisenhart, W273
       Symphony No. 3, W56

1973   Cantata on Poems of Edward Lear, W97
       The Courtship of Yongly Bongly Bo, W150

1974   Family Portrait, W198

1975   Hurray!, W7
       Parson Weems and the Cherry Tree, W8 & W199

1976   Suddenly an Eagle, W325

1979   Go to Sleep, Gabriel Liebowitz, W151
       The Peace Place, W98
       What Is It?, W152

1980   The Cat, W153

1981   Anne-Marie Soullière: Something of a Beauty, W58 & W289
       Barbara Epstein: Untiring, W283
       Bill Katz: Wide Awake, W58 & W274
       Buffie Johnson: Drawing V.T. in Charcoal, W290
       Christopher Cox: Singing a Song, W58 & W282
       Craig Rutenberg: Swinging, W291
       Dead Pan: Mrs. Betty Freeman, W58 & W284
       For Lou Harrison and His Jolly Games 16 Measures (Count'em), W201
       Franco Assetto, Drawing V.T., W286
       Gerald Busby: Giving Full Attention, W278
       John Wright, Drawing, W285
       Karen Brown Waltuck: Intensely Two, W58 & W288
       Morris Golde: Showing Delight, W281
       Noah Creshevsky: Loyal, Steady, Persistent, W58 & W279
       Norma Flender: Thoughts About Flying, W275
       A Prayer to Venus, W99
       Richard Flender: Solid Not Stolid, W58 & W276
       Round and Round: Dominique Nabokov, W287
       Sam Byers: With Joy, W58 & W280
       Scott Wheeler: Free-Wheeling, W58 & W277
       A Short Fanfare, W202
       Theme for Improvisation, W200
       Thoughts for Strings, W57

1982   Cantantes Eamus, W100
       David Dubal in Flight, W58 & W298
       Dennis Russell Davies: In a Hammock, W58 & W294
       Dr. Marcel Roche: Making a Decision, W297
       Doña Flor: Receiving, W296
       Eleven Portraits for Orchestra, W58
       Molly Davies: Terminations, W293
       Paul Sanfacon: On the Ice, W292
       Rodney Lister: Music for a Merry-Go-Round, W295

1983   Bell Piece, W203

Charles Fussell: In Meditation, W308
Cynthia Kemper: A Fanfare, W204
Fanfare for Peace, W101
Glynn Boyd Harte: Reaching, W305
Lily Hastings, W205
Louis Rispoli: In a Boat, W303
Malitte Matta: In the Executive Style, W304
Mark Beard: Never Alone, W302
Peter McWilliams: Firmly Spontaneous, W299
Phillip Ramey: Thinking Hard, W307
Power Boothe: With Pencil, W301
Senza Espressione: Bennett Lerner, W306
Vassilis Voglis: On the March, W300

1984 Boris Baranovic: Whirling, W312
      Brendan Lemon: A Study Piece for Piano, W309
      Four Saints: An Olio for Chamber Orchestra, W59
      Jay Rozen, W207
      John Houseman: No Changes, W310
      Lines: For and About Ron Henggeler, W311
      A Pair of Portraits: "A Double Take" and "Major Chords," W60
      A Portrait of Two, W206
      Southern Hymns, W102
      Tony Tommasini: A Study in Chords, W313

1985 Christopher Beach Alone, W314
      Danyal Lawson: Playing, W315
      Stockton Fanfare, W208

Alphabetical List of Compositions

The "W" number following each title, e.g. W123, refers to the "Works and Performances" section of this volume.

Acadian Songs and Dances from "Louisiana Story," W31
Agnus Dei (1924), W66
Agnus Dei (1925), W69
Air de Phèdre, W119
Alternations (port. of Maurice Grosser), W210
Androcles and the Lion, W333
Antony and Cleopatra, W332
Aria (port. of Germaine Hugnet), W250
At the Beach, W33, W185
At the Spring, W134
Autumn: Concertino for Harp, Strings, and Percussion, W49
Awake or Asleep (port. of Pierre Mabille), W252

The Baby Maker, W324
Le Bains-bar, W168
Ballet Music from III:2 of "Lord Byron," W197
Barcarolle (port. of Georges Hugnet), W238
Barcarolle for Woodwinds, W19, W183
The Bard (port. of Sherry Mangan), W233
Bayou, W4
The Bell Doth Toll, W135
Bell Piece, W203
La Belle en dormant, W123
Benedictus, W70
Le Berceau de Gertrude Stein, W112
Bertha, W345
A Bride for the Unicorn, W327
The Bugle Song, W77, W128
Bugles and Birds (port. of Pablo Picasso), W20, W243

Canons for Dorothy Thompson, W18
Canons with Cadenza (port. of André Ostier), W256
Cantabile (port. of Nicolas de Chatelain), W21, W253
Cantantes Eamus, W100
Cantata on Poems of Edward Lear, W97
Capital Capitals, W109

Five Songs from William Blake, W37, W130
Five Two-Part Inventions, W163
For A Happy Occasion, W190
For Lou Harrison, W201
Four Saints: an Olio for Chamber Orchestra, W59
Four Saints in Three Acts, W1
Four Songs to Poems of Thomas Campion, W84, W129, W187
Free-Wheeling (port. of Scott Wheeler), W58, W277
A French Boy of Ten (port. of Louis Lange), W231
From Byron's "Don Juan," W52
From "Sneden's Landing Variations," W149
Fugue (port. of Alexander Smallens), W23, W257
Fugue and Chorale on "Yankee Doodle," W28
Fugues and Cantilenas, W42

Giving Full Attention (port. of Gerald Busby), W278
Go to Sleep, Alexander Smallens, Jr., W125
Go to Sleep, Gabriel Liebowitz, W151
Go to Sleep, Pare McTaggett Lorentz, W126
The Goddess, W321
The Grass Harp, W338

Hamlet, W331
The Harvest According, W5
Helen Austin at Home and Abroad (port.), W226
The Holly and the Ivy, W90, W132
Homage to Marya Freund and to the Harp, W270
Horse Eats Hat, W330
How Will Ye Have Your Partridge Today?, W95
The Hunt (port. of A.E. Austin, Jr.), W222
Hurray!, W7
Hymn (port. of Josiah Marvel), W223
Hymn for the Pratt Institute, W96
Hymns from the Old South, W80

If Thou A Reason Dost Desire to Know, W137
In a Bird Cage (port. of Lise Deharme), W234
In a Boat (port. of Louis Rispoli), W303
In the Executive Style (port. of Malitte Matta), W304
In a Hammock (port. of Dennis R. Davies), W58, W294
In Meditation (port. of Charles Fussell), W308
Injunction Granted, W329
Insistences: Portrait of a Lady (port. of Louise Crane), W259
Intensely Two (port. of Karen Brown Waltuck), W58, W288
Invention: Theodate Johnson Busy and Resting (port.), W242

James Patrick Cannon, Professional Revolutionary (port.), W262
Jay Rozen (port.), W207
The John Mosher Waltzes, W16, W224
John Peel, W138
Journey to America, W323

King John, W340
King Lear, W337
Kyrie Eleison, W81

Lamentations, W193
The Life of a Careful Man, W335
Lily Hastings, W205
Lines: For and About Ron Henggeler (port.), W311
The Lively Arts Fugue, W41
Look, How the Floor of Heaven, W136
Lord Byron, W6
The Louisiana Story, W320
A Love Scene (port. of Betty Freeman), W58, W284
Loyal, Steady, Persistent (port. of Noah Creshevsky), W58, W279
Lullaby Which is Also a Spinning Song (port. of Howard Putzel), W245

Macbeth, W328
Madame Dubost chez elle (port.), W213
Making a Decision (port. of Marcel Roche), W297
Man of Iron (port. of Willy Eisenhart), W273
Mass for Solo Voice, W46, W88, W144
Mass for Two-Part Chrous and Percussion, W74
The Mayor LaGuardia Waltzes, W17
Measure for Measure, W341
Meditation (port. of Jere Abbott), W24, W227
The Merchant of Venice, W343
Metropolitan Museum Fanfare, W53
Missa Brevis, W67
Missa pro defunctis, W87
Mostly About Love, W142
The Mother of Us All, W3
Much Ado About Nothing, W344
Music for a Merry-Go-Round (port. of Rodney Lister), W295
My Master Hath a Garden, W91
My Shepherd Will Supply My Need, W75, W141

The Nativity as Sung by the Shepherds, W94
Never Alone (port. of Mark Beard), W302
Never Another, W82
Nine Etudes for Piano, W188
No Changes (port. of John Houseman), W310

O My Deir Hert, W62
Ode to the Wonders of Nature, W50
Oedipus Tyrannos, W336
An Old Song (port. of Carrie Stettheimer), W220
On the Ice (port. of Paul Sanfacon), W292
On the March (port. of Vassilis Voglis), W300
Ondine, W339
Oraison Funèbre de Henriette-Marie de France, W118
Othello, W342

A Pair of Portraits, W60
Pange Lingua, W195
Parades (port. of Florine Stettheimer), W261
Parson Weems and the Cherry Tree, W8, W199
Passacaglia, W158
Pastoral (port. of Jeane Ozenne), W214
Pastoral (port. of Tristan Tzara), W249
Pastorale (port. of Aaron Copland), W25

Pastorale on a Christmas Plainsong, W155
The Peace Place, W98
Percussion Piece (port. of Jessie K. Lassell), W26, W260
Persistently Pastoral (port. of Aaron Copland), W266
Piano Sonata No. 1, W169
Piano Sonata No. 2, W170
Piano Sonata No. 3, W173
Piano Sonata No. 4 (port. of Peggy Guggenheim), W244
Pigeons on the Grass Alas, W124
Pilgrims and Pioneers, W47, W323
Playing (port. of Danyal Lawson), W315
The Plow that Broke the Plains, W316
Poltergeist (port. of Hans Arp), W236
Portrait of Claude Biais, W230
Portrait of F.B., W116
A Portrait of R. Kirk Askew, W217
A Portrait of Two, W206
Portraits for Violin Alone, W166
Portraits for Violin and Piano, W172
Power Among Men, W322
Praises and Prayers, W146
A Prayer to Venus, W99
Preciosilla, W110
Prelude and Fugue (port. of Agnes Rindge), W225
Prelude for Organ, W157
Prelude for Piano, W154
Prisoner of the Mind (port. of Schuyler Watts), W264

Reaching (port. of Glynn Boyd Harte), W305
Remember Adam's Fall, W133
The River, W317
Round and Round (port. of Dominique Nabokov), W287
Russell Hitchcock, Reading, (port.), W215

Saints' Procession, W72
Sanctus (1921), W63
Sanctus (1926), W71
Scenes from the Holy Infancy According to St. Matthew, W76
Scottish Memories (port. of Peter Monro Jack), W263
Sea Coast (port. of Constance Askew), W216
Sea Piece with Birds, W38
The Seine at Night, W29
Senza Espressione (port. of Bennett Lerner), W306
Serenade for Flute and Violin, W175
Seven Choruses from the "Medea" of Euripides, W73
Shakespeare Songs, W139
A Short Fanfare, W202
Showing Delight (port. of Morris Golde), W281
Le Singe et le léopard, W117
Singing a Song (port. of Christopher Cox), W58, W282
Les Soirées Bagnolaises, W115
A Solemn Music (for band), W34
A Solemn Music and a Joyful Fugue (for orchestra), W45
Solid, Not Stolid (port. of Richard Flender), W58, W276
Solitude (port. of Lou Harrison), W268

Two Sentimental Tangos, W9, W159

Untiring (port. of Barbara Epstein), W283

La Valse Grégorienne, W111
Variations on Sunday School Tunes, W165
Variations for Koto, W194
Vernal Equinox, W103

Walking Song, W189
Wedding Music (port. of Jean Watts), W265
Welcome to the New Year, W79
What Is It?, W152
Wheatfield at Noon, W32
When I Survey the Bright Celestial Sphere, W93
Whirling (port. of Boris Baranovic), W312
Wide Awake (port. of Bill Katz), W58, W274
With Fife and Drums (port. of Mina Curtiss), W258
With Joy (port. of Sam Byers), W58, W280
With Pencil (port. of Power Boothe), W301
With Trumpet and Horn (port. of Louise Ardant), W235

Young and Alone (port. of Maurice Bavoux), W232

Index

Roman numerals refer to pages in the "Preface," Arabic numerals to the "Biography," and numbers preceded by "W," "D," "T," "B," and "A" refer respectively to citations in "Works and Performances," "Discography," "Bibliography by Thomson," "Bibliography about Thomson," and "Archival Resources [Appendix I]."

Madrigal Singers, W76
Mahler, Fritz, W15
"Major Chords," See A Pair of Portraits
Making a Decision (port. of Marcel Roche), W297
Man of Iron (port. of Willy Eisenhart), W198, W273
Mandel, Alan, B72; D45
Mandel, Nancy, B72
Mangan, Sherry, D45; W113, W140, W233
Mann, Erika, T76
Mannes, Leopold, 4
Margrave, Wendell, B73
Marino, Amerigo, D25, D41
Marisol, B65
Markevitch, Igor, T69, T135
Marlowe, Sylvia, D45, D63; W188, W269
Marriner, Neville, D4, D41, D53
Marrocco, W. Thomas, B127
Marthe-Marthine, D47; W106, W110, W111, W113
Mase, Raymond, W198
Mason, Marilyn, D77
Mass for Solo Voice, W46, W88, W144
Mass for Two-Part Chorus and Percussion, B186; W74
Massi, R. Wood, xiii
Massimo, Leone, T122, T135
Masters, Edgar Lee, B28
Matta, Malitte, W304
Matthews, Benjamin, D24; W1
Matthews, Edward, D23
Matthews, Inez, D23
Maxwell, Linn, D34
Mayor LaGuardia Waltzes, The, B177; W17
Measure for Measure, B143; W139, W341
Meckna, Michael, 9; B159
de Medina, Juanita, D47; W166
Meditation (port. of Jere Abbott), W24, W227
Mellers, Wilfred, B160; T126
Mendel, Arthur, B147
Menotti, Gian-Carlo, B168; T75
Merchant of Venice, The, W139, W343
Merkling, Frank, B74
Messiaen, Olivier, T121
Mester, Jorge, D19
Metcalf, Addison, T119

Metéhen, Roger, W121, W174
Metropolitan Museum Fanfare, D30; W53, W261
Metropolitan Opera (New York), 8; T159; W316
Meyer, Nicholas, W14
Michel, François, B241
Mikhashoff, Yvar, D22, D41, D45, D50, D60, D71; W213, W215, W220
Milhaud, Darius, 5; T9, T28, T100, T135
de Mille, Agnes, 7; W5
Miller, Bessie, xiii
Miller, Gilbert H., T190
Mills, Fred, D65
Mills College, B34; W201
Miracle, Anne, W172
Missa Brevis, 5; D31; W67
Missa pro defunctis, 7; B50, B109, B128, B177; D32; W81, W87
Mitchell, David, W6
Mock, Alice, W107
Mokry, Ladislav, B240
Moldenhauer, Hans, A14
Moore, Douglas, T30, T132
Moore, Marianne, D75; W147
Morel, Jean, W107
Morgenstern, Sam, T189, T190
"Morning Star, The," See Three Hymns from the Old South
Mosbacher, Carl, W86
Mosher, John, W2, W16, W224
Moskovitz, Harvey, D59
Mostly About Love, B4; D33; W142
Mother of Us All, The, 7, 8; B31, B33, B37, B43, B67, B75, B77, B89, B97, B116, B128, B146, B149, B152, B157, B164, B168, B177, B190; D34, D35; T67; W3, W34
Movshon, G., B75
Mozart, Wolfgang Amadeus, T37
Mozart Festival Orchestra, W47
Much Ado About Nothing, T108; W139, W344
Mueller, Erwin, xiv
Mueller, John Henry, B276
Municipal Orchestra of Valencia, W49
Murray, Robert Leigh, 3
Music for a Merry-Go-Round (port. of Rodney Lister), W295
Music Reviewed, 1940-1954, T191
Music, Right and Left, T192
Musical Scene, The, A13; B137;

ABOUT THE AUTHOR

MICHAEL MECKNA is an Assistant Professor of Music History at Ball State University, Indiana. He is the editor, with R. N. Freeman, of *Austrian Cloister Symphonists* and has contributed articles to *The New Grove Dictionary of Music in the U.S.*, *Music Journal*, and *American Music*.